CUTTING EDGE

PRE-INTERMEDIATE

photocopiable resources by Chris Redston

TEACHER'S RESOURCE BOOK

jane comyns carr

with sarah cunningham   peter moor

Contents

Introduction

Cutting Edge Pre-Intermediate is a course aimed at young adults studying general English at a pre-intermediate level. It provides material for up to 120 hours' teaching, according to how much photocopiable material is used from the *Teacher's Resource Book*. It is suitable for students studying in either a monolingual or multilingual classroom situation.

STUDENTS' BOOK **CLASS CASSETTES**	*Cutting Edge Pre-Intermediate Students' Book* is divided into sixteen modules, each consisting of approximately 6–8 hours of classroom material. In each module you will find: • **grammar** – two *Language focus* sections • **vocabulary** – including a *Wordspot* section in alternate modules • **reading** and/or **listening** – with extended speaking activities • **Real life** (everyday survival language) and/or **writing** • **Do you remember?** – quick spot-check revision In addition there are **Consolidation sections** after Modules 6, 11 and 16. At the back of the book you will find: • **Communication activities** • a list of **Irregular verbs** • a detailed **Language summary** • **Tapescripts** – for material on the Class Cassettes **Mini-dictionary**: in the back cover pocket of the *Students' Book* is the *Cutting Edge Pre-Intermediate Mini-dictionary*, which contains definitions and examples for approximately 1,500 words and phrases from the *Students' Book*.
WORKBOOK **STUDENTS' CASSETTE**	*Cutting Edge Pre-Intermediate Workbook* is divided into sixteen parallel modules, consisting of: • additional **grammar** practice • additional **vocabulary** practice • **Vocabulary booster** sections • **skills work** – *Listen and read* and *Improve your writing* sections • **pronunciation** • **spelling** There is an **Answer key** at the back of the *Workbook*. The optional **Students' Cassette** features the *Listen and read* texts, exercises on pronunciation and some grammar exercises.
TEACHER'S RESOURCE BOOK	*Cutting Edge Pre-Intermediate Teacher's Resource Book* consists of five sections: • **Introduction** and **Teacher's tips** on: – Making speaking Tasks work – Responding to learners' individual needs – Helping students with pronunciation – Working with lexical phrases – Making the most of the *Mini-dictionary* • **step-by-step teacher's notes** for each module – including alternative suggestions for different teaching situations, detailed language notes and integrated answer keys. • photocopiable **Resource bank** – including learner-training worksheets, communicative grammar practice activities, vocabulary extension activities, and three **Tests** to follow Modules 6, 11 and 16.

The thinking behind *Cutting Edge Pre-Intermediate*

Cutting Edge Pre-Intermediate Students' Book has a multi-layered syllabus, which includes a comprehensive grammar and vocabulary syllabus, incorporating systematic work on listening, speaking, reading and writing. It takes an integrated approach to pronunciation, and includes learner-training and revision. We are particularly interested in helping learners to take an active approach in their lessons, and in encouraging them to use the language they know, even at this relatively low level. To do this, we realise that learners need guidance and preparation, and so we aim to take them step by step through new language and tasks, providing them with the support they need in order to communicate successfully.

Lexis

VOCABULARY SECTIONS/WORDSPOTS/REAL LIFE

The first step to successful communication is a good vocabulary, so there is a strong emphasis on lexis in *Cutting-Edge Pre-Intermediate*. As well as knowing individual words, learners need to know how to use them. Often this involves knowing the collocations of the word, and looking at phrases and 'chunks' of language. The *Vocabulary* sections in the *Students' Book* focus consistently on this kind of lexis, particularly the regular *Wordspot* sections, which look at the most useful collocations of high-frequency words like *feel* or *look*. Students will find useful everyday phrases in the regular *Real life* sections too – these focus on areas such as telephoning, directions, social chit-chat, etc.

MINI-DICTIONARY

It is important that learners are active in improving their own vocabulary, so *Cutting Edge Pre-Intermediate* has its own *Mini-dictionary* containing all the words from the *Students' Book* that we anticipate students might want to check, with graded explanations and examples that are intended to clarify meaning. In the *Mini-dictionary* students can find out about phrases and collocations involving the key word, as well as the pronunciation, any irregularities and common learner errors. The following icon [md] occurs whenever it might be useful to refer to the *Mini-dictionary*.

VOCABULARY BOOSTER/PERSONAL VOCABULARY

We encourage learners to improve their vocabulary independently in other ways too. There are regular *Vocabulary booster* sections in the *Workbook*, which students can study by themselves. These extend simple concrete areas of vocabulary (such as parts of the body, sports and activities) via pictures and pronunciation practice. In the *Students' Book* there are *Personal vocabulary* boxes on the task pages, where students are encouraged to ask the teacher for the words and phrases they need to express their own experiences.

LEARNER-TRAINING

Of course, many students need to develop the skills necessary to use a monolingual dictionary, notice collocation or study vocabulary independently. To this end, the *Resource bank* in this *Teacher's Book* contains *Learner-training worksheets* to accompany each module of the *Students' Book*. These also focus on skills such as recording vocabulary and guessing meaning from context.

Grammar

LANGUAGE FOCUS SECTIONS/GRAMMAR ANALYSIS

To enable learners to use the language confidently, we also aim to provide a sound basis in grammar. Each module has two *Language focus* sections, which first contextualise and introduce the new language, then take the students step-by-step through the important rules before they practise using it. To encourage an active approach, the *Grammar analysis* boxes in each section ask students to work out some of these rules themselves, from the sample language they have seen. We aim to make this as straightforward as possible. The *Language summary* at the back of the book summarises the rules in greater detail and provides extra information and examples.

COMMUNICATIVE PRACTICE

All new language is practised actively in meaningful contexts, through personalisation and other communicative pairwork activities. Many information gap-type activities have additional material in the *Communication activities* at the back of the book. Further practice is provided via a range of photocopiable activities in the *Resource bank*, and systematic written practice in the *Workbook*.

Speaking Tasks

Many lower-level learners do not feel confident about expressing themselves in English, even though they have a growing passive knowledge. We aim to develop their confidence in communicating by setting regular speaking Tasks – one in each module of the book.

EXTENDED SPEAKING ACTIVITIES

In these tasks the focus is on an end product or outcome rather than on 'practising the language'. However, it is likely that learners will need some of the language they have encountered in the module, in order to accomplish the Task. The Tasks involve more extended communication than the practice activities, and require students to do many of the things that they may have to do in real life: ask and give personal information; tell an anecdote; discuss a plan or a problem; describe places or people.

STAGING OF TASKS

Of course, most low-level students cannot 'just do' this without support. For this reason, each Task includes a *Preparation* stage, with a model for students to follow, and a *Useful language* box that they can draw on. We encourage students to prepare what they will say before they speak, and to ask the teacher for any personal vocabulary that they may need to express themselves.

TEACHER'S NOTES

The teacher's notes provide step by step guidance through the Tasks, and suggestions for adapting them to the particular teaching situations. There is also a special *Teacher's tips* section in this book to provide more general guidelines.

Other important elements in *Cutting Edge Pre-Intermediate*

Listening

Cutting Edge Pre-Intermediate places a strong emphasis on listening. Listening material includes:
*   short extracts and mini-dialogues to introduce and practise new language.
*   longer texts (interviews, stories, songs and conversations) for more extensive listening. Sometimes these are models for tasks.
*   opportunities to check answers to exercises via listening.
*   words and sentences to model pronunciation.

In addition, the *Workbook* has an optional *Students' Cassette*, which includes:
*   extensive *Listen and read* texts.
*   pronunciation work on sounds.
*   models for new vocabulary.
*   some grammar exercises.

Reading

There is a wide range of reading material in the *Students' Book*: both short extracts to contextualise new language (often stories or quizzes); and more extensive reading texts, often in the form of newspaper articles. As well as comprehension checks, reading exercises include vocabulary work and discussion.

There are additional reading texts in alternate modules of the *Workbook* and these include simple comprehension and vocabulary work.

Writing

Writing skills are developed through:
*   regular *Writing* sections covering real-life situations such as writing postcards, filling in forms, formal and informal letters.
*   *Optional writing* sections following on from many of the Tasks – these give students an opportunity to write about what they have discussed.
*   *Improve your writing* sections in the *Workbook*, which provide further practice of the tasks in the *Students' Book* as well as work on specific sub-skills such as paragraphing, punctuation and linkers.
*   *Spelling* sections in the *Workbook*, which cover important patterns like *-ed* endings, double letters, etc.

Pronunciation

Pronunciation work in the *Students' Book* is integrated into the sections which present new language (*Grammar*, *Vocabulary* and *Real life*) and covers sentence and word stress, weak forms, intonation and a number of key difficult sounds like / ʒ: / or / ə /. The *Workbook* focuses on problem sounds, often in relation to spelling.

Pronunciation work is presented in *Pronunciation* boxes so as to stand out clearly. A range of activity types is used and there is an equal emphasis on understanding and reproducing the language. Pronunciation sections in both the *Students' Book* and the *Workbook* are accompanied by exercises on the cassette, which provide models for students to copy.

This *Teachers' Book* includes a *Teacher's tips* section on *Helping students* with pronunciation.

Revision

Cutting Edge Pre-Intermediate places a strong emphasis on revision. The *Students' Book* revises and recycles language in the following ways:
*   a *Do you remember?* quiz at the end of thirteen modules provides quick spot-check revision of the main areas covered in the module.
*   a *Consolidation* unit at the end of Modules 6, 11 and 16 combines grammar and vocabulary exercises with listening and speaking activities which recycle material from the previous five (or six) modules.
*   three photocopiable tests in the *Resource bank* for use after Modules 6, 11 and 16.
*   constant opportunities for learners to re-use what they have learnt in the *Task* sections of each module.

We hope that you and your students will enjoy using *Cutting Edge Pre-Intermediate*.

Teacher's tips

Making speaking Tasks work

❶ Treat Tasks primarily as an opportunity for communication

Remember the main objective is for students to use the language that they know (and if necessary learn new language) in order to achieve a particular communicative goal, not to 'practise' specific language. Although it is virtually impossible to perform some of the Tasks without using the language introduced earlier in the module, in others students may choose to use this language only once or twice, or not at all. Do not try to 'force-feed' it. Of course, if learners are seeking this language but have forgotten it, this is the ideal moment to remind them!

❷ Make the Task suit your class

Students using this course will vary in age, background, interests and ability. All these students need to find the Tasks motivating and 'do-able', yet challenging at the same time. Do not be afraid to adapt the Tasks to suit your class if this helps. The teacher's notes contain suggestions on how to adapt certain tasks for monolingual and multilingual groups, students of different ages and interests, large classes, and weaker or stronger groups. There are also ideas for shortening Tasks, or dividing them over two shorter lessons. We hope these suggestions will give you other ideas of your own on how to adapt the Tasks.

❸ Personalise it!

All the Tasks in *Cutting Edge Pre-Intermediate* have a model to introduce them. Sometimes these are recordings of people talking about something personal, for example the first time they did something important. However, finding out about you, their teacher may be more motivating, so you could try providing a personalised model instead. If you do this, remember to:
- plan what you are going to say, but do not write it out word for word, as this may sound unnatural.
- bring in any photos or illustrations you can to help to bring your talk alive.
- either pre-teach or explain as you go along any problematic vocabulary.
- give students something to do as they are listening (the teacher's notes give suggestions on this where appropriate).

This approach may take a little courage at first, but students are likely to appreciate the variety it provides.

❹ Set the final objective clearly before students start preparing

Do not assume that students will work out where their preparations are leading if you do not tell them! Knowing, for example, that their film review will be recorded for a class radio programme may make a big difference to how carefully they prepare it.

❺ Pay attention to seating arrangements

Whether you have fixed desks or more portable furniture, when working in groups or pairs always make sure that students are sitting so that they can hear and speak to each other comfortably. Groups should be in a small circle or square rather than a line, for example. Empty desks between students may mean that they have to raise their voices to a level at which they feel self-conscious when speaking English – this can have an adverse effect on any pairwork or groupwork activity.

❻ Give students time to think and plan

Planning time is very important if low-level students are to produce the best language that they are capable of. It is particularly useful for building up the confidence of students who are normally reluctant to speak in class. The amount of time needed will vary from Task to Task, but normally about five to ten minutes.

This planning time will sometimes mean a period of silence in class, something that teachers used to noisy, communicative classrooms can find unnerving. Remember that just because you cannot hear anything, it does not mean that nothing is happening!

It may help to relieve any feelings of tension at this stage by playing some background music, or, if practical in your school, suggest that students go somewhere else to prepare – another classroom if one is available.

Students may well find the idea of 'time to plan' strange at first, but, as with many other teaching and learning techniques, it is very much a question of training.

❼ Provide students with the language they need

As students are preparing, it is important that you make it clear that they can ask you about language queries, so that when they perform the Task they are able to say what they personally want to say.

USEFUL LANGUAGE BOXES

Each Task is accompanied by a *Useful language* box containing phrases which can be adapted by individual students to express different ideas and opinions, rather than anything very specific. Sometimes the *Useful language* boxes include structures which have not yet been covered in the grammar syllabus. However, the examples used can be taught simply as phrases – it is not intended that you should launch into major grammatical presentations here!

The phrases in the *Useful language* boxes can be dealt with at different points in the lesson:

* before students start the *Preparation for the Task*.
* during the preparation phase on an individual basis.
* after the Task in the feedback stage.

(*See Teacher's tips: responding to learners' individual language needs, number 9 on page 9.*)

❽ Give students an opportunity to 'rehearse'

This will not be necessary for the simpler Tasks, but for more complicated Tasks, or with less confident students, it can make a big difference. It will help fluency, encourage students to be more ambitious with their language, and possibly iron out some of their errors. This rehearsal stage can take various forms:

* students tell their story, etc. in pairs before telling it in groups or to the whole class.
* students discuss issues in groups before discussing them as a class.
* students go over what they are going to say 'silently' in their heads (either during the lesson, or at home if the Task is split over two lessons).

❾ Insist that students do the task in English!

It may not be realistic to prevent students from using their own language completely, but they should understand that during the performance of the Task (if not in the planning stage, where they may need their mother tongue to ask for new language) they <u>must</u> use English. At the beginning of the course, it may be useful to discuss the importance of this, and the best ways of implementing it. Students will be more tempted to use their own language if they find the Task daunting, so do not be afraid to shorten or simplify Tasks if necessary. However, planning and rehearsal time will make students less inclined to use their first language.

❿ Let the students do the talking

If students are hesitant, it is easy (with the best of intentions!) to intervene and speak for them. Some students will be only too happy to let you do this, and before long they won't even attempt to formulate full sentences, knowing that you will usually do it for them. Don't worry if they have to think for a little while before they can string

their words together, they will get better at this eventually, but only if they get the opportunity to practise!

⓫ Give your feedback at the end ... and make it positive!

Students of this level are bound to make a lot of errors in any kind of extended communication, and you may feel that you need to deal with these. It is usually best not to interrupt however, but to make a note of any important points to deal with at the end. Keep these brief though, and remember that at low levels any kind of extended speaking is a considerable challenge. Keep the emphasis on praise and positive feedback, and hopefully your students will be eager to do this kind of speaking task again!

(*See Teacher's tips: responding to learners' individual language needs* on pages 8–9)

Responding to learners' individual language needs

❶ Encourage students to ask about language

Students who take an active approach to their own learning are far more likely to succeed than those who sit back and expect the teacher to do it all for them. Make students aware of this, and convey to them your willingness to deal with their queries. Circulate during pair and individual work, making it clear that you are available to answer questions. Even if you cannot answer a query on the spot, let students know that you are happy to deal with it.

❷ Be responsive, but do not get side-tracked

One danger of this approach is that a teacher may get side-tracked by dominant students who want all their attention, leading to frustration and irritation among others. If you feel that this is happening, tell these students that you will answer their questions later, and move quickly on. Make sure that you keep moving round during pair/group/individual work. Keep a 'bird's-eye' view of the class, moving in to help students if they need it rather than spending too much time with one pair/group/individual.

❸ Encourage students to use what they already know

There is also a danger that students will become over-dependent on you, perhaps asking you to translate large chunks for them, which they are very unlikely to retain. Always encourage students to use what they know first, only asking you if they really have no idea.

❹ Have strategies for dealing with questions you cannot answer

Have at least one bilingual dictionary in the classroom (especially for specialised/technical vocabulary) for students to refer to, although you may still need to check that they have found the right translation. If students ask for idioms and expressions, make sure you keep it simple – in most cases you will be able to come up with an adequate phrase even if it is not precisely the phrase the student wanted. Finally, if all else fails, promise to find out for the next lesson!

❺ Note down important language points to be dealt with later

Note down any important language points that come up during Tasks and discussions and build in slots to go over these later on. Write the errors onto the board or OHT, and invite students to correct them/think of a better word, etc. Remember that it is also motivating (and can be just as instructive) to include examples of good language used as well as errors. Feedback slots can either be at the end of the lesson, or, if time is a problem, at the beginning of the next.

❻ Select points for these correction slots carefully

Students are more likely to retain a few well-chosen points in these correction slots than a long list of miscellaneous language points. The following are useful things to bear in mind:

*   *Usefulness*: many items may only be of interest to individual students – only bring up general language with the whole class.
*   *Quantity/Variety*: try to combine one or two more general points with a number of more specific/minor ones, including a mixture of grammar, vocabulary and pronunciation as far as possible.
*   *Level:* be careful not to present students with points above their level or which are too complex to deal with in a few minutes.
*   *Problems induced by students' mother tongue*: correction slots are an excellent opportunity to deal with L1 specific errors (false friends, pronunciation, etc.) not usually mentioned in general English courses.
*   *Revision:* the correction slots are a very good opportunity to increase students' knowledge of complex language covered previously, as well as to remind them of smaller language points.

❼ Don't worry if you can't think of 'creative' practice on the spot

If students encounter a genuine need for the language as they try to achieve a particular goal, it is more likely to be remembered than if it is introduced 'cold' by the teacher. In many cases, elaborate practice may be unnecessary – what is important is that you are dealing with the language at the moment it is most likely to be retained by the student. With lexis and small points of pronunciation, it may be enough to get students to repeat the word a few times and write an example on the board, highlighting problems.

❽ *Some simple 'on the spot' practice activities*

If you feel more work is needed, the box below includes some well-known activities which are relatively easy to adapt 'on the spot' (you can always provide a more substantial exercise later). A few examples should be enough for students to see how the structure is formed, and to increase awareness of it. These activities are also useful for practising phrases in the *Useful language* boxes.

> a *Choral and individual drilling*
>
> b *Questions and answers*: ask questions prompting students to use the language item in the answer. For example, to practise the phrase *famous for* ask questions such as:
> What's Monte Carlo famous for?> *It's famous for its Casinos.*
> What's Loch Ness famous for? > *It's famous for the Loch Ness Monster.*
>
> c *Forming sentences/phrases from prompts*: for example, to practise the construction *it's worth ... -ing* provide the example: *The National Gallery is worth visiting*, then give prompts like this:
> ROYAL PALACE / SEE > *The Royal Palace is worth seeing.*
> THIS DICTIONARY / BUY > *This dictionary is worth buying.*
>
> d *Combining shorter sentences/phrases*: give two short sentences and ask students to combine them with a more complex construction. For example, to practise *too ... to*:
> She's very young. She can't do this job. > *She's too young to do this job.*
> He's too old. He can't drive a car. > *He's too old to drive a car.*
>
> e *Dictate sentences for students to complete*: dictate a few incomplete sentences including the phrase or structure, which students complete themselves, then compare with other students. For example, to practise *it takes ... to,* dictate:
> *It takes about three hours to get to ... It only takes a few minutes to ... It took me ages to ...*

❾ *Using the* Useful language *boxes*

The *Useful language* boxes are intended to help students with language they need to perform the Tasks. It is important to get students to do something with the phrases in order to help students pronounce them and begin to learn them. Here are some suggestions:

- You can write the useful language on an overhead transparency. Give a definition/explanation to elicit each phrase and then uncover it.
- Give some group and individual repetition if necessary, first with students looking at the phrase and then covering it up to encourage students to remember it.
- When you have looked at all the phrases, give students a minute to try and memorise them and then turn off the OHP, and students in pairs can try to say them to each other, or to write them down.
- If the *Useful language* box has a lot of questions, you could write the answers on the board and see if students can provide the questions. Don't write the questions. Give group and individual repetition practice of each question as needed, continually going back to earlier questions to see if students can remember them. At the end, students can look at the questions in the book.
- Elicit each phrase, as above, and write them up on the board until you have all the useful language up. Then ask students in pairs to read the phrases aloud to each other, and when they finish they should start again. Meanwhile you can start rubbing off individual words from the phrases and replace them with a dash. Start with smaller words, so that you leave the main information words. Keep rubbing off more and more words until all that's left is dashes! See how much students can remember of this missing language.
- Write the phrases on cards, and cut the phrases into two e.g. *I was ten at the time*, and students in groups can try to match the two halves. They can then check the *Useful language* box and you can give group and individual practise.

Helping students with pronunciation

When people say 'you speak good English', very often they are reacting to your pronunciation – it is very important in creating a confident first impression as a speaker of a foreign language. Although most students today are learning English for communication in an international context (so the perfect reproduction of British vowels, for example is not essential), a high frequency of pronunciation errors can make students hard to understand, and listeners, whether native speakers or not, may just switch off. Setting high standards for pronunciation (even if you are not aiming for native-speaker-like production) is probably the best practical way to achieve the right kind of comprehensibility. And the ideal time to lay the right foundations for this is at low levels.

❶ Give priority to pronunciation ... but be realistic

Don't wait for a *Pronunciation* box to come along in the *Students' Book*. Integrate pronunciation work whenever students have a problem. 'Little and often' is a particularly good principle with pronunciation.

On the other hand, think about what you want to achieve: clarity and confidence are what most students need, rather than perfection in every detail. Individuals vary widely in what they can achieve, so don't push too much when a particular student is getting frustrated or embarrassed. Leave it and come back to it again another day.

A humorous, light-hearted approach also helps to alleviate stress!

❷ Drill ...

Choral and/or individual repetition is the simplest pronunciation activity to set up and possibly the most effective. It can help to build confidence, and is often popular with low-level students as long as you don't over do it (see above). There are models on the cassette that students can copy for most key language in *Cutting Edge Pre-Intermediate*.

❸ ... but make sure students can <u>hear</u> the correct pronunciation before you ask them to reproduce it

Even if students cannot yet produce the target pronunciation, it will improve their listening skills if they can at least hear it; and it goes without saying that you cannot reproduce something that you haven't heard clearly! There are various ways of doing this. At low levels it is often helpful to repeat the word or phrase two or three times

yourself, before you ask students to say it. Sometimes you need to isolate and repeat individual syllables or sounds, and exaggeration of features like stress and intonation is helpful. Or you can contrast the correct pronunciation with what the students are producing: either with the way that that word or syllable is pronounced in their own language, or with a similar sound in English.

❹ Pay particular attention to words with problematic spelling

One of the biggest problems for learners of English is the relationship between sounds and spelling. Highlight and drill problem words on a consistent basis. Think about teaching students the phonemic alphabet – this gives them a valuable tool for finding out problematic pronunciation themselves, and for recording it. You can use the list of sounds on page 4 of the *Workbook* to teach it – but only teach a few symbols at a time, and make constant use of them, otherwise students will soon forget them again.

❺ Focus on the sounds which most affect students' comprehensibility and provide practical guidance about how to produce them

Consonants (particularly at the beginning and ends of words) are probably more important than vowels here. Use any tips you know for helping students to reproduce them. You might focus them on a similar sound in their own language then help them to adapt it, or use a trick like starting with /u:/ to get students to produce the /w/ sound. Anything that works is valid here! Sometimes it is useful to contrast the problem sound with the one that students are mistakenly producing, via a 'minimal pair' (*tree* and *three*, etc.). Say the pair of words several times, then ask students to say which they can hear, before asking them to produce the words themselves.

❻ Pay attention to schwa /ə/

This is one vowel sound that you shouldn't ignore. It is by far the most common vowel sound in English, occurring in a very high percentage of multi-syllable words. Using it correctly will help students to speak faster, and will greatly increase their comprehensibility. At the beginning of the course, make sure that students can produce this sound, and focus on it whenever it occurs in new words. Be careful not to stress it accidentally though – syllables with schwa in them are not normally stressed. To avoid this, drill new words starting with the stressed syllable, then add the schwa sounds either before or afterwards, for example:

/ə/   /ə/
ten ... atten ... attention

Consistently marking schwa sounds when you write words on the board will also help:

/ə/   /ə/
attention

❼ Focus consistently on word stress ...

This is an easy area in which to correct students effectively. Get into the habit of focusing on word stress whenever you teach a new word with potential problems. If students have problems, try one of the following ideas when you drill:

*   exaggerate the stress.
*   clap, click your fingers, etc. on the stressed syllable.
*   mumble the stress pattern, before saying the word: mm-MM-mm > attention.
*   isolate the stressed syllable first then add the other syllables.

Don't forget to mark stressed syllables when you write new words on the board, by underlining or writing a blob over them, and encourage students to do the same when they write in their notebooks. Make sure that students know how word stress is marked in the *Mini-dictionary*.

❽ ... and sentence stress

Sentence stress is one of the most important elements in helping students to be easy to understand when they speak, just as punctuation makes their written work more comprehensible. Try to focus on it little and often, for example when you teach a new structure or phrase. You can use the same methods as for word stress to help students to hear and reproduce the sentence stress.

❾ Make students aware of weak forms and word linking

As students become more advanced these features will also contribute to comprehensibility and fluency, and at any level they are important for the purposes of listening. As you teach new phrases and structures, draw students' attention to weak forms and linking as appropriate, and give students the opportunity to practise them. You can use the same method as for schwa sounds if they have problems. However, do not worry too much if students do not produce these weak forms, etc. spontaneously – this is more likely to come naturally when students are more fluent. All you can do at this stage is to sow the seeds for the future.

❿ Make students aware of intonation

Intonation is a source of worry to many teachers and consequently students. Teachers worry that their students (or they themselves) cannot hear it and that whatever they do, their students don't seem to 'learn' it. In reality, there are few situations in which wrong intonation leads to serious misunderstanding. Where problems do occasionally occur is in the area of politeness, and sounding sufficiently enthusiastic (although even here, in real life many other factors – such as facial expression – can counteract 'wrong' intonation!).

In *Cutting Edge Pre-Intermediate* we focus on these limited areas for intonation work. Again the key idea is 'awareness': you probably won't 'teach' students the right intonation overnight, but by focusing on this problem you can help them to see the importance of it. They are more likely to improve their overall intonation via plenty of exposure to natural-sounding English, and this is something that will take time. If students have problems hearing and reproducing the intonation patterns that you choose to focus on, try some of the following ideas:

*   exaggerate the intonation pattern, before returning to a more normal model.
*   hum the intonation pattern before repeating the words (incidentally this is very useful for hearing intonation patterns yourself, if you have difficulty).
*   use gestures to show the intonation pattern (rather like a conductor).
*   Mark the intonation on the board using arrows.

Remember though, that if students are getting frustrated, or cannot 'get' the correct intonation, it is probably best to leave it and come back to it another time!

Working with lexical phrases

❶ Become more aware of phrases and collocations yourself

Until recently, relatively little attention was given to the thousands of phrases and collocations that make up the lexis in English, along with the traditional one-word items. If necessary, look at the list of phrase-types, and start noticing how common these 'pre-fabricated chunks' are in all types of English. They go far beyond areas traditionally dealt with in English-language courses – phrasal verbs, functional exponents and the occasional idiom, although of course they incorporate all of these.

1 **Collocations**: (common word combinations) including:
   - nouns + verbs (work long hours, have a drink)
   - adjectives + nouns (old friends, bad news)
   - adverbs + verbs (work hard, will probably)
   - verbs + prepositions/particles, including phrasal verbs (think about, grow up)
   - adjectives + prepositions (famous for, jealous of)
   - other combinations of the above (go out for a meal, get to know)
2 **fixed phrases**: such as: Never mind!, On the other hand ... , if I were you ... , Somone I know, etc.
3 **semi-fixed phrases**: (that is phrases with variations), such as: a friend of mine/hers/my brother's; both of us/them/my parents; the second/third/tenth biggest in the world, etc.
4 **whole sentences which act as phrases**: such as: How are you? He's gone home, I'll give you a hand, I agree to some extent.

Such phrases blur the boundaries between 'vocabulary' and 'grammar' – in teaching these phrases you will find that you are helping students with many problematic areas that are traditionally considered to be grammar, from the use of articles and prepositions, to the use of the passive and the Present Perfect. Many common examples of these structures are in fact fixed or semi-fixed phrases. We are not suggesting that work on chunks should entirely replace the traditional grammatical approach to such verb forms, but that it is a useful supplement.

❷ Make your students aware of phrases and collocations

Students should also know about the importance of such phrases. They may look at a phrase like leave home and assume that they know it (because the two constituent words look 'easy'), although in fact they are unable to produce the phrase for themselves when appropriate. Learner-training worksheet C on page 135 of the Resource bank aims to develop students' awareness of such collocations.

❸ Feed in phrases on a 'little but often' basis

To avoid overloading students and ensure that your lexical input is useful, teach a few phrases relating to particular activities as you go along. For example, in a grammar practice activity, instead of simple answers such as Yes, I do or No, I haven't, feed in phrases like it depends or I don't really care. The same is true of discussions about reading/listening texts and writing activities.

❹ Introduce phrases in context, but drill them as short chunks

Phrases can be difficult to understand and specific to certain situations, so it is important that they are introduced in context. However, students may retain them better if you drill just the phrase (for example, have lunch, go for a walk) rather than a full sentence with problems which might distract from the phrase itself. The drilling of such phrases can be a valuable opportunity to focus on pronunciation features such as weak forms and linking.

❺ Point out patterns in phrases

Pointing out patterns will help students to remember phrases. Many do not fit into patterns, but you can often show similar phrases with the same construction, like this:

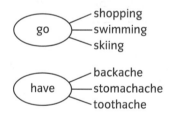

❻ Keep written records of phrases as phrases

One simple way to make your students more aware of collocation is to get into the habit of writing word combinations on the board wherever appropriate, rather than just individual words. The more students see these words together, the more likely they are to remember them as a unit. Rather than just writing up housework or degree write up do the housework or get a degree. In sentences, collocations can be highlighted in colour or underlined – this is particularly important when the associated words are not actually next to each other in the sentence. Remind students to write down the collocations too, even if they 'know' the constituent words.

❼ Reinforce and recycle the phrases as much as you can

This is particularly important with phrases which, for the reasons given above, can be hard to remember. Most revision games and activities teachers do with single items of vocabulary can be adapted and used with phrases. You may find the following useful in addition:

- **Making wall posters**: help students remember collocations by making a wall poster with a diagram like those in the *Wordspot* sections in the *Students' Book*. Seeing the phrases on the wall like this every lesson can provide valuable reinforcement. There are many other areas for which wall posters would be effective, for example common passive phrases, or common offers with *I'll* ... Always write the full phrase on the poster (*get married* not just *married*) and remove the old posters regularly as they will lose impact if there are too many.

- **A phrase bank**: copy the new words and phrases from the lesson onto slips of card or paper (large enough for students to read if you hold them up at the front of the room) and keep them in a box or bag. This is a good record for you as well as the students of the phrases that you have studied – you can get them out whenever there are a few spare moments at the beginning or end of a lesson for some quick revision. Hold them up and, as appropriate, get students to give you:

  - an explanation of the phrase
  - a translation of the phrase
  - synonyms
  - opposites
  - the pronunciation
  - situations where they might say this
  - a sentence including the phrase
  - the missing word that you are holding your hand over (for example, *on* in the phrase *get on well with*)
  - the phrase itself, based on a definition or translation that you have given them.

Making the most of the *Mini-dictionary*

❶ Build up students' confidence with monolingual dictionaries

Some students may never have used a monolingual dictionary before. *Cutting Edge Pre-Intermediate Mini-dictionary* is designed to help students make the transition from bilingual to monolingual dictionaries. The explanations are graded to pre-intermediate level, and the dictionary focuses on the meanings of words as they are used in the *Students' Book*, so students should have little difficulty in finding the information they are looking for. (See the introduction to the *Mini-dictionary* for a detailed explanation of which words and phrases have been included.) If students lack confidence, the following ideas may help:

- discuss with them the value of using a monolingual dictionary. Point out that they will avoid misleading translations, that it may help them to 'think in English', and that they will be increasing their exposure to English.
- look up words together at first, reading out and discussing the explanations as a class. Use the *Mini-dictionary* 'little and often' for limited but varied tasks (for example, for finding the word stress or dependent preposition of a new item of vocabulary).
- encourage students to use the *Mini-dictionary* in pairs and groups as well as individually so that they can help each other to understand the explanations and examples. Circulate, making sure that they understand definitions.

❷ Explain the different features of the *Mini-dictionary*

Many students do not realise how much information they can find in a dictionary, so point out all the features given, such as parts of speech, phonemic script, irregular verb forms, etc. *Learner-training worksheet* A, B, E, I and K in the *Resource bank* introduce students to these areas.

❸ Discourage over-use of the *Mini-dictionary*

There are many other important strategies for improving vocabulary as well as dictionary skills, such as guessing meaning from context, sharing information with other students and listening to the teacher. Encourage your students to use a balance of approaches.

Discourage over-use of the *Mini-dictionary* during reading activities, by focusing students' attention initially on 'key' words in the text, rather than 'anything they don't understand'. If students are really keen to look up other words, you can allow time for this at the end.

❹ Vary your approach

If you always use the *Mini-dictionary* in the same way, students may get tired of it before long. Try using the *Mini-dictionary* in the following ways instead for a change:

a **Matching words to definitions on a handout**: make a worksheet with the new words in column A and their definitions from the *Mini-dictionary* mixed up in column B. Students match the words with the definitions.

b **Matching words to definitions on cards**: the same idea can be used giving each group two small sets of cards with definitions and words to match.

c **I know it / I can guess it / I need to check it**: write the list of new words on the board, and tell students to copy it down marking the words ✔✔ if they already know it, ✔ if they can guess what it means (either from context, or because it is similar in their own language) and **?** if they need to look it up. They then compare answers in pairs to see if they can help each other, before looking up any words that neither of them know.

d **Look up the five words you <u>most</u> need to know**: instead of pre-teaching the vocabulary in a reading text, set the first (gist-type) comprehension activity straightaway, instructing students not to refer to their *Mini-dictionary* at this point. Check answers or establish that students cannot answer without some work on vocabulary. Tell them that they are only allowed to look up five words from the text – they have to choose the five that are most important to understanding the text. Demonstrate the difference between a 'key' unknown word in the text and one that can easily be ignored. Put students in pairs to select their five words, emphasising that they must not start using their *Mini-dictionary* until they have completed their list of five. After they have finished, compare the lists of words that different pairs chose and discuss how important they are to the text, before continuing with more detailed comprehension work.

e **True / False statements based on information in the Mini-dictionary**: write a list of statements about the target words on the board, then ask students to look them up to see if they are true or false, for example:
The phrase ... is very informal – true or false?
The phrase means ... – true or false?

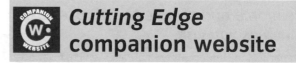

Cutting Edge companion website

Cutting Edge has its own dedicated website, with a wide variety of resources for you and your students, to complement each level of the course. The site is updated regularly, taking into account your comments and suggestions. Help make *www.longman-elt.com/cutting edge* your site by exchanging ideas and opinions with other *Cutting Edge* users, and with the authors and publishers.
For teachers:
• Resources to download and use in class
• Teaching tips
• Language and Culture
• Perfect Partners (recommended Penguin Readers)
• Discussion forum and ideas share
For students:
• Interactive activities with instant feedback
• Links, unit by unit, to supplement the course
• Language and Culture
• Perfect Partners
• Opportunities for real communication
In addition to general *Cutting Edge* resources, there are specific web materials for each module. Here is a sample of web resources for *Cutting Edge Pre-Intermediate*:
Module 1: Start the course with the *Cutting Edge Pre-Intermediate* online quiz.
Module 2: Explore the links on the website, which take you to the vast resources of words to songs on the Internet.
Module 3: Go to the Resources section for extra material to help your students with error correction.
Module 4: Find out more about festivals around the world by using the selected links to sites of interest.
Module 5: Let your students compare their favourite famous people online.
Module 6: Encourage your students to send a *Cutting Edge* card to their friends.
Module 7: Opportunities to talk to the stars on the Internet.
Module 8: Go to the Resources section to compare different views from around the world.
Module 9: Practise the language of shopping online.
Module 10: Students can tap into the Internet's vast resources to find out what their dreams mean.
Module 11: Go to the Perfect Partners section and see this term's selection of Penguin Readers.
Module 12: See all the latest fashions online.
Module 13: Which is the job for you? Take your students to the Companion Website to find out their ideal career.
Module 14: Take your students on a virtual magical mystery tour with these fascinating links.
Module 15: Use these online resources with your students, and see how much money they can make!
Module 16: Finish the course with these online games.

module 1

Vocabulary and speaking (PAGE 6)

Leisure activities

See *Teacher's tips: working with lexical phrases* on pages 12–13.

1 **a)** Focus students on the pictures, then on the words/phrases in the box. Students work individually or in pairs to match the pictures to the correct words from the box. Check answers with the class.

Introduce students to the *Mini-dictionary* here, showing them how to find one or two of the words and pointing out how the stress is marked in the dictionary entries.

> **ANSWERS**
> **The activities shown in the pictures are:**
> playing the guitar, entertaining friends, surfing the Internet, going shopping.

Check the meaning of the other words/phrases in the box. Practise the new words/phrases by repetition drilling, marking the stressed syllables on the board. Pronunciation to check: *sunbathing* /ˈsʌnbeɪðɪŋ/, *guitar* /ɡɪˈtɑː/, *entertaining* /ˌentəˈteɪnɪŋ/, *surfing* /ˈsɜːfɪŋ/.

b) Before you start this activity, point out that the *-ing* form is used for the names of activities, but students should use the Present Simple to say what activities they do and when. Focus students on the example and highlight the use of *a lot* and *never* for expressing frequency. Include *sometimes* and *often* if your students are familiar with these adverbs. Put students in pairs or small groups for the discussion.

2 Words to check: *survey, fit, healthy*. Students work individually before discussing answers in pairs and with the class.

> **ANSWERS**
> The answers depend on students' age/criteria. The only statement which is **not** true from the survey is the second one.

3 **a)** *If you have a mono-nationality class*: encourage students to prepare different lists in groups, for example for all ages, for older people, for young people, for people who live in cities, for people who live in the country, etc.

If you have a multi-nationality class: encourage students of the same nationality to work together. Circulate. Answer vocabulary questions and check that students are using the *-ing* form correctly.

b) Either regroup students so that each student in the new group has a different list, or ask one student from each group to present their list to the class.

4 **a)** Show students how useful word locusts are for recording word combinations (collocations) particularly because they can add new collocations at a later date. Students complete the diagrams in pairs or groups before checking with the class.

> **ANSWERS**
> - *going to*: a restaurant
> - *going for a*: drink, drive, walk
> - *going + -ing*: dancing, shopping
> - *playing*: computer games, the guitar, football
> - *watching*: television
> - *listening to*: the radio, cassettes/CDs

b) Do an example with the class first, for example *going to the cinema*. Give students a minute or two individually or in pairs to think of ideas, then discuss answers with the class.

> **POSSIBLE ANSWERS**
> - *going to* the cinema, theatre, beach
> - *going for a* ride
> - *going* swimming, riding, sailing
> - *playing* the piano (and other instruments)
> - *playing* cards, tennis (and other games and sports)
> - *watching* a film, a football match
> - *listening to* music, a concert

c) Start with one of the ideas from the Additional suggestions box below as an example. Give students a minute or two to think of ideas of their own. If they are having difficulty, explain/demonstrate one or two more.

> **Exercise 4c: additional suggestions**
>
> Ideas for remembering word combinations.
> - *Correct your partner*. Students close their books. Read out the word combinations randomly, sometimes correctly, sometimes incorrectly (*going to gym, listening the radio, playing the cards*). Students shout out the correct answer when you make a mistake. Students then continue the activity in pairs or small groups.
> - Students think of a typical week and, as quickly as they can, write down all the activities that they do. In pairs, they read out their lists and compare answers.
> - Students test each other in pairs. For example one student says *going to the*. The other student answers *going to the gym*.
> - Students choose one set of word combinations to learn every day. They could keep them on a piece of paper in their pocket/bag, to look back at and check.

- Students make a poster of the word combinations for the classroom wall or for their room at home. They look at the poster to remind themselves of the combinations, and add new ones as they find them.

ADDITIONAL PRACTICE

Workbook: Vocabulary booster: sports, page 9; Vocabulary (Phrases with *go* and *play*), page 9

RB **Resource bank:** 1A *Get to know the Students' Book*, page 118; *Learner-training worksheet A* (Using the *Mini-dictionary*: introduction), page 119.

Reading (PAGE 8)

1 Students discuss their ideas as a class or in pairs.

2 Words to check: *national passion.*
Encourage students to match the pictures to the three parts of the article as quickly as possible. Set a time limit of one minute.

ANSWERS
1 Surfing capital of the world: c
2 The music of the people: a
3 A day in the *banya*: b

3 Students work individually to complete the table. Compare answers in pairs before checking with the class.

ANSWERS

	When?	Who?	Why?
surfing	any sunny day	young people	it's their passion, the national passion
samba	on Saturday night and at Carnival	everybody	because it's fun, and a good way to meet people
the *banya*	any time of day	everybody	to relax, to talk to people

4 Personalise this by telling the class **your** answers to these questions first. Then put the students in pairs or groups to discuss their answers.

Exercise 4: additional suggestion

Students write a paragraph about the most typical leisure activities of their country. Refer them back to the paragraphs in the text as models. Suggest that they brainstorm ideas for their writing by answering the following questions: *What exactly is the activity? Where do people go to do it? When do they do it? What kind of people do it? Why do they like it?* Students then show their ideas to a partner for comments, before they write the paragraph.

Language focus 1 (PAGE 9)
Question forms

1 Check students understand the difference between a sport and a game. Put them in pairs or groups to discuss the questions.

2 Focus students on the pictures and pre-teach: *a race, a dice, a racket, a referee, toss a coin, a draw.* Put students in groups to do the quiz and set a time limit of five minutes.

Give three points to any group which has answered all the questions after five minutes. Then give one point for each correct answer (see Exercise 3).

3 [1.1] Ask a spokesperson from each group to give the answer to each question before you play the recording. Stop the recording before the next answer and repeat the procedure.

ANSWERS
See tapescript Module 1, recording 1 on page 158 of the *Students' Book.*

Grammar analysis

Wh- questions

1 Students work individually or in pairs. As you check answers, highlight the difference between *what* and *which: what* = many possible answers, *which* = only a few possible answers.

ANSWERS
a a person *Who* **b** a place *Where*
c a thing *What* or *Which* **d** a time *When*
e the reason for something *Why*
f the way you do something *How*

2 As you check the answers, elicit some other examples of compound question words, to show students how common they are, for example *How much...? What time...? Which day...?*

ANSWERS
e How long f What kind g which country
h How many j which sports

Word order in questions

Point out that:

* in questions where the subject is known, the verb *be* and other auxiliary verbs go before the subject.

* the subject can be a phrase like *the Barcelona Olympics* or a pronoun like *they*.

ANSWERS

	Question words	verb/ auxiliary	subject (+ main verb)
d	Where	does	the sport of judo come from?
e	How long	does	an ice hockey match last?
f	What kind of ball	do	they use in the game of rugby?

If you wish, point out that the question word can also be the subject. Highlight the fact that, in this case, the word order is the same as in a statement.

The white player (subject) starts (verb) in a game of chess.

Who (subject) starts (verb) in a game of chess?

Tell students to look at the *Language summary A/B* on page 149 of the *Students' Book* for more information.

PRACTICE

1 📼 [1.2] Before starting this activity, you may wish to highlight/model the structure *It takes (me)* . . .

Students work in pairs or groups on the matching activity. It could be done as a race. Emphasise that the questions come in a different order on the recording. Students may need to listen more than once to get all the answers.

ANSWERS
a 1 On Sunday mornings.
  2 Some people from college.
  3 In the local park.
  4 It's fun, and it's good exercise.
b 1 Twice a week.
  2 Two hours.
  3 Tuesdays and Thursdays.
  4 Two.
c 1 Nearly half past three.
  2 Monday.
  3 The sixteenth, I think.
  4 About ten pounds.

Pronunciation

See *Teacher's tips: helping students with pronunciation* on pages 10–11.

📼 [1.3] Show students how the main stress falls on the words carrying information, for example *long, lessons, who, play* and that the auxiliary verbs are squashed in between them. Do this by drilling the information words first, then adding the auxiliary.

long … lessons? > How long are the lessons?

Who … play? > Who do you play with?

Play the recording. Stop after each question for students to repeat. Help students to hear the rhythm by clapping/tapping on the stressed syllables.

ANSWERS
See tapescript, Module 1, recording 3 on page 158 of the *Students' Book.*

If your students need more pronunciation practice at this point, ask them to choose five questions from Exercise 1 to ask a partner, paying attention to their pronunciation.

2 Demonstrate using the example. Get a student to ask you the question and answer about yourself. Then ask students if they need to change the first statement. Put students in pairs or groups to prepare their questions. Circulate and monitor their use of question words.

Get a student from each pair to ask you a question in turn. Give students time in their pairs to change the statements as necessary. Check with the class.

If you prefer, students can prepare their questions to ask a student from another pair. When the questions are ready, they swap partners.

ADDITIONAL PRACTICE

Workbook: Question forms, pages 5–6

RB **Resource bank:** 1B *Me too!* (Present Simple and question words), page 120

Language focus 2 (PAGE 10)

Present Simple

1 Discuss briefly what students know about the lifestyles of the people who do the sports in the pictures. Words to check: *weigh, earn.*

2 📼 [1.4] Emphasise that students don't need to understand everything they hear. They need to pick out the relevant pieces of information. Students discuss the final question in pairs, or as a class.

ANSWERS
Toshi: a, e, g, i, k
Ania: b, d, f, h
Dan: c, j

Grammar analysis

Present Simple

1 To check students understand the meaning of the Present Simple, write up some more examples from Exercise 1 on the board, for example *lives in a small apartment, enjoys her lifestyle.* Ask students which things are habits and which are generally true.

2 Elicit the question and negative forms of the examples and write them on the board. Alternatively, to save time, refer students to the *Language summary* on page 149 of the *Students' Book.* Highlight:

- the *-s* on the third person in the positive form.
- the use of *do/does* in negative and question forms, with the main verb remaining in the infinitive without *to.*
- the contractions *don't* and *doesn't.*
- the short answer forms:
  Yes, I/you/we/they do. No, I/you/we/they don't.
  Yes, he/she does. No, he/she doesn't.

How often?

1 Do an example first, then give students time individually or in pairs to think of more words. Emphasise the position of these phrases: they cannot go between the subject and the verb ~~We every day go swimming~~. Note that these phrases are more emphatic if placed at the beginning of a sentence.

> **POSSIBLE ANSWERS**
> **every** week, day, year, morning, afternoon, evening, night
> **on** Mondays (and all other days of the week)
> once **a** day, month, year
> twice **a** month
> three times **a** year

2 Write the adverbs in the correct order on the board (*always, usually, often, sometimes, occasionally, never*). Ask students for some more example sentences with *often, sometimes, occasionally, always.* Show them that these adverbs are often used in combination with other time phrases, for example *I usually go shopping on Saturdays.* Practise the pronunciation of *usually* /ˈjuːʒuəli/ and *occasionally* /əˈkeɪʒənli/ with a repetition drill.

PRACTICE

1 The focus here is on word order. Students work individually then check answers with the whole class.

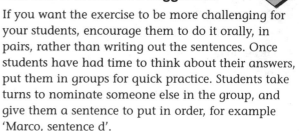

Exercise 1: alternative suggestion
If you want the exercise to be more challenging for your students, encourage them to do it orally, in pairs, rather than writing out the sentences. Once students have had time to think about their answers, put them in groups for quick practice. Students take turns to nominate someone else in the group, and give them a sentence to put in order, for example 'Marco, sentence d'.

ANSWERS
a All of them train for many hours every day.
b Ania and Toshi don't earn much money.
c Ania usually gets up at 7.00.
d She never goes to bed before midnight.
e Toshi lives in a special training camp called a *heya.*
f He often sleeps on the floor.
g He receives lots of fan letters every week.
h Dan doesn't play in every match.
i He owns two sports cars.
j He misses his family in Romania.
k He phones his mother about four times a week.

2 **a)** Before you start this activity, do a couple of examples on the board, reminding students that *do you?* is used with a verb, and *are you?* is used with an adjective. Put students in groups. Refer Group A to page 139 and Group B to page 145 in the *Students' Book.* Circulate and help with vocabulary as students discuss and complete the questions. Words to check: *get up/get ready, be healthy/be unfit, wake up/be awake, be sleepy/be energetic.*

b) Pair up A and B students. Ask a stronger pair to demonstrate an example. When students have finished, ask two or three students to tell the class briefly how energetic or healthy their partner is.

Exercise 2: alternative suggestion
For strong classes, give each group the title (for example *How healthy are you?*) and one example question only. Ask them to invent five more. You could also give prompts like *drink/sleep/smoke* and *How many ...? How often ...?*

ADDITIONAL PRACTICE

Workbook: Present Simple, page 7; Frequency, page 8
RB **Resource bank:** 1C *Connected lives* (Present Simple questions with *'How often ... ?'* and adverbs of frequency), page 121

Compile a fact file about your partner

See *Teacher's tips: making speaking Tasks work* on pages 6–7 and *responding to learners' individual language needs* on pages 8–9.

Preparation for task (PAGE 12)

1 Focus students on the pictures. Either discuss the question as a class or put students in pairs to discuss. Elicit ideas about Zoe's life. For example *she's very busy, she meets lots of people, she has an interesting life.* Ask if any students use the Internet to find out about people they like, and elicit *website.*

2 Give students two minutes to read the website to see if their ideas were correct. Encourage them to mark anything interesting/unusual. Ask students to close their books and work in pairs to remember as much as they can about Zoe. Words to check: *a typical day, shopaholic.*

> **Preparation for task: alternative suggestions**
>
> a *If you have access to the Internet:* print a selection of fact files from websites about people that your students will be interested in. Put students in groups and give each group copies of a different fact file to read and remember as much as they can. Then students mingle, telling each other about the person. Students can use these fact files to prepare their questions for Exercise 3.
>
> b *If enough of your students have access to the Internet:* ask them to bring in some fact files from websites about people they like. Distribute the fact files so that there is one between two, and give each pair a few minutes to read and discuss their fact file. Students then mingle and tell each other about their fact file.

3 Focus students on the *Useful language* box and do a couple more examples with the class. Put students in pairs to work on the questions and remind them to write them down, as they will need to refer to them later. Circulate and help with question formation. Make a note of any questions that are causing problems. Go over these with the class when students have finished.

Task (PAGE 13)

1 Make sure students understand that they are going to interview someone they don't know well in the class. Get them to decide at this point who it will be, to avoid

confusion later. Elicit or give ideas for other topics, for example *favourite school subject, 'pet' hates, favourite TV programme/sport/book/magazine/newspaper, best friend.*
a)–b) Allow at least ten minutes for students to work individually on their questions and answers. They should spend some time thinking about their answers, and ask you for personal vocabulary.
If some students are ready before others, help them individually with the intonation of their questions, for example the importance of sounding interested.

2 **a)** Put students in pairs to interview each other and complete the fact file. As they do this, circulate and note down errors/useful language for analysis and correction later. Concentrate on the use of question forms and the Present Simple.

b) *Either*: put students in groups of 4–8 to tell each other about their partner. *Or*: with smaller groups, ask one student from each pair to report back. After this feedback, write on the board examples of language students used well and/or errors. Ask students in pairs to note the examples of good language use and/or correct the errors. Go through the answers with the class.

> **Task: alternative suggestions**
>
> a *If you want to provide more language input before the task:* do the Real life section before students start preparing their questions and answers.
>
> b *If you are short of time:* ask students to read the fact file for homework and come to class prepared to tell a partner what they can remember about it.
>
> c *If your students already know each other well:*
>
> - students pretend to be someone else in the class and answer all the questions as if they are that person. Their partner guesses at the end who they are.
>
> - students answer the questions as if they are ten or twenty years older.
>
> - an English-speaking visitor comes to the class (the director of studies, another teacher) and students interview him/her.
>
> - students interview other English-speaking staff in the school. Students could prepare a magazine about the school.
>
> - students interview people in another class, with roughly the same level of English. This could lead to other joint activities between the classes, for example writing and replying to letters, presentations of tasks, more interviews.

Optional writing

Students make any corrections to the fact file they completed during the Task. The fact files can be displayed on the wall, or put together in a class magazine. If your school has contacts with a school in another country, you could use the fact files as introductions for a penpal system. Alternatively, you could start a website for the class with the fact files. For more ideas see the *Cutting Edge* website: www.longman-elt.com/cuttingedge

Real life (PAGE 13)

Questions you can't live without

1 Discuss with the class who/where the people are in the pictures. Put students in pairs to allocate questions to pictures. Emphasise that there will be more than one question for each picture, and that students should decide which they would actually ask, and which they would hear.

POSSIBLE ANSWERS
a What time is it? Where's the nearest (bank)? Do you speak English?
b Where are you from? What's your date of birth? How long are you going to stay? How do you spell ... ?
c Anything else? Can we have the bill, please? Where are the toilets, please?
d How do you spell ...? Sorry, could you repeat that, please?
e Can I help you? How much does this cost?
f Where are you from? Which part of (Poland) are you from?

2 a) [1.5] Students listen and write the letter for the appropriate situation.

ANSWERS
1 c (In a restaurant.)   2 a (In the street.)
3 e (In a shop.)

b) Play the recording for students to tick the questions. Students compare answers as a class.

ANSWERS
1 Can I help you, (madam)? Where are the toilets, please? Can we have the bill, please?
2 Do you speak English? Where's the nearest (underground station)? Where are you from? And how long are you going to stay?
3 How much does this cost? Anything else?

Pronunciation

See *Teacher's tips: helping students with pronunciation* on pages 10–11.

Although *wh-* questions do not **always** go down at the end, this is a useful general rule for students. They can sound surprised or disbelieving if their voice goes up.

1 [1.6] Play the first three or four examples for students to listen to. Then play the recording, pausing after each question for them to copy the intonation. If they have trouble hearing the falling intonation, get them to add a person's name to the end of the question, for example *Where are you from, Doctor Jones?* This will help them to hear the voice falling after the final stress, (*from* in this case).

ANSWERS
See tapescript Module 1, recording 6 on page 158 of the *Students' Book*.

2 Put students in pairs to practise. Encourage students to: read a line, look up, speak. This will help stop them stumbling over the words and encourage natural rhythm.

3 Give students five to ten minutes to plan and practise their conversations. Encourage them to give an unexpected twist, for example the customer in the bank gives very strange answers, the people on the plane realise they are related. Choose one or two pairs who have done well to act out their conversation.

Do you remember? (PAGE 14)

ANSWERS
2 a) Who b) What c) How long
   d) When e) What
3 a) What is the national sport of your country?
   b) How do you spell your surname?
   c) How many teachers are there in your school?
   d) Who starts and stops a football match?
   e) What time does your English class start?
   f) What sort of music do you listen to?
4 a) Demi Moore receives a lot of fan letters.
   b) I don't **always get up** late at the weekends.
   c) correct
   d) She **writes** to her grandparents **every week**.
      OR **Every week she writes** to her grandparents.
   e) My boyfriend doesn't **earn** much money.
5 b) Who is **on** a diet ... – Toshi
   c) Who goes **for** a run ... – Dan
   d) ... money **from** his parents ... – Toshi
   e) Who lives **with** her ... – Ania

Language focus 1 (PAGE 15)

Past Simple

1 Before you start the activity, check students know the film genres listed. Give students names of some well-known films and ask them which genre each one belongs to. Put students in pairs or groups to discuss the questions. After the discussion, ask one or two people to report back on any interesting points.

2 Check students understand *feature film* (a full-length film that tells a story). Ask for one or two examples. To stop students looking at the text while guessing the answers, write the questions on the board or on an overhead projector transparency, or get students to cover the text with a notebook.

3 Give students a time limit to check their answers, to prevent them from completing the gaps at this stage.

ANSWERS
a 1906   **b** Australia   **c** a gangster film

4 Words to check: *stole, robbed, wore, armour, disappeared, scene, close-up, success, box office.* This text is challenging in terms of vocabulary. Pre-teach the unfamiliar words yourself, or get students to use the *Mini-dictionary*. (See *Teacher's tips: making the most of the Mini-dictionary* on page 14.) Encourage students to read through the whole text to get the gist of it, before they attempt to complete the gaps. Check comprehension with the following questions: *How much did the film cost/make? How many actors played Kelly?* Students then complete the gaps individually or in pairs.

5 🔊 [2.1] Play the recording through once and encourage students to listen for as much information as they can the first time. Then play the recording again, pausing as necessary for students to check/change answers.

ANSWERS

2 told	10 cost
3 stole	11 played
4 robbed	12 didn't think
5 wore	13 disappeared
6 were	14 had to
7 became	15 could
8 hated	16 opened
9 lasted	17 was

Grammar analysis

To clarify the use of the Past Simple before looking at the form, use the following examples from the text: ***made** the first feature film ... in 1906* (= single finished action); ***stole** horses and cattle* (= repeated action); *people ... **hated** the government at that time* (= state).

If this is revision for your class, students can work on questions 1, 2 and 3 in pairs.

1 As you elicit the answers, focus on the spelling of *hated* and *robbed*. Encourage students to tell you the rules/give you more examples. Refer them to the spelling rules in the *Language summary* on page 150 of the *Students' Book* if they are not sure.

ANSWERS
Regular verbs add *-ed* to form the Past Simple.
Examples from Exercise 4: disappeared, hated, robbed, lasted, played, opened.

2 As you check the answers, refer students to the irregular verbs list on page 148 of the *Students' Book*. Emphasise that the verb forms simply have to be learnt. Ask if students have ideas for how best to learn the verbs and/or suggest some ideas such as:

● choose ten verbs to learn every week.

● at the end of every day remember all the 'irregular' things you did, for example ***went** to work, **bought** a book, **had** coffee with ...*

ANSWERS
made – make   told – tell   stole – steal   wore – wear
were – be   cost – cost   had to – have to/must
could – can   was – be

3 Elicit a table for the negative and question forms of the verbs onto the board. Alternatively, students check by referring to the table in the *Language summary* on page 150 of the *Students' Book*. Highlight:

● the use of *did* for all persons (not with *be*).

● the fact that the main verb remains in the infinitive without *to*.

● the contraction *didn't*.

● the inversion for the question form of *be,* and the formation of the negative *was/were not.*

If necessary, explain that *could* operates like *was/were* and *had to* operates like a normal verb using *did ... have to.*

ADDITIONAL PRACTICE

RB **Resource bank:** *Learner-training worksheet B*, page 123

PRACTICE

1 Before you start the activity, check these words using the pictures in the quiz: *degree, vending machine, space.* Give students a few minutes to discuss their answers in pairs or groups. Then refer them to page 139 in the *Students' Book.*

2 **a)** Put students into pairs or groups, A and B. Refer A to page 139 and B to page 143 in the *Students' Book.*

b) Do an example of your own with the class first. For example write *When/first underground system/open?* on the board and elicit the full question. Give students at least five minutes to work on the form of the questions and answers, either individually or in their groups. Circulate and help with any problems.

c) Before students ask and answer their questions, help them with pronunciation. Drill one or two examples, demonstrating how to sound interested by using a higher pitch at the beginning of the question. Set up a scoring system. If a student answers a question correctly, they get three points. If they answer wrongly, their partner gets two points. Give them plenty of time to ask all their questions. Feed back briefly on which answers were surprising/which nobody knew, etc. and who got most points.

Pronunciation

1 Give students a few minutes to check the infinitives and meaning of the verbs. Either explain unfamiliar verbs yourself or ask students to look in the mini-dictionary. Check students understand *rhyme* and demonstrate using the first pair of verbs. Point out that words which have similar spellings are not always pronounced the same, for example *know* and *now.* Students work individually or in pairs to decide which pairs rhyme.

2 🔲 [2.2] Play the recording once for students to check their answers, then again for students to repeat the verbs. Encourage students to check the pronunciation of any new past forms they meet in the mini-dictionary. Highlight the fact that the *-ed* ending on regular verbs is pronounced /ɪd/ **only** when the infinitive ends in *-t* (*started*) or *-d* (*ended*). This will help students to see that verbs like *appeared* and *played* are **not** pronounced /əˈpɪrɪd/ and /pleɪɪd/.

ANSWERS
The pairs which rhyme are: a, d, f, g, h, i, j.

3 Demonstrate the activity with a student, then put students in pairs. Encourage them to check the pronunciation with you if they are uncertain.

Pronunciation, Exercise 3: alternative suggestion

Put students in groups with a ball. One student says the infinitive of the verb and throws the ball to another, who has to give the Past Simple. That student then says another infinitive form and throws the ball to someone else, etc. After a minute or two, introduce the rule that anyone who answers wrongly drops out, until there is only one student left.

3 **a)** Demonstrate the activity using the board. Write up three things you did yesterday and invite students to guess which one is not true. Give students a few minutes to write notes. Circulate and help with vocabulary.

Exercise 3a: additional suggestions

To make the exercise more challenging, and/or to have each student in the pair working on ideas, write up the following:

● Things you ate/wore yesterday.

● Things you did on your last holiday.

● Good things that happened to you last year.

● Things you did on your last birthday.

b) Focus students on the example in speech balloons. If necessary, get a student to demonstrate one of his/her own examples with you. Tell students to change over after each set of three things. This can also be done as a mingling activity, where students move on to the next person after each set of three things.

ADDITIONAL PRACTICE

Workbook: Past Simple, pages 11–12

RB **Resource bank:** 2A *Dead famous* (Past Simple *yes/no* questions and short answers), page 124

Language focus 2 (PAGE 17)

Time phrases often used in the past: *in, on, at, ago*

Elicit and number the time phrase which is least recent. Students work individually or in pairs. If you want to encourage some discussion, ask students to try to remember and tell each other something about each time/date.

ANSWERS
These will depend to some extent when your lesson takes place: in the eighteenth century, 100 years ago, in the 1980s, in 1998, in November of last year, on 1st January this year, four months ago, last weekend, on Monday morning, yesterday afternoon, ten hours ago, at eight o'clock this morning

Grammar analysis

Refer students back to the time phrases in the box. Give them a few minutes individually or in pairs to complete the rules. As you elicit the answers, ask students for more examples for each rule.

ANSWERS
1 a at b on c in d Ø
2 *the summer ago* is wrong, because *ago* is used for a period of time from the present to the past, showing how far in the past something happened

PRACTICE

1 [2.3] Do this as a written or an oral exercise. *Either:* play the recording while students write their answers. Ask them to compare their answers in pairs and try to remember what each question was. *Or:* stop the recording after each question and ask students to tell each other their answers in pairs, without writing.

2 Words to check: *rent, stay up, perform in a play/concert.* If students play the game in groups or teams, they take turns to ask someone else in the group, or someone from the other team. You may want to use a scoring system, especially if you run this as a team game. If a student talks for twenty seconds without stopping, and uses a time phrase, they get three points. If they cannot keep going for twenty seconds, or they fail to use a time phrase, the opposing team gets a point. Have some brief feedback on any good examples of language use, or problems with the time phrases or Past Simple.

ADDITIONAL PRACTICE

Workbook: Time phrases often used in the past, page 13
RB Resource bank: 2B *The Millionaire's Ball* (Past Simple and time phrases), page 126

Vocabulary (PAGE 18)

Words to describe feelings

See *Teacher's tips: working with lexical* on pages 12–13 and *making the most of the Mini-dictionary* on page 14.

1 Students work in pairs or groups to match the words to the pictures. Some of the words are similar in meaning, so students may not agree on all the answers. Encourage any useful discussion.

ANSWERS
a nervous, frightened, worried
b disappointed, worried, bored, fed up
c excited
d excited, in a good mood, surprised

Vocabulary: language notes
- If *nervous is a* 'false friend' for your students, check it carefully with examples. You can feel *nervous* before an exam because you are worried about it and can't relax.
- *Nervous* and *worried* are similar in meaning, but *nervous* implies an element of fear, whereas *worried* implies that you are unhappy and cannot stop thinking about the problem.
- *Fed up* is quite informal and means that you are annoyed or bored with something and want the situation to change: *I'm really fed up with this weather.*

2 This exercise checks that students have understood the meaning of the words. Write them in two lists on the board.

ANSWERS
a **positive feelings:** excited, in a good mood, relaxed
b **negative feelings:** nervous, disappointed, worried, bored, guilty, frightened, angry, embarrassed, fed up
surprised can be positive or negative

3 Words to check: *a queue, miss a train/bus, a spider.* Emphasise that students need only write a word or phrase, not a whole sentence, as their answer. Give them a few minutes individually to answer the questions. Suggest that students take turns to ask and answer, and that they choose questions at random, to keep the pace going. Feed back briefly on any unusual answers.

Pronunciation

[2.4] Students listen, write the words and mark the stress patterns. Ask students to group words with similar stress patterns together. Write them on the board to check.

ANSWERS

●•
nervous
worried
guilty
frightened
angry
fed up

•●•
excited
embarrassed

•●
relaxed
surprised

••●•
disappointed

●
bored

••●•
in a good mood

ADDITIONAL PRACTICE

Workbook: Vocabulary (Words to describe feelings), page 13

Listening (PAGE 18)

The first time ever I saw your face

1 Start the discussion by telling students about the last CD or cassette you bought. Give students a few minutes in pairs or groups to discuss the questions.

2 a) Ask students how many of them like love songs, and elicit some examples of favourites. Write the title of the song on the board and do an example. Put students in pairs to discuss the words. Students may well be able to make a case for **all** the words being in the song, which is fine. Encourage them to explain why. Feed back briefly on some of their ideas.

b) [2.5] Play the song (students keep the song itself covered) for students to check their answers.

> **ANSWERS**
> **The words from the box are:** the sun, the moon, gifts, dark, endless, joy, the Earth, trembling, captive, command.

c) Tell students to look at the song and play the first two lines only, demonstrating what they have to do. Play the song through and let students discuss their answers in pairs before checking with the whole class.

> **ANSWERS**
> **The lines which are different are:**
> I thought the sun rose in your **eyes**
> To the dark and the endless **skies**
> I **felt** the Earth move in my hand
> That was **there** at my command
> And I **knew** our joy
> And last till the end of **time**

3 a)–b) Students discuss the words and questions in pairs or groups. Choose one or two students to report back to the class.

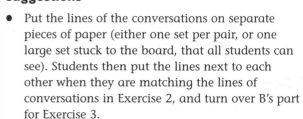

> **Song: additional discussion questions**
>
> If appropriate, continue the discussion with questions like:
> - How did you feel when you heard the song?
> - Do you believe in love at first sight?
> - Do you think first impressions are important?

Wordspot (PAGE 19)

feel

See *Teacher's tips: working with lexical phrases* on pages 12–13.

1 Explain that in each of these Wordspot sections students are going to look at a word with several meanings which is used a lot in English.
Do an example with the class, then give students time individually or in pairs to study the diagram. Circulate to help and assess the level of knowledge. Elicit more examples for each category in the diagram, and highlight the following:

- *feel* is followed by an adjective when referring to a person or a thing. *He feels stupid. The room felt hot.*
- *feel* is followed by *about* when it means *have an opinion* (or *think*).
- *feel like* is quite informal and is followed by a noun or an *-ing* form.

With a mono-nationality class, translation might be helpful to check the meaning by comparison with the students' own language.

2 a)–b) [2.6] Students work individually or in pairs to match the sentences. They then listen to the recording to check.

> **ANSWERS**
> 1 d   2 g   3 a   4 f   5 h   6 c   7 e   8 b

3 Give students a few minutes to study the conversations. Put them in pairs to practise.

> **Exercises 2 and 3: alternative suggestions**
>
> - Put the lines of the conversations on separate pieces of paper (either one set per pair, or one large set stuck to the board, that all students can see). Students then put the lines next to each other when they are matching the lines of conversations in Exercise 2, and turn over B's part for Exercise 3.
> - Instead of remembering B's part in Exercise 3, students invent their own lines (trying to use a phrase with *feel*).

Tell a first time story

See *Teacher's tips: making speaking Tasks work* on pages 6–7 and *responding to learners' individual language needs* on pages 8–9.

Preparation for task (PAGE 20)

1 Start by telling students how many of the 'firsts' **you** remember. Ask them to guess which ones they are. Students then work individually for a few minutes, ticking the appropriate boxes on the list.

2 a) Give students a minute or two to discuss their ideas.

b) Students stay in their pairs to predict ideas for the story. The words in boxes are key to the stories, so check that students understand them all. Choose a student from one or two pairs to tell the class their ideas.

c) 🔲 [2.7] Before playing the recording, emphasise that students do not need to understand the stories in detail at this stage, just the general idea.

> **ANSWERS**
> See tapescript Module 2, recording 7 on page 159 of the *Students' Book*.

3 Choose whether to play one or both of the stories again depending on how strong your class is, and how much time you have. Give students time to discuss their answers in pairs.

> **ANSWERS**
> **a When?/Where?**
>
> | David | Jayne |
> |---|---|
> | he was 11, on a school trip | she was 19, working in a sandwich shop |
>
> **b Who else?**
>
> | David | Jayne |
> |---|---|
> | children on the trip, the teacher | the gorgeous-looking male customer, other customers |
>
> **c What happened?**
>
> | David | Jayne |
> |---|---|
> | The teacher left the passports at the service station and had to go back. He ate cream cakes and was very sick. | She cut her hand and got blood on his sandwich. He came back and asked her out for a pizza. |
>
> **d How/feel?**
>
> | David | Jayne |
> |---|---|
> | he doesn't say – worried about the passports, probably | nervous about the man and stupid about the sandwich |

> **Preparation for task: alternative suggestion**
>
> ● To personalise this stage, you could tell the story of one of your 'firsts'. Speak from notes, and if possible bring in maps, photos, souvenirs, etc. to illustrate your story. Students answer the same questions as for the recording (Exercise 3 a–d).

Task (PAGE 21)

1 Refer students back to the list of 'firsts' that they ticked in Preparation for task. Explain that you want them to choose one to speak about. Elicit any ideas for other important 'firsts' that were not on the list. Encourage students to spend some time thinking, and to make notes to help them remember and structure what they want to say. Show students what you mean by notes with an example on the board: *first pet – 8 or 9 – mum and dad bought – puppy – fell in love – so sweet – got up five every day – ran home from school – played with puppy all the time.*

2 Circulate, feeding in language, and prompting less confident students with questions: *Why was it important for you? Why did you feel worried?* etc.

3 Focus students on the *Useful language* box. They could spend a minute or two thinking how to improve their story by the addition of any of the phrases in part a and practising the listener's phrases in part b. Students then practise telling their story to their partner. Deal with any problems and questions. Encourage students to give each other feedback at this stage: what they liked about the story, any parts which were difficult to understand, etc.

4 The size of the groups will depend on the size of your class and on how long your students can concentrate on listening to other people's stories. While you are listening to the stories, collect examples of good language use and/or errors for comment and correction later. When the groups have finished, ask one person from each group to report on the funniest/saddest/nicest story.

Task: alternative suggestions

a *If any of your students really cannot think of a personal first or do not want to talk about themselves:* they could tell the story of another person's first, a friend or family member, or a person from a book or a film.

b *If any of your students lack the confidence or ability to speak at any length:* they could prepare two or three shorter stories to tell.

c *If you want to record students telling their story:*

- students record their stories in a language laboratory, then change places and listen to each other's stories.

- students record their story on cassette at home, then give you the cassette for correction, in the same way as a piece of written homework (comments and corrections can be written on a separate piece of paper).

- groups work in different rooms and record their three/four stories, to listen to and comment on later (this is obviously more suitable for smaller classes).

Writing (PAGE 22)

Linking ideas in narrative

1 **a)** Words to check: *coach, youth hostel, a silver ring.* Students work individually or in pairs before checking with the whole class.

ANSWERS
(a) 1 (b) 6 (c) 7 (d) 2 (e) 9 (f) 6 (g) 3 (h) 8 (i) 4

b) *Either:* students underline the linking words in their books. *Or:* write the complete text on the board or an overhead projector transparency, and go through the text with the class. Clarify the following:

- *and* is used to join two clauses, *I went to London and stayed for six months.*

- *because* introduces a reason, *I stayed at home because I was ill.*

- *so* follows a reason, *I was ill **so** I stayed at home.*

- *then* is used to show sequence, *I went to the supermarket, **then** to the post office.*

- *but* introduces information which contrasts or is unexpected, *The weather was terrible **but** we had a good time.*

If your students seem fairly familiar with the words, point out *first* (used at the beginning of a sequence of events) and *unfortunately* (used to introduce something negative).

To give students some controlled practice of the linking words, put them in A and B pairs. B closes his/her book and A reads Marcos' story, saying 'beep! instead of the linking words. B calls out the correct word as soon as he/she can. A and B change over.

2 Refer students back to the notes they made for their story in the Task. The notes can be used to help them structure their writing. Encourage students to plan their writing. If there is time, they can write a first draft in class, then write a second draft for homework. This will enable you to give them some help in the initial stages.

ADDITIONAL PRACTICE

Workbook: Linkers: *but, so, because, then,* page 16
RB **Resource bank:** 2C *Invent a story* (Past Simple and linkers), page 128

Do you remember?
(PAGE 22)

ANSWERS
2 b) I think the course started about two weeks **ago**.
 c) He was here at eight o'clock **this** morning.
 d) Where did you go for your holidays **last** year?
 e) Clothes were very different in **the** 1970s.
3 a) I **feel** very cold and tired.
 b) Do you **feel like** a drink?
 c) This bread **feels** hard: are you sure it's fresh?
 d) Do you **feel like having** a snack?
4 a) We couldn't go **because** Sue was ill.
 b) The bus didn't come **so** I got a taxi to the station.
 c) They loved the film **but** I didn't.
 d) No – you put the sugar in first, **then** you add the cream.

Language focus 1 (PAGE 23)

Can, can't, have to, don't have to

1 🔲 [3.1] Write the names of the people on the board. Play the recording once and elicit as many answers as possible to the first two questions. Play the recording again to check/fill in the gaps. Students discuss in pairs or as a class whose reasons are closest to their own, explaining **why**.

2 Students work in pairs to choose the verbs. Play the recording again for them to listen and check their answers. Feed back with the whole class.

Grammar analysis

Give students a few minutes individually or in pairs to do question 1, before checking with the whole class. As you check the answers, highlight:

- the use of the infinitive without *to after can.*

- *can* does not change in the 3ʳᵈ person, but *have to* does, *he/she has to.*

- negative forms and their contractions, *can't, don't/doesn't have to.*

- question forms, *Can ...? Do I/Does he/she have to ...?*

ANSWERS
it is possible = can
it is not possible = can't
it is necessary = have to
it is not necessary = don't have to

Note

Must is not treated here, to avoid confusion at this level. *Have to* can be used safely by students instead. However, if students ask about *must,* explain that:

- *must* and *have to* are very similar in meaning.

- *mustn't* and *don't have to* are different in meaning: *mustn't = can't* (it's prohibited), *don't have to = it's not necessary* (but you can if you want).

2 To check students understand the difference between ability and permission/prohibition, give them some more examples and ask them to divide the examples into the two categories, for example
a) *You can't use your dictionary in the exam. She can speak four languages. I can't swim.*
b) *You can come in now.*

ANSWERS

a	can't	e	don't have to
b	can	f	have to
c	don't have to	g	can't
d	can't	h	can

PRACTICE

1 🔲 [3.2] Students work individually or in pairs to complete the gaps. More than one answer is grammatically possible in many cases, but students should write the most logical one. Words to check: *population, alphabet, subtitles.* Play the recording for students to check. If you wish, pause the recording **before** each sentence for students to call out their ideas (to add an element of competition). Feed back briefly on answers students found surprising.

Pronunciation

See *Teacher's tips: helping students with pronunciation* on pages 10–11.

1 🔲 [3.3] Play the recording or say the sentences yourself at natural speed. Drill the sentences, paying attention to the following:

- *can* is unstressed. Help students by first drilling *They choose which language ...* Then show them how *can* is squashed in between *They* and *choose.*

- *can't* is stressed.

2 Students work individually deciding what they can/can't do on the list. They then practise saying the sentences carefully to themselves first. Students then tell each other what they can/can't do.

Students can make a note of each other's answers, then report back briefly on what everyone in the group can/can't do.

Pronunciation: additional suggestions

Ask students if there is anything on the list which they do/don't have to do. Get them to explain why. Students should pay attention to the pronunciation of *have to.* For example:

I have to remember new people's names because it is very important in my job. I don't have to drive – I can use public transport.

2 a) ▭ [3.4] Words to check: any names of school subjects on the list which your students do not know. Let students look at the list before playing the recording. Encourage students to make notes rather than writing full sentences. For example *primary/secondary school – have to study RE/PE – once a week.*

ANSWERS
- Students have to study RE and PE at least once a week in primary and secondary schools.
- Children have to study one hour per day of Maths and English in primary school.
- They don't have to study Geography and History after the age of fourteen.
- Students have to pass Maths GCSE or they can't go to university.
- Students can stop studying some subjects after the age of fourteen.
- They have to stay at school until the age of sixteen.

b) If necessary, give students prompts to think about before writing their sentences: *primary/secondary school subjects, exams, leaving school, going to university.*

If you have a mono-nationality class: students work on their sentences in pairs, then compare with other pairs.

If you have a multi-nationality class: students work individually or with students from the same country. They then compare with students from other countries.

ADDITIONAL PRACTICE

Workbook: *can/can't, have to/don't have to,* pages 17 and 18

Reading and vocabulary (PAGE 25)

1 Words to check: *successful, motivation, praise, realistic, develop an 'ear' for something.* Give students a minute or two to decide on their four ideas. Put them in pairs to discuss and give reasons for their choice.

2 Although there will be some unfamiliar words, be careful not to pre-teach the words in Exercise 3. The words in Exercise 1 are sufficient for students to do the activity.

Do an example with the class, referring them back to the ideas in Exercise 1. Students compare answers in pairs.

ANSWERS

hard work = A/T	getting praise from your teacher = T
enjoying learning = A/T	
really believing that you will be successful = A	being realistic about the progress you can make = A
having a good teacher = A/T	developing an 'ear' for language = A
really wanting to learn (motivation) = A/T	reading and listening to lots of English = T
studying lots of grammar = T	

3 Do an example or two with the class. Students work individually or in pairs before checking with the whole class.

Ideas for helping students to guess meaning from context

- Tell students to look at the parts of speech in the definitions (for example *to become angry* is a verb, *often* and *carefully* are adverbs) and to check that the word they choose in the text is the same part of speech.

- Do one or two examples with sentences containing nonsense words. Ask students to tell you as much as they can about the word. For example *He had some **smirkles** in his pocket. Smirkle* is a countable noun, and an object small enough to be in someone's pocket.

ANSWERS

a	you won't get very far	e	on their own
b	get frustrated	f	make fools of
c	notice		ourselves
d	systematically		

Exercise 3: additional activity

Either write up the words in the box and the text below on the board or put them on an overhead projector transparency. Students use the words/phrases in the box to complete the summary of what Alistair and Teresa say. Proceed as follows:

- Ask students to check what part of speech the words in the box are.

- Show students that they can predict what kind of word goes in each gap by looking at the language around it. For example *is* after a gap can mean a noun is missing, *to* before a gap can mean a verb is missing.

- Tell students which of the words in the box are used twice: *hard, motivation, a good teacher, successful.*

- Students work individually or in pairs, then check with the class.

hard	motivation	better	imagine
a good teacher	successful	stupid	enjoy
on their own			

Alistair believes that (1) _____ is the most important thing if you want to learn a language. He also thinks that you have to really believe that you will be (2) _____. He thinks it is a good idea to (3) _____ yourself speaking the language really well. He says that you need to work

(4) _____ but you should also try to
(5) _____ yourself. We also need to 'develop
an ear for the language', and he believes that some
people do this (6) _____, but others need
(7) _____ to help them.

Teresa agrees that (8) _____ is the most
important thing, and believes that you have to work
very (9) _____. Not many people can learn a
language successfully without (10) _____,
she believes. Adults sometimes feel
(11) _____ when they start to learn a foreign
language because they speak like children, but if
they continue to study, many of her students become
very (12) _____ language learners, and some
learn to speak English (13) _____ than she
does!

ANSWERS

1 motivation   2 successful   3 imagine   4 hard
5 enjoy   6 on their own   7 a good teacher
8 motivation   9 hard   10 a good teacher
11 stupid   12 successful   13 better

4 Students discuss this question in small groups, or as
a class.

ADDITIONAL PRACTICE

Workbook: Vocabulary booster: things in a school, page
20; Vocabulary (Word - building), page 21

RB **Resource bank:** 3A *The secret of successful language
learning* (Vocabulary extension–word building), page 129

Vocabulary and speaking (PAGE 26)

Studying new vocabulary

See *Teacher's tips: working with lexical phrases* on pages
12–13 and *making the most of the Mini-dictionary* on
pages 13–14.

1 Introduce the topic. Ask students how easy/difficult
they find learning vocabulary and why, or tell them a
personal anecdote about your own experiences of learning
vocabulary in a foreign language. Students discuss in pairs
then feed back with the class. Highlight the position of the
pronoun *it* in *look **it** up, write **it** down*. Show students that
you can say *write down **the word***, but *write down **it*** is
wrong. Pronunciation to check: *explains, guess*.

Exercise 1: additional suggestion

Put the sentences on separate pieces of paper (one
set per pair or group). Students physically put them
in order. Tell students to turn over all the pieces
except the first one, and to turn them back one by
one, trying to remember the next phrase before they
turn the paper over. This acts as a drill of the phrases.

2 Give students a minute or two to think about their
answers. Elicit examples. Then put students in pairs or
small groups to discuss the questions. Ask one or two
students to report back on their answers.

3 Elicit or give a couple of examples *(look up an address,
an important date, a recipe)*. Put students in pairs or
groups to discuss the rest.

POSSIBLE ANSWERS

b **You can check:** your telephone messages, your
diary, an address, a phone number.
c **You can find out:** someone's name/phone
number/address, why someone did something.
d **You can guess:** the price/weight of something,
why someone did something.
e **You can practise:** a language, your part in a
play.
f **You can write down:** someone's name/phone
number, instructions.

Language focus 2 (PAGE 26)

Should/Shouldn't

Words to check: *join a club, get a part-time job.* Give
students a minute to read the text and check they
understand the situation. Stephanie has won a language
course in Edinburgh, and wants advice about how to
continue learning outside the classroom.
Put students in pairs or small groups to discuss the
best/worst advice and to think of any more ideas. If
students are studying or have studied in an English-
speaking country, they can draw on their own experience.
Ask one or two students to report back.
Avoid discussing *should* at this point. Students deduce from
the context that it's a way of giving someone your opinion
about what to do.

Grammar analysis

Give students a minute or two individually or in pairs to look
at questions 1 and 2. As you check the answers, highlight:

● *should* is less strong than *have to* (and *must*, if students
ask about it) and is used to talk about what is a good
idea/the right thing to do. This general meaning is more
useful to students than limiting it to *should* = advice.

- *should* operates like *can*. It does not change in the 3rd person and it is followed by an infinitive without *to*.
- the 'l' in *should* is silent, /ʃəd/.
- the fact that we often use *Perhaps ...* or *I think ...* in front of *should*, to make it less direct.

ANSWERS
1 The best explanation of *should* is *this is a good idea/the right thing to do*.
2 The negative form is *should not* (contracted to *shouldn't*). The meaning is *this is **not** a good idea/not the right thing to do*.
The question form is *Should I...?*

Practice: additional activity

Students work with a partner to answer one of the questions below. Emphasise that they should use *should/shouldn't* in their answers.

Either: think of three pieces of advice for someone who wants to practise their English outside the classroom in their own country.

Or: think of some more advice for someone going to stay in Britain or another English-speaking country. (The advice can be about things as well as language learning: money, things to take with you, etc.)

Elicit an example before putting students into pairs or small groups to discuss their ideas. The first alternative here is for students studying in their own country, the second is for students studying in an English-speaking country. If some of your students have experience of both situations, get some pairs/groups to discuss the first alternative, and some the second. They then exchange ideas.

Ideas for advice

a *In the student's own country*:
- Listen to radio programmes in English (for example on the BBC World Service).
- Find newspapers, etc. in English in the library.
- Subscrbe to an English magazine.
- Find a cinema which shows English films in the original version with subtitles.
- Find a speaking partner (in your class or another class) and arrange to meet for an hour or so every week to speak English.

b *In an English-speaking country*:
- Make friends with students from other countries, rather than your own country, so that you have to speak English.
- Don't forget to take some warm clothes and an umbrella.

- Arrange a conversation exchange with an English-speaking person. Meet for an hour. Speak for half an hour in English, half an hour in your language.
- Don't take too much cash. Take traveller's cheques and a credit card.

PRACTICE

1 **a)** Start by asking students when they last had to study for an exam, how they prefer to study and how organised they are. Give students a minute or two to find the things in the box in the picture. Encourage comments about how successful Bruce is in his studies!

b) Discuss the sentences briefly with the class. Emphasise that whether students agree with the sentences or not depends on their view of the right/wrong thing to do.

c) Students discuss their ideas in pairs, then make a written list. Circulate and help with vocabulary.

Students compare ideas with other pairs or with the whole class. Encourage them to give reasons for their ideas.

POSSIBLE ANSWERS
He should tidy his room.
He should organise his notes and books.
He should empty the ashtray.
He shouldn't play computer games/read the newspaper when he's studying.
He should have a short break every hour or two hours (to read the newspaper or play a computer game).
He should get dressed before he starts studying.
He should put his telephone answering machine on.
He shouldn't phone friends when he's studying.
He shouldn't listen to loud music when he's studying.

2 Words to check: *be annoyed with someone, do something secretly, overweight, put on weight, miss a meal*. Give students a few minutes to read about the situations and to think about what the people should/shouldn't do. Then put them in pairs to discuss their ideas.

Exercise 2: alternative suggestions

- *Students imagine they are a famous person with a problem situation:* give them a few minutes to prepare what they are going to say. Then put them in groups to tell each other about the problem and to give advice.
- *If you have access to an English magazine with a problem page* (those written for teenagers are best in terms of language level): collect some examples of letters and distribute them, one per student or one between two. Students read their letter, then mingle and tell each other about the problem and ask for advice.

ADDITIONAL PRACTICE

Workbook: *should/shouldn't*, page 18

RB **Resource bank:** 3B *Parents and children* (*can, can't, have to, don't have to, should, shouldn't*), page 130

Make a list of guidelines for a language class

See *Teacher's tips: making speaking Tasks work* on pages 6–7 and *responding to learners' individual needs* on pages 8–9.

Preparation for task (PAGE 28)

1 **a)** Focus students on the picture. Make sure they understand the situation, especially the idea of classroom guidelines which have been negotiated and agreed between teacher and students. Emphasise that they are only going to hear about the guidelines **for the teacher** (the ones for the students come later). Elicit ideas for the first topic: how much the teacher should speak English/the students' language. Students work individually to predict what was agreed about the other topics.

b) 🔊 [3.5] Students listen and make notes. They then compare answers in pairs and/or with the class.

ANSWERS
1 The teacher should speak English as much as possible, and only use the students' language if it's really necessary.
2 The teacher should give homework after every lesson, but not too much.
3 The teacher should try to make the lessons interesting.
4 The teacher should try to answer questions. If they don't know the answer, they can find out for the next lesson.
5 The teacher should use the coursebook, but bring in other materials from time to time.
6 The teacher should correct important mistakes.

2 Students discuss the questions in small groups or as a class. If students are reticent, explain that it is useful for the teacher to know what students think: it can be beneficial for their learning, class dynamics, etc.

Task (PAGE 29)

1 Do the first option if your students responded well to the material in the Preparation for task section. Do the second if your students were uncomfortable with the idea of a class contract, or if it is inappropriate for your teaching circumstances. Alternatively, students choose which to do, and have different groups within the class working on different options. Put students in groups of four or five to discuss their ideas. Circulate and help with vocabulary.

2 Focus students on the *Useful language* box. Point out some useful collocations like: *make a mistake, do homework/tests.* You may prefer to do this after the Task so as not to interrupt the discussion.

Encourage students to agree on and write out their list of guidelines. Warn them that a spokesperson from the group will be asked to present their list to the class in the next stage. Ask them to write the list on an overhead projector transparency or a poster-size piece of paper that everyone can see. At this stage collect examples of good language use and/or errors for analysis and correction after the Task.

3 Ask the spokesperson from each group to present their list to the class. Tell the other students in the groups to make a note of which guidelines were the same. Then set up a class discussion and/or vote to decide on the ten most important guidelines.

Task: alternative suggestions

a *If you are short of time:*
   Either: spread the Preparation for task and Task over two lessons. This also gives students time to think of ideas between lessons.
   Or: leave out the listening in the Preparation for task and spend a few minutes discussing the ideas of class guidelines and setting up the Task.

b *If you have a large class, or your students are not confident about speaking in front of the class:* instead of having 'spokespeople' present the lists to the class, regroup the students (into groups of three/four) with others who have made different lists, and ask each person to present their list to the rest of the group.

Optional writing

Encourage students to collaborate in their groups to write up their guidelines on poster-size paper. If the groups already made a poster in Exercise 2 of the Task, they can refine it by adding colours, pictures, etc. Put the lists round the classroom wall and encourage students to walk around and look at them. Alternatively, students write up the list on a normal size piece of paper and stick it in the front of their notebooks. The lists can be reviewed at a later stage in the course, to see how well everyone is keeping to the guidelines.

Real life (PAGE 29)

Making requests and asking for permission

1 **a)** Ask students to look briefly at the conversations. Establish that all the conversations take place in a classroom, and what each person wants. Ask students to guess the missing words in pairs, or as a class, but tell them not to write yet.

ANSWERS
1 The student wants the teacher to speak more slowly.
2 The student wants to leave early.
3 The student wants to borrow a dictionary.
4 The student wants to change seats.

b) [3.6] Play the recording. Pause after each conversation for students to write in the missing words. Students compare answers in pairs and/or as a class.

ANSWERS
1 could you speak more, Thank
2 is it OK if I leave, go ahead, telling me
3 Can I borrow it, here you are
4 Do you mind if I, What's the problem
In 1, the speaker is making a request, asking someone else to do something. *Could you speak …?*
In **2, 3,** and **4** the speakers are asking for permission, asking if they can do something. *Is it OK if I leave …? Can I borrow …? Do you mind if I change …?*
The responses used are: *Sure, go ahead. OK (then). Yes, all right.*

Note
Although strictly speaking the positive response to *Do you mind if I …?* is *No*, in practice English speakers are inconsistent about this. They simply make it clear through the other words they use whether the response is positive or not.

Pronunciation

See *Teacher's tips: helping students with pronunciation* on pages 10–11.

1 [3.7] Play the recording or say the examples yourself. Students will sound more polite if they start on a higher pitch.

2 Play or say the examples again, pausing for students to repeat. If necessary, extend this controlled practice by giving students prompts to substitute in the examples. For example:
T: *use your pen* > S: *Can I use your pen, please?*

T: *say that again* > S: *Could you say that again, please?*

2 Give students five to ten minutes to choose the situations and prepare their conversations. If you are short of time, ask them to prepare two conversations. Check the use of *keep* + verb *–ing* to talk about repetitive/annoying behaviour. Circulate and help with vocabulary. Depending on time, choose two or three pairs to act out their conversations. Other students tick the situations from the list that they are acting out and/or the request/permission phrases that they use.

ADDITIONAL PRACTICE

Workbook: Short answers with modal verbs *can, should, have to*, page 19

Do you remember? (PAGE 30)

ANSWERS
1 a) **find out** someone's age
   b) **make** a mistake
   c) **pass** an exam
   d) **interrupt** the teacher
   e) **write down** a word
3 *the students:* a) b) f)
   the teacher: c) d) e)
4–5 a) Could you open the window, please? – Yes, it's very hot in here, isn't it?
   b) Do you mind if I smoke? – No problem, go ahead.
   c) Can I borrow your newspaper, please? – Sure, here you are.
   d) Could you phone again later? – OK. About eight?
   e) Is it OK if I use your printer? – Oh, I'm sorry, it's not working at the moment.

module 4

Vocabulary and speaking (PAGE 31)

Dates and special occasions

See *Teacher's tips: working with lexical phrases* on pages 12–13.

1 First check that students can say the months of the year in English. Get them to recite them from December backwards. Revise ordinal numbers briefly as students will need them for saying dates. Then practise by getting students to ask each other, 'What's the third/fifth/eleventh month of the year?' Put students in pairs or groups to discuss the questions. Then feed back on which months are the most/least popular and why.

2 a) *If you have a mono-nationality class*: go through the days with the class, making sure they understand them all. Ask students to tick the ones celebrated in their country.
If you have a multi-nationality class: there will be more scope for cross-cultural comparison in small groups.

Note
1 Students may have All Saints' Day, rather than Halloween which is now a secular occasion in Britain/the USA, when children play games and dress up as witches, etc.
2 May Day is also known as Labour Day in some countries. Chinese New Year is discussed later in the module.

Put students in pairs or small groups to discuss the order that the days happen in their country/countries. Do an example on the board first: *X is in April /X is at the beginning of May /X is on the 20th June*. Ask students to number them, for example St Valentine's Day = 1.

b) [4.1] Students number the days 1–10 as they listen to the recording. Put them in pairs or small groups to compare answers and discuss the differences between Britain/the USA and their country/countries.

> **ANSWERS**
> See tapescript Module 4, recording 1 on page 160 of the *Students' Book*.

> ## Pronunciation
> See *Teacher's tips: helping students with pronunciation* on pages 10–11.
>
> 1 Highlight the two ways of writing and saying the dates. Elicit some more dates from students, and demonstrate the written and spoken forms.
> 2 [4.2] Play the recording or say the dates yourself and point out the difference between the voiced sound /ð/ in *the* and the unvoiced sound /θ/ in *fourth, fourteenth, thirty-first, twenty-fifth*. Students listen again and repeat the dates.

3 Check students understand the word *celebrate*. Put them in pairs or small groups to discuss/explain the special days and to make a list.
If you have a mono-nationality class: expand the discussion. Which days do the students like best/least? Which days are most important/not really celebrated in their families?
If you have a multi-nationality class: make sure there is a mix of nationalities in the groups. Ask a couple of students to report back to the class on days from other countries.

4 a) Do an example *You visit relatives at Christmas*. Then give students a few minutes to think about what they do. Students compare answers in pairs or small groups.

Note
Remind students of the usefulness of word locusts (*Students' Book* Module 1, page 7) for collecting phrases with a common verb: *have a party, have the day off work, have a special meal*.

b) Elicit one or two more examples (*you have a party for someone's birthday, you buy flowers when someone is in hospital*). Students discuss in pairs or small groups. Feed back on two or three of the best ideas.

ADDITIONAL PRACTICE

Workbook: Vocabulary booster: special occasions, page 25; Vocabulary (Things people do on special occasions), page 26

Language focus 1 (PAGE 32)

Present Continuous (and Present Simple)

1 Students look at the picture and discuss briefly what they think it is like working for a fashion magazine. If any of your students do work for a magazine, ask them to say something about it. Words to check: *choose something, earn money*. Do the first example with the class. Students then work individually or in pairs to decide what the three people do in their jobs. Students may disagree with each other about the answers. That is fine, if they are having a useful discussion.

> **ANSWERS**
> **Juliet:** a, c, f
> **Imogen:** b, e, g
> **Carlos:** d, h
> *Ideas for: What else do they do?*
> **Juliet:** goes to a lot of meetings.
> **Imogen:** types letters, organises meetings and appointments for Juliet.
> **Carlos:** travels a lot.

2 Remind students about the topic of special occasions. Set the context: it is the May Day holiday. Explain that students are going to find out about the three people from *Glitz* magazine, who have got the day off. Tell students to read the paragraph about Imogen. Establish that she is relaxing at home with her husband.

Grammar analysis

First ask students to look back at the text in Exercise 2, and underline all the examples of the Present Simple (in one colour) and Present Continuous (in a second colour). Then proceed with the exercises in the *Analysis* box.

1–2 Give students a few minutes individually or in pairs to do the questions. As you check the answers, highlight:

- the use of the Present Continuous both for actions happening in a present period (*this year, this week, this term*) which may be less familiar for students, and for actions in progress at this moment.

- the contracted form of *be*.

- the inversion of the subject and *be* to form a question.

- short answer forms: *Yes, he is. No, he isn't.*

- the spelling of the present participle, for example *making, running* (see *Language summary* on page 151 of the *Students' Book* for the complete rules).

ANSWERS
1 **a** they **meet** friends / Imogen **likes** her job / she **doesn't want** to be a PA / she **wants** to have her own design company
   b Imogen **is spending** her day off / (they'**re**) **relaxing**
   c **She's finding** the course really useful.
2 See page 151 of the *Language summary* for formation of questions and negatives.

3 Contrast the examples of state verbs with sentences containing verbs expressing activity or processes like *do, go, work*. Point out that state verbs are often used with feelings and the senses: *love, hate, know, think.*

PRACTICE

1 Start by getting students to predict from the pictures what Carlos and Juliet are doing. Words to check: *wedding anniversary.* Students work individually or in pairs before checking with the whole class.

ANSWERS
1 is spending 2 lives 3 doesn't see 4 are celebrating
5 spends 6 doesn't like 7 is looking 8 wants

2 Do an example with the class first, to show that there are no set answers here. Students work in pairs before checking with the whole class.

POSSIBLE ANSWERS
She's spending her day off with: her family, her mother and her husband and baby.
At the weekends she usually: goes shopping, does housework.
Today she's: painting, decorating her house. She isn't shopping.
Her husband is: reading a newspaper, looking after the baby, relaxing.
She doesn't: like her job, like her life. **He doesn't:** help her, like decorating.
One day she wants to: go and live by the sea, go abroad, leave her husband.

Exercises 1 and 2: alternative suggestion
Students work in pairs or groups on *either* Carlos *or* Juliet. They then regroup and exchange information trying to remember as much as they can, rather than simply reading the sentences aloud.

3 **a)** Do number 1 with the class. Show students that first they need to choose the correct form of the verb, and then finish the sentence with information about themselves. Encourage students to think of ideas of their own. Words to check: *comic, novel, try hard to, busy, tired.* Students either write sentences, or just think about them, before they tell their partner.

b) Students compare answers, making a note of any that are the same. Highlight the phrases with *both* and *neither*, then ask a student from each pair to report back to the class. *We're both learning/trying to … Both of us like/speak … Neither of us likes/is wearing …*

ADDITIONAL PRACTICE

Workbook: Present Continuous/Present Simple, pages 23–24
RB **Resource bank:** 4A *Party guests* (Present Continuous and Present Simple), page 131

Wordspot (PAGE 34)

day

See *Teacher's tips: working with lexical phrases* on pages 12–13.

1 [4.3] Elicit suggestions for the first gap, then students work individually or in pairs to predict the others. Suggest that students write in pencil, so that they can change any answers when they listen to the recording. Play the recording and check answers as a whole class.

ANSWERS
a these b the other c off, every d after tomorrow
e One f out

2 Ask students to copy the diagram into their notebooks, so there is enough room to write. Students should have a separate section in their notebooks for the Wordspots, so they can refer to and add to them easily. Students work individually or in pairs before checking with the whole class.

ANSWERS
a the other day b these days
c the day after tomorrow, one day d every day
e a day off, a day out

Note
One day can refer to the future or the past: *One day he left work early and ...*
A day out means a day when you go somewhere for pleasure, like the beach or a place of interest.

3 a) [4.4] Play the first question on the recording. Elicit some other possible answers, for example:
I visited my aunt and uncle. Emphasise that students only need to write a word or a short phrase. Play the recording.

b) Suggest that students exchange pieces of paper to look at each other's answers. Tell students to try to remember the phrases with *day*, even if they can't remember the exact question from the recording.

Listening (PAGE 34)

New Year in two different cultures

1 Put students in pairs or groups to discuss the questions. *For mono-nationality classes*: students discuss what people usually do in their country. They can tell the class about any customs from other countries they know. *For multi-nationality classes*: students tell each other about different customs in the different countries.

2 Students look at the photos of Karen and Johnny. Ask if anyone knows any of the customs relating to their New Years. Put students in pairs and give them a few minutes to decide who mentions what. Students check unknown words in the *Mini-dictionary* or with you. Words to check: *mushrooms and oysters, envelopes*.

3 a) [4.5] Put students in pairs or small groups to listen and mark the phrases with **K** or **J**.

Play the recording once. Remind students that they only need to understand enough to do the activity. They do not need to understand everything. Play the recording again for students to check their answers. Students discuss answers in pairs or as a class.

ANSWERS
mushrooms and oysters = J
new clothes = J   cleaning the house = K
little red envelopes of money = J   fruit cakes = K
the front and back door = K

b) Emphasise that students only need to make notes for this activity. Give them more support by writing prompts on the board. For example:
● food ● good luck ● children/adults
● when are the celebrations? ● clothes ● the house
Play the recording through again. Give students time to compare answers in pairs or small groups before checking with the class.

POSSIBLE ANSWERS
Similarity: in both cultures people eat special food, to bring them good luck and lots of money.
Differences: 1 Chinese New Year involves children, but Scottish New Year is more for adults because most of the customs happen at midnight. 2 Scottish New Year is on 31st December, whereas Chinese New Year is either at the end of January or the beginning of February. 3 Scottish people clean the house to bring good luck, whereas Chinese people wear their new clothes.

c) Put students into pairs or small groups. If possible, these should be different pairs or groups from Exercise 1. Students compare Chinese and Scottish New Year to their country/countries.

Language focus 2 (PAGE 35)

Present Continuous for future arrangements

1 Words to check: *rent*. Give students a minute or two to think about/discuss which verb goes in each gap, but emphasise that they should not write yet.

2 [4.6] Play the recording, pausing after each person to give students time to write. Students compare answers in pairs and/or as a class. They then discuss whose plans are most interesting.

Grammar analysis

Write a couple of examples of the Present Continuous from
the recording on the board. Highlight:

- the use of the Present Continuous for future
  arrangements. This often means that you have arranged
  it with another person or told them about it.

- the fact that the future time is usually given (*this New
  Year*) or is understood from the context.

Note

Although many grammar books distinguish between the use
of Present Continuous for future arrangements and *going to*
+ verb for future plans, in practice the Present Continuous **is**
often used for plans, for example *I'm staying in and
washing my hair tonight*. However, the Present Continuous
is not used for general intentions, for example *I'm going to
study hard this year*. Avoid discussing this unless a student
asks you about it. *Going to* is covered in Module 6.

PRACTICE

1 Words to check: *something unusual, go abroad.* Do
one or two examples of possible questions with the
class. Drill them, demonstrating appropriate intonation for
questions. Give students a few minutes to think about their
questions and practise saying them.

2 Demonstrate how to fill in the answers next to *Name
and Notes* (see Exercise 1 above). Tell students to stand
up and move around the class, talking to as many different
people as they can. Give them ten minutes. They should not
speak to the same person more than twice.

Exercise 2: alternative suggestion

If you have a large class and it is not possible for
your students to move around, put them in groups of
four to six to ask each other their questions. They
can then pair up with someone from another group
to compare answers at the next stage.

3 Students compare answers in pairs or small groups
and/or with the whole class.

ADDITIONAL PRACTICE

Workbook: Present Continuous for future arrangements,
page 24

RB Resource bank: 4B *I'm having lunch with Madonna*
(Present Continuous for future arrangements), page 133

Prepare and talk about a personal calendar

See *Teacher's tips: making speaking Tasks work* on pages
6–7, and *responding to learners' individual language
needs* on pages 8–9.

Preparation for task (PAGE 36)

1 Elicit an example of an important date, for example
your birthday, the day you start a new job. Put
students in pairs or groups to think of others.

2 a) 📼 [4.7] Tell students that they will hear the
recording twice. The first time, they should write only
the dates mentioned, in column 1. Emphasise that they will
not hear a date for every month. Play the recording through
without stopping. Students then compare answers.

b) Tell students they only need to write a word or a date for
each gap in column 2. Play the recording again. Students
compare answers in pairs and/or as a class.

Preparation for task: alternative suggestions

a *If you want to make the material more personal:*

- instead of using the recording, give a short
  talk about **your** personal calendar. Invite
  students to ask questions about anything they
  are interested in, or don't understand.

- if possible, invite another English-speaking person to the class (another teacher or a student from a higher level class). Students listen to the two of you discussing your personal calendars and make notes.

b *If you are short of time:* instead of using the recording, make a calendar which has already been completed with dates and notes to give students a model. Discuss it with the class. Show students how the notes are expanded to longer utterances when speaking.

Task (PAGE 36)

1 Students draw a blank calendar in their notebooks. Remind students to include dates from the past and future arrangements, as well as events that happen every year. Circulate, helping with vocabulary and making sure that students are just writing notes.

2 Ask students to look at part a of the *Useful language* box and give them a few minutes to think about what they will say. If appropriate, point out phrases like *that's the day when*, *the most important date is* and remind students of the different tenses they need to use. Encourage students who finish early to practise telling you about some of their dates.

3 Put students in pairs or small groups. Ask students to look at part b of the *Useful language* box. Drill some examples of questions to help students with their intonation. Students take turns to talk about their calendars. Students listening make notes so that the group can decide afterwards which was the most interesting thing, and report back to the class.

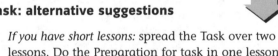

Task: alternative suggestions

a *If you have short lessons:* spread the Task over two lessons. Do the Preparation for task in one lesson, then ask students to prepare their own calendar for homework. Exercises 2 and 3 of the Task, with feedback, can then be done in the next lesson.

b *If you have young students who cannot think of enough dates of their own for the calendar:*

- tell them to make it their family's calendar, so they include important dates for their parents, sisters/brothers, etc.

- tell them to think of a famous person they like and to fill in the calendar as if they are that person, inventing dates if necessary.

Real life (PAGE 37)

Phrases for special occasions

1 Words to check: *anniversary, illness, operation.* Students look at the pictures and predict what the people are saying before looking at the phrases in the box. Students work in pairs or groups, then check with the whole class.

POSSIBLE ANSWERS
New Year: Happy New Year! Good health! The best of luck for the New Year. Cheers!
Birthday: It's lovely, thank you very much. Happy birthday! Many happy returns!
Illness: Thanks for coming. I hope you feel better soon! Good luck! The best of luck for your operation.
Christmas: It's lovely, thank you very much. Merry Christmas!
Wedding: Thanks for coming. Congratulations! I hope you'll be very happy! Good luck! The best of luck for the future.
Wedding anniversary: Happy anniversary! Thanks for coming. Congratulations! Good health! Cheers!

Note
Happy birthday! and *Many happy returns!* mean the same. *Cheers!* and *Good health!* are only used when making a toast. *Good health!* is quite formal.

Pronunciation

[4.8] Play the recording. Pause after each phrase for students to repeat and copy the intonation.

2 [4.9] Play the recording, pausing for students to write the best phrase(s). Alternatively, to give more speaking practice, pause the recording and ask students to call out their answers.

ANSWERS
a Happy birthday! Many happy returns!
b Congratulations!
c Cheers! Good health!
d It's lovely, thank you very much.
e Happy New Year!
f Good luck!
g I hope you feel better soon.
h Thanks for coming.

3 Refer students to page 161 in the *Students' Book* and put them in pairs to practise. Encourage them to: read a line, look up, speak. This will stop them stumbling over the words too much and encourage natural rhythm.

Give students a few minutes to invent and practise their own conversations. Invite three or four pairs to act out their conversations. The other students decide what the situation is in each case.

Writing (PAGE 38)

A letter of invitation

1 Check the meaning of *engagement*. Give students a minute to read the letter and decide what kind of invitation it is. Get students to tell you where they found the relevant information in the letter.

> **ANSWER**
> It is an invitation to an engagement party.
> The relevant information is in para. 2.

2 Students work in pairs or groups to match each paragraph to its purpose.

> **ANSWERS**
> **how she can get to the party:** para. 3
> **personal news about Marina:** para. 1
> **the reason/details:** para. 2
> **how to reply:** para. 4

Exercise 2: additional activity

Students look at the following sentences from another invitation.

a We're going to a new restaurant called Moonlighting.

b Are you still doing that evening course in Russian?

c Can you call me one evening next week to let me know if you're coming?

d I booked the table for 8.30.

e I'm having a party for twenty-first birthday, and I hope you can come.

f The restaurant's not far from the station. It's about five minutes' walk.

g I finished my university exams last week. I hope I did OK!

h Go straight down Bearnside Road, then first left into North Street.

Students then match the sentences to the paragraph of Marina's letter in Exercise 1.

Highlight any useful words or phrases at this stage:
Actually/Anyway/I'm writing to tell you about/I really hope you can come/We'd love to see you/It's about five minutes walk/Let me know.

> **ANSWERS**
> a = para. 2   e = para. 2
> b = para. 1   f = para. 3
> c = para. 4   g = para. 1
> d = para. 2   h = para. 3

---

3 If you have time, students could plan their letter and write a rough draft in class. They then write the final draft for homework. Put students in small groups to think of an imaginary occasion and write their letters to people in other groups. Students who have access to e-mail could e-mail their invitations to each other for homework (and reply!).

ADDITIONAL PRACTICE

Workbook: Improve your writing, page 28

RB Resource bank: *Learner-training worksheet C* (Noticing and recording collocations), page 135

Do you remember? (PAGE 38)

> **ANSWERS**
> **1** ●●● February   ●● August   ●● July
>
> ●●● October   ● May
> November   June
> December
>
> **2** You send someone a card for *a birthday, Christmas, a wedding anniversary.*
> You spend a lot of money *at Christmas, when you go on holiday, when you move house.*
> You say congratulations *when someone gets engaged/married, when someone passes an exam.*
> You give a present *for someone's birthday, for Christmas, to say thank you.*
> **3** a) visit your relatives   b) dress up   c) earn some money   d) answer the phone   e) take some photographs   f) do the photocopying
> **4** a) sitting   b) driving   c) studying   d) making   e) writing   f) travelling
> **5** a) 's making   b) visits   c) isn't spending   d) 's earning   e) Do you know   f) am celebrating
> **6** a) different: *one day* refers to the future *the other day* refers to the past
> b) the same
> c) the same
> d) different: *a day off* is a day not working, *a day out* is a trip somewhere for pleasure
> e) the same

module 5

Language focus 1 (PAGE 39)

Comparatives and superlatives

1 Students look at the photograph and discuss the similarities between the sisters.

2 [5.1] Check that students understand the questions, then play the recording. Students compare answers in pairs and/or with the whole class.

ANSWERS
Sophie and Emma are very similar.
No, Emma is different from her two sisters.

3 Words to check: *fair hair, forehead, both, organised.*
Play the recording again. If necessary, pause after each sentence for students to write. Students compare answers in pairs and/or with the whole class.

ANSWERS
a oldest, taller than   b similar   c look like   d eyes
e different from   f more, than   g than, birthdays

Grammar analysis

1 Give students a few minutes to find the comparative/superlative of the adjectives individually or in pairs. Refer them to the examples of comparatives and superlatives in Exercise 3. Write the table on the board. As you check the answers, elicit one or two more examples for each rule, and highlight:

- the spelling rules for 1-syllable adjectives.
- the different rules for 2-syllable adjectives ending in -*y* and other 2-syllable adjectives.
- the use of *the* with all superlatives.

See *Language summary* on page 151 of the *Students' Book* for more information.

ANSWERS

	adjective	comparative	superlative
1 syllable	tall	taller	the tallest
	slim	slimmer	the slimmest
	pale	paler	the palest
2 syllables ending in -*y*	pretty	prettier	the prettiest
	friendly	friendlier	the friendliest
2/3 or more syllables	organised	more organised	the most organised
	modern	more modern	the most modern
irregular forms	good	better	the best
	bad	worse	the worst

2 Give students a minute or two to match the beginnings and ends of the sentences. Write the complete sentences on the board. Give students time to look at and to

remember them. Rub out the prepositions and get students to test each other in pairs.

ANSWERS
a older **than**   b the tallest **in**   c the same **as**
d similar **to**   e different **from**   f looks **like**

3 Use examples to highlight the use of *more* (and *the most*) with nouns, for example *X has **more** pens than Y/Z, X has **the most** pens in the class*, etc.

Note
If students ask you about *less*, explain that *less* is used with uncountable nouns and *fewer* with countable nouns.

PRACTICE

1 Words to check: *warm/cool, bright/dark, top.* Focus students on the example. Students work individually on their sentences, then compare answers in pairs or small groups.

Exercise 1: alternative suggestion

Students write their sentences with *This person* at the beginning, instead of the student's name. Then they read out their sentences in groups and the other students guess who they are talking about in each case.

2 Go through the example with students, showing them other alternatives. For example *My brother is the tallest person in my family. My grandmother is the oldest person in my family*, etc. Students work individually on their sentences.

3 Demonstrate this by talking about your own family, then asking students what they can remember. If possible, bring in some family photographs to pass round while you are talking, and ask students to do the same.

Pronunciation

1 [5.2] Students work individually or in pairs to put the sentences in order. Play the recording and check the answers with the class.

ANSWERS
See tapescript Module 5, recording 2 on page 161 of the *Students' Book*.

2 [5.3] Play the recording or say the phrases yourself. Highlight the /ə/ sound in *than, from, to* and

as. Show students the following stress patterns and drill them if necessary.

●●● – *older than, different from, similar to*

●●● – *the nicest, the biggest, the same as*

Play or say the sentences from Exercise 1 for students to repeat, rather than asking them to read from the page, as this will affect their rhythm.

ADDITIONAL PRACTICE

Workbook: Comparatives and superlatives, pages 29–30; Prepositions in comparative phrases: *as, than, from, like, in, to*, page 30

RB Resource bank: 5A *Put these in order* (Comparatives and superlatives), page 136

Reading and vocabulary (PAGE 40)

1 **a)** If possible, bring in some photographs of famous men and women to prompt students for this discussion. Start by telling students who **you** think is the most attractive man/woman and why. Students discuss in pairs or groups, then report back briefly on how similar/different their ideas are.

b) Write the saying on the board and explain *beholder* (old-fashioned word meaning *person who is looking*). Give students a few minutes to discuss their ideas in pairs. Feed back briefly with the class. Ask if students agree with the saying and if they have similar sayings in their own language(s). Ask students to explain the sayings.

2 **a)** Focus students on the pictures and do an example with the class. Students discuss the questions in pairs or groups, and/or as a class.

b) Tell students to read the text quickly, to see if their ideas in Exercise 2a were correct. Give them a time limit to prevent them from reading too intensively, and reassure them that they are going to read the text again in a few minutes. Words to check: *tanned/to have a suntan, pale, lead, poisonous, wig, on a diet, brave, to compete.*

> **Exercise 2b: alternative suggestion**
>
> Students read the text and number the pictures 1–5 in the order that they are mentioned.

3 Go through the example, getting students to find the relevant part of the text and to explain why the answer is true. Tell students to put **?** if there is nothing in the text to suggest that the answer is true. Students work individually or in pairs before checking with the whole class.

ANSWERS
a true ('until the 1920s')
b true ('lead is poisonous')
c we don't know
d true ('they would need to spend …')
e we don't know
f true ('a true gentleman showed …')
g true ('big is beautiful')

4 **a)** Elicit one or two more examples for different sections, for example *hair – long*. Put students in pairs or small groups to find more examples in the text. Copy the diagram onto the board for feedback.

ANSWERS
height: *tall* (para. 5)
build: *slim* (para. 1), *athletic* (para. 5), *fat* (para. 7)
hair: *long* (para. 1), *shiny* (para. 1), *a wig* (para. 3)
skin: *tanned* (para. 1), *pale* (para. 2)
age: nothing in the text
general appearance: *gorgeous* (in the title), *natural-looking* (para. 1), *beauty* (paras. 2 and 4), *fashionable* (para. 2), *attractive* (para. 5)
other: *a long neck* (para. 4), *make-up* (para. 6)

b) Ask students to think of any relevant words and refer them back to all the exercises in Language focus 1 on pages 39–40 of the *Students' Book* for more words to do with appearance. Limit this to one or two more words per category, to prevent feedback from taking too long. Encourage students to work in small groups, since it is a good opportunity for them to teach each other.

POSSIBLE ANSWERS
height: short   **build:** big   **hair:** dark/fair, short
skin: no more words   **age:** old/young
general appearance: pretty
other: blue eyes, big/small hands, nose

>
> **Exercise 4b: alternative suggestions**
>
> ● Allocate a different section of the diagram to each group. Ask them to report back to the class, explaining any unfamiliar words.
>
> ● Ask each group to make a poster of the diagram, including the words from the text and all the others they found/thought of. Put the posters on the walls of the classroom and give students time to walk around and look at them. Students ask the people who made the poster about any words that are unfamiliar.

Pronunciation

1 Show students that a syllable is a part of the word with a pronounced vowel sound in it using a couple of examples. Demonstrate that although *teres* in *interesting* looks like two syllables because there are two vowel sounds, it only counts as one because the first 'e' is not pronounced. Put students in pairs to decide the number of syllables.

2 [5.4] Play the recording once through for students to check their answers. Play the recording again for students to repeat, or drill the words yourself.

ANSWERS
one syllable: tanned
two syllables: gorgeous, well-dressed, ancient,
three syllables: ordinary, fashionable, old-fashioned, traditional

ADDITIONAL PRACTICE

Workbook: Vocabulary (Describing appearances), page 32

Language focus 2 (PAGE 42)

Describing what people look like

Before you start the activity, get students to brainstorm any questions they already know for asking about appearance. Do not correct any mistakes at this point, but simply answer the questions.

1 Words to check: *wavy* /ˈweɪvi/, *untidy* /ʌnˈtaɪdi/, *average* /ˈævərɪdʒ/. Do an example first, then students work individually or in pairs before checking with the whole class.

Note
Differences in meaning and form are covered in the *Analysis* box. Students will also see more examples in Exercise 3a to help them work out the differences.

ANSWERS
a I don't know exactly, but I think he's in his forties.
b He's about average height, I think.
c White.
d He's quite slim, and attractive, but he looks a bit untidy sometimes.
e It's dark and wavy, and he's going grey.
f I think they're brown.
g No, he hasn't.

2 Give students a moment or two to look at the photos and discuss the questions with the class.

ANSWER
Richard Gere

3 a) Put students in pairs to match the answers to the questions in Exercise 1. Check answers with the whole class. Pronunciation to check: *overweight* /ˌəʊvəˈweɪt/, *straight* /streɪt/, *middle-aged* /ˌmɪdlˈeɪdʒd/, *tidy* /ˈtaɪdi/.

ANSWERS
a He's middle-aged, about 55. He's in his twenties.
b About 1.80 m I suppose. He's not very tall.
c He's black.
d He's quite good-looking but a bit overweight. He looks a bit strange. He looks very ordinary – average height, average build. He's very tidy and well-dressed.
e It's short and dark. It's completely white.
f They're greyish.
g He's got a moustache, but not a beard.

b) Put students in pairs to decide which phrases match the film stars, and think of ways to describe their appearance.

Grammar analysis

Give students a few minutes individually or in pairs to complete the gaps in question 1. Ensure they don't look back at the examples in Exercises 1 and 3. As you check the answers, write the sentences on the board so you can refer to them later. Highlight:

● the word order in the questions: *What colour is ...?* not *What is colour ...?*, *Has he got ...?* not *He has got ...?*
● the possessive adjective: *He's in his twenties. She's in her thirties. I'm in my forties.* etc.
● the singular form of question e: *What is her hair like?*
● the plural form of question f: *What do they look like?*

Drill any questions/answers which your students find difficult. For example *What ... like?* vs. *What ... look like?*

ANSWERS
1 a What, is, It's b How, is c Has, got, got
  d How, is, in her e are, like, They're
  f does, look like, looks
2 e asks for a description/opinion of something
  f asks about appearance

PRACTICE

1 Students work individually or in pairs, before checking with the whole class.

ANSWERS
a What's your new dress like?
b What colour are her eyes?
c Has he got long hair?
d They're in their teens.
e What does her husband look like?
f What do her children look like?
g He's got glasses and a beard.

2 If possible, bring in a selection of photographs of famous people for this activity. Student A thinks of one of the people in the photographs. Student B guesses who it is. Set up the following scoring system:
B scores points according to how many questions are asked before getting the right answer – 10 points after one question, 9 points after two questions and so on, down to 1 point after ten questions. If B fails to guess after ten questions, A gets 3 points.

ADDITIONAL PRACTICE

Workbook: Describing what people look like, pages 30–31

RB Resource bank: 5B *An alien family* (Vocabulary for describing people's appearance), page 137

Wordspot (PAGE 43)

look

See *Teacher's tips: working with lexical phrases* on pages 12–13.

1 Do the first sentence with the class. Students then work individually or in pairs. Check with the class.

> **ANSWERS**
> section a: a, c, e, i section b: b, f section c1: d
> section c2: j section d: g section e: h
> Although *see* and *look* are not interchangeable, the idea of 'turning your eyes to something' is the same.

2 Do an example with the class and give students a few minutes to complete the questions individually, before comparing answers in pairs or small groups.

ADDITIONAL PRACTICE

Workbook: Vocabulary (*look*), page 32

Describe a suspect to the police

See *Teacher's tips: making speaking Tasks work* on pages 6–7 and *responding to learners' individual language needs* on pages 8–9.

Preparation for task (PAGE 44)

1 Discuss the questions with the class. Elicit *thief* and *steal something* as one of the possible crimes that the man committed.

> **Preparation for task: additional suggestion**
>
> If there have been any crime stories of interest in the news recently, you could bring in the newspaper pictures/ headlines for discussion and vocabulary.

2 Set the scene, telling students that thieves have stolen a valuable painting from an art gallery. Check the words *description, suspect, lift* and *witness* then put students into A and B groups. Within each group, students work in smaller groups of two to four. Give them time to read their cards and check that they understand what they have to do. Make sure that As look at the pictures on page 146 for only two minutes and choose the suspect. Bs must not look at the pictures! Tell As to look at part a of the *Useful language* box. Bs look at part b. Circulate and help with vocabulary. Encourage students to make a note of their description/questions, to help them with the Task later.

ADDITIONAL PRACTICE

Workbook: Vocabulary booster: parts of the face and body, page 33

Task (PAGE 45)

1 Put students in A/B pairs and check that they understand what to do. Make it clear that B (the police officer) can choose whether to make written notes about the suspect or to use the blank outline to draw the face. For the latter, students should reproduce the face outline, larger, in their notebooks. Demonstrate how B can use questions to check the accuracy of the drawing. Circulate and collect examples of good language use/errors, for analysis and correction later.

2 **a)–c)** As students finish the first part of the Task, direct them to the pictures of suspects on page 140. Make it clear that B (the police officer) has a maximum of **two** chances to choose the right picture. If the first guess is wrong, A can explain **why**, but not point to the correct picture until B has had a second guess.

3 Feed back briefly on how many guesses the police officers needed. Ask two or three students to comment on the accuracy of the witness' description. This leads naturally into analysis and correction of the language used during the Task. Put the language you collected onto the board or an overhead projector transparency. Give students time in pairs to decide which are good examples of language use, and which need correction.

> **Task: alternative suggestion**
>
> a *Role-play:* if your students enjoy acting out roles, give the police officers and the witnesses role cards with different characteristics, so they can act out the interview 'in character'. Examples for the

police officer: *It is late in the day. You are tired and you want to go home./You are a new officer and you don't want to make any mistakes. Examples for the witness: You don't remember the man very well, but you want to help the police officer as much as possible./You have a very good memory and you want to know if there is a reward for helping the police to catch the thief.*

Optional writing

Give students a model for this. Write a description of one of the other suspects on the board or an overhead projector transparency for students to read and choose the correct picture. When students have written their description, tell them to swap with a partner, to guess who it is.

ADDITIONAL PRACTICE

Workbook: Improve your writing (Writing a description), page 34

Real life (PAGE 45)

Social chit-chat

1 Students read the definition of *chit-chat.* Ask students if the people in the first picture know each other, whether they are friends, and what topic(s) from the list they might talk about. Students then discuss the other pictures in pairs, or continue the discussion as a class.

2 🔊 [5.5] Tell students to tick the topics in the box when they hear them.

> **ANSWERS**
> **Conversation a**: the weather, plans for the day, family
> **Conversation b**: health, family
> **Conversation c**: reasons for your visit, where you're from, family
> **Conversation d**: what you did at the weekend, sport

3 🔊 [5.6] Look at the first answer with the class and elicit some possible questions: *It's a nice day, isn't it? It's lovely weather today, isn't it?* Students predict the other questions. They can do this orally or write their questions on a separate piece of paper. Students then write the actual questions in their books as they listen to the recording. Play the recording. Pause after each question.

> **ANSWERS**
> See tapescript Module 5, recording 5 on page 161 of the *Students' Book.*

Pronunciation

See *Teacher's tips: helping students with pronunciation* on pages 10–11.

🔊 [5.7] Play the recording or say the questions yourself. Point out that the speakers use a higher pitch at the beginning of the question, which makes them sound interested. Demonstrate this by giving an example of a question with very flat intonation, then contrast it with the same question, sounding interested. Play the recording again for students to repeat.

4 **a)** Put students in pairs to prepare their conversations. Suggest that they practise the conversation first, so that they can act it out without reading from a script.

b) As each pair acts out their conversation, tell the other students to think about the three questions in Exercise 4a. They can then answer the questions when the conversation is finished.

> **Exercise 4: alternative suggestion**
>
> *If you have a large class:* put students in groups of six, (three pairs) to act out their conversations. This will be less time-consuming than having each pair act out to the whole class. Position yourself so that you can listen in to parts of conversations from all the groups, then do some general feedback on the language afterwards.

Do you remember? (PAGE 46)

> **ANSWERS**
> 1 a) 1 the nicest 2 nearer 3 bigger 4 the most unusual 5 the most useful
> 2 a) attractive b) overweight c) tanned
> d) dark e) short
> 3 a) look b) Has c) to d) from e) like
> 4 a) beauty b) attractive c) fashionable
> d) to describe
> 5 a) 1 Did you have a good holiday?
> 2 Have you got any plans for tomorrow?
> 3 Did you see any films at the weekend?
> 4 So are you here on business?
> 5 Are you feeling OK today?
> 6 How's the family?
> 7 Is this your first time in (New York)?

ADDITIONAL PRACTICE

RB **Resource bank:** *Learner-training worksheet D* (Recording new vocabulary), page 139

module 6

Language focus 1 (PAGE 47)

Intentions and wishes: *going to, planning to, would like to, would prefer to*

1 Focus students on the pictures. Establish that all the people have *time off* from work or school/college. Check that students understand the questions and put them in pairs or small groups for the discussion.

2 Personalise the topic of the quiz by referring back to the pictures and telling students what **you** prefer to do in your free time. Check that students understand the title of the quiz: *a live wire* = someone who is very active and has a lot of energy; *a couch potato* = someone who spends a lot of time sitting and watching television. Get students to predict which of these their partner is. Students do the quiz in pairs, taking turns to read out the questions and make a note of each other's answers.

3 Keep the discussion light-hearted by suggesting that students decide if their partner is a live wire, a couch potato, or something in between, for example *a semi-live wire, a busy couch potato*. Elicit an example of a resolution about free time. Students discuss the questions in groups.

Grammar analysis

1 Write sentences a and b on the board and elicit one or two more examples from the quiz for each verb form, for example *I'm going to tidy my desk/watch a film on TV.* Highlight:

- the fact that in both sentences the person has thought about the plan, but in sentence b they have thought **more** about it, and possibly **how** to do it, for example when to meet the friends.
- the negative form: *I'm not going to/I'm not planning to.*
- the question form: *(What) are you going to ...? (What) are you planning to ...?*
- *I'm going (to the cinema)* is usually preferred to *I'm going to go (to the cinema)* because it sounds less awkward.

Note

Students may ask about the difference between this verb form and the Present Continuous, which was covered in Module 4. Remind them that the Present Continuous is used for future arrangements, and that another person is often involved (you have made the arrangement with them). There is, of course, some overlap here, since *I'm planning to meet a few friends* could also involve some form of arrangement. It really depends on how the speaker sees the event.

2 Write sentences c and d on the board. Elicit another example from the quiz for each verb form, for example:

I'd prefer to join a health club. I'd like to go on a cycling holiday. Highlight:

- *would like* is a less direct, and therefore more polite, way of saying *want*.
- *would prefer* means *want something more than something else*.
- the question forms: *Would you like ...? Would you prefer ...?*
- the negative forms: *wouldn't like* and *wouldn't prefer* (although the latter is not very common).

3 Elicit that the infinitive is used with all four verb forms.

ANSWERS

1 Sentence b shows that the person has thought more about the plan and how to do it.

2 Sentence d means 'I want to do this'. Sentence c means 'I want to do this more than something else'.

3 The infinitive, for example *to phone, to win* is used after these verb forms.

PRACTICE

Note

You may wish to do the *Pronunciation* box at this point, **before** students start the Practice activities.

1 **a)** Go through the examples with the class. Give students time to look through the list of verbs and phrases. Point out that resolutions can be positive and negative. Words to check: *argue, spend time* + verb *-ing, keep in touch with, stop* + verb *-ing.*

b) Elicit an example of a resolution from a good student, or give one of your own. Put students in pairs or small groups to compare and discuss their resolutions. Feed back briefly on some of the more unusual resolutions.

2 Establish the idea of going away for a day or weekend If possible, bring in pictures/pamphlets from places of interest near your school, and find out where your students have been recently. Do the first question from the table with the class, then give students a few minutes to prepare the others. Put students in groups of three to ask their questions.

Pronunciation

See *Teacher's tips: helping students with pronunciation* on pages 10–11.

1 🔊 [6.1] Tell students to write the letters a–d in their notebooks and point out that a contraction counts as two words. Play the recording, stopping after each sentence for students to count and write down the number of words.

ANSWERS
See tapescript Module 6, recording 1 on page 161 of the *Students' Book*.

2 Say the phrases yourself, showing students that the stress falls on the main verbs, for example *planning/have, going/see* and that *to* is therefore weak. Drill the phrases.

3 Play the recording again or say the sentences yourself for students to repeat. Extend this pronunciation work by drilling the question forms of the phrases in Exercise 2 and helping students with their intonation.

ADDITIONAL PRACTICE

Workbook: Intentions and wishes (*going to* and *planning to*), page 35

RB **Resource bank:** 6A *Talk about the future* (*going to; would like to; would prefer to; will/won't*), page 140

Vocabulary and speaking (PAGE 49)

Holidays

See *Teacher's tips: working with lexical phrases* on pages 12–13.

1 **a)** Before you start the activity, elicit one or two examples of the important features of a holiday. Put students into pairs or small groups to discuss their (four) most important features.

b) Encourage students to describe what they can see in each picture, and whether they are positive or negative aspects of holidays. Get students to use language they know, rather than stopping to teach words like *delay* and *building site*, since these are covered in Exercise 2.

2 **a)** Do an example with the class, then give students a few minutes to divide up the rest of the phrases.

b) Put students in pairs or small groups to compare their answers and think of more ideas. Give them a limit of two or three extra ideas per category, to prevent the activity becoming too long. As you check the answers, drill the phrases if necessary.

Exercise 2b: alternative suggestion

When you put students into groups to compare answers, give each group a set of cards with the phrases on, and some blank pieces of card. Students can then physically move the phrases into groups, and can write their own ideas on the blank cards to

add to the groups. Students then take turns to turn over some of the phrases in each group, and ask their partners to remember them.

3 **a)** Start by giving students an example of a holiday of your own. Ask if any of them have had a similar experience.

b) Students tell their stories in pairs or small groups and see how many experiences they have in common.

ADDITIONAL PRACTICE

Workbook: Vocabulary (Holidays), page 37

Listening and speaking (PAGE 50)

The holiday from hell

1 Give students a minute or two to read the brochure and ask them why it is a 'dream' holiday.

2 Put students into pairs, A and B. Give them time to prepare what they are going to say, before acting out the conversation. Get one or two pairs to act out their conversations for the class.

Exercises 1 and 2: alternative suggestion

For stronger groups, put students into A and B pairs, and tell As to look at the brochure, and Bs to close their books. As prepare what to say about the holiday, while Bs think of questions to ask them.

3 **a)** [6.2] Establish that Mark and Rosa have now come back from the holiday and are talking on a TV programme about how terrible it was. Refer students back to the problems in Exercise 2 on page 49 of the *Students' Book* and tell them to underline any they hear. Feed back briefly with the whole class.

ANSWERS
The plane was delayed and there was bad weather (a hurricane), so they had to fly to another city.

b) Encourage students to predict the second part of the story, either as a class, or in groups.

Emphasise that students do no need to understand the details of the story yet, just enough to get a general idea about whether their predictions were correct. Play Part 2 and give students time to discuss what they heard in pairs or groups, before checking as a class.

ANSWERS
The hotel that Mark and Rosa went to was awful. The sea was dirty, there was no beach, there were problems with the swimming pool and the food.

4 Before playing each part of the story again, give students time to look at the sentences. Words to check: *a five-star hotel, sandy beach, ants, lettuce.* Play the recording and give students time after each part to compare answers in pairs. Encourage students to explain **why** the answers are true or false in Part 2.

> **ANSWERS**
> **Part 1**
> **a** over £1,000   **b** May, the weather's beautiful in May   **c** there was bad weather in the Caribbean
> **d** 12   **e** there was a hurricane   **f** the capital city
> **Part 2**
> **a** false   **b** false   **c** false   **d** true   **e** true
> **f** false   **g** true   **h** true

5 **a)** Remind students of the conversations they acted out before listening to the story of the holiday.

Before you start the activity, elicit or give some language for the friend to use while they are listening to Mark/Rosa's story, for example *Oh no, really? You're joking! I don't believe it!* and suggest that they could give advice about what to do next, for example *I think you should …*

b) Students discuss the question as a class.

Exercise 5b: additional suggestions for writing practice

Students write a letter of complaint to the travel agency who organised Mark and Rosa's holiday.
● *Either*: elicit the whole letter from the students and write it on the board. Discuss with them the best way to word each paragraph. Students then write up the letter for homework.
● *Or*: give students a gapped letter. They complete the gaps with relevant information about what happened on the holiday, then compare with other students.

ADDITIONAL PRACTICE

RB **Resource bank:** 6B *Holiday crossword* (Holiday vocabulary), page 141

Language focus 2 (PAGE 51)

Predictions: *will* and *won't*

Check that students understand the context and emphasise that they need to choose only the statements which are true of their capital city in August. *If you have a mono-nationality class:* students compare their choices in small groups and explain why they made those choices. *If you have a multi-nationality class:* students compare choices in mixed nationality groups and see how similar or different they are.

Grammar analysis

1 Go through the three options and elicit/explain that sentences a–h all describe things you expect to happen, they are predictions.

2 Write a positive and a negative example on the board and highlight:
● the use of *will* in a positive sentence and *won't (will not)* in a negative one.
● *will/won't* are followed by the infinitive of the verb without *to*.
● the use of the contraction *'ll* particularly after personal pronouns, *it* and *there*.
● the question form *Will I …?*
● the use of *be able* instead of *can* after *will/won't*.

Consolidate by getting students to change the form of the other sentences: change sentence d into the positive, sentence f into the negative, sentence g into a question.

> **ANSWERS**
> **1** **b** is the correct answer
> **2** **a** *will/won't* + infinitive without *to*
>   **b** Will it be very hot?
>   **c** You can't find a hotel.

PRACTICE

Note
You may wish to do the *Pronunciation* box at this point before going on to the Practice activities.

1 Put students in pairs and tell them that A is Matt and B meets him during a visit to London. Matt asks about coming to stay in B's capital city. Focus students on the example, and suggest some other topics, for example accommodation, clothes to take. Students act out the conversation in pairs. Feed back briefly on any errors you heard in the use of *will/won't* during this activity.

2 **a)** Establish that if Matt stays longer in the country, he may want to do some of the things in the box. Students match the parts of the questions individually or in pairs before checking with the class.

> **ANSWERS**
> 1 Will I have to make an appointment?
> 2 Will I have to leave a tip?
> 3 Will I have to pay?
> 4 Will I need to book a seat?
> 5 Will it be crowded?
> 6 Will it be expensive?
> 7 Will the people be able to speak English?
> 8 How long will it take?
> 9 What documents will I need?
> 10 Will there be anywhere to sleep?

b) Do an example with the class. Put students in pairs to choose questions for two of the situations, for example *open a bank account: Will I have to make an appointment? What documents will I need?*
Demonstrate the conversation first with a strong student, then put students into pairs to act out their conversations.

Pronunciation

See *Teacher's tips: helping students with pronunciation* on pages 10–11.

1 Students complete the gaps individually or in pairs.

2 [6.3] Play the recording once for students to check their answers. Play it again or say the sentences yourself for students to repeat.

> **ANSWERS**
> **a** You'll   **b** You'll   **c** There'll   **d** It'll   **e** It'll

Students then practice further in pairs. One gives a prompt, for example *hot* and the other responds with a prediction *It'll be hot.*

ADDITIONAL PRACTICE

Workbook: Predictions (*will* and *won't*), page 36; Pronunciation (*'ll, will* and *won't*), page 36

Plan your dream holiday

See *Teacher's tips: making speaking Tasks work* on pages 6–7 and *responding to learners' individual language needs* on pages 8–9.

Preparation for task (PAGE 52)

1 **a)** Focus students on the advertisements and check that they know where the places are. If you have access to a world map, make this more realistic by getting students to find the places on the map.

b) *Either*: check these words with the class and elicit which holiday they relate to. *Or*: put students in pairs to check the words in their mini-dictionary and match them to the relevant holiday. Pronunciation to check: *safari* /səˈfɑːri/, *cruise* /kruːz/, *canal* /kəˈnæl/, *self-catering accommodation* /selfˈkeɪtərɪŋəˌkɒmədeɪʃən/, *excursion* /ɪkˈskɜːʃən/.

> **ANSWERS**
> **African Wildlife Safari**: a safari lodge, the dry season, an ostrich
> **European City Tour**: a cruise, a canal
> **The Florida Experience**: a theme park, a motel, self-catering accommodation, dolphins and killer whales, sailing
> **All three holidays**: an excursion

2 Encourage students to predict the answers to the questions. Do this as a class, or in small groups.

Task (PAGE 53)

1 Establish the idea of a dream holiday. Refer back to *Students' Book* page 50, Listening and speaking, if necessary. Put students in small groups to decide on one of the three holidays. It is important that the students in each group agree on the same holiday. If students in any group really cannot agree, regroup them with students who have the same preference. Alternatively, simply allocate the holidays to different groups.

2 **a)** Refer students to pages 140, 146 and 144.

b) Explain that in each fact file there are some choices to be made, for example how long you spend in each city on the European Tour. Direct students to part a of the *Useful language* box and remind them of *I'd like/prefer to ...*

Point out the language for suggestions: *How about* + verb *-ing/We could* + verb. You may prefer to do this after the Task, to avoid interrupting the discussion.

Give students ten to fifteen minutes to discuss the fact file and complete the table.

3 Before putting students with new partners, warn them that they are going to ask each other about their holidays and explain what they have planned. Direct them to parts b and c of the *Useful language* box, and point out that *going to* is used in the questions and answers because they are talking about plans. Give students a few minutes to think about how they will present their holiday, and what questions they will ask their partners. While students explain their holidays to their new partners, circulate and collect examples of good language use and/or errors for analysis and correction later. Ask three or four students to report back on the best things about their partner's holiday.

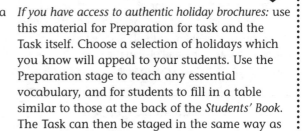

> **Task: alternative suggestions**
>
> a *If you have access to authentic holiday brochures:* use this material for Preparation for task and the Task itself. Choose a selection of holidays which you know will appeal to your students. Use the Preparation stage to teach any essential vocabulary, and for students to fill in a table similar to those at the back of the *Students' Book*. The Task can then be staged in the same way as above.
>
> b *If you want to make Exercise 3 into a role-play:* A takes the role of a travel agent, and tries to sell their holiday to B. A attempts to persuade B to change their mind and choose the holiday A has described. Students then change partners, and

change roles, so B is now the travel agent. In feedback, students report back on who was the most persuasive travel agent.

Writing (PAGE 53)

Write a postcard

Introduce the topic by discussing with the class whether they like writing postcards, how many they usually send, any interesting postcards they have received, etc.

1 **a)** Do the first pair as an example. Students then work on the rest individually or in pairs before checking with the whole class.

ANSWERS
Phrases suitable for a postcard to a friend:
a Hi Tim! b Here we are … c It's lovely and sunny d The food is really tasty e We're staying in … f … when we get home g Bye for now! h There are plenty of clubs and things to do

The other phrases are not suitable because they are too formal. Some are more appropriate to a formal letter, and some are in the style of a holiday brochure.

b) Students copy the phrases onto the postcard, then compare answers in pairs before checking with the whole class.

ANSWERS
1 Hi Tim!
2 Here we are
3 we're staying in
4 It's lovely and sunny
5 The food is really tasty
6 when we get home
7 There are plenty of clubs and things to do
8 Bye for now!

2 Give students a moment or two to read the list of things to include in their postcard. They then work individually or in pairs to write it. Suggest that they address their postcard to someone else in the class. Put the postcards up on the classroom walls for everyone to read.

Exercise 2: additional suggestion
To make the activity more realistic, bring in a selection of blank postcards collected from friends, colleagues, etc for students to write on.

ADDITIONAL PRACTICE

Workbook: Improve your writing (More postcards), pages 39–40.

Consolidation modules 1–6 (PAGES 54–55)

ANSWERS
A 2
　(1) are looking for　(2) sees　(3) shouldn't
　(4) should　(5) want　(6) think　(7) can't
　(8) can　(9) live　(10) are asking　(11) should
　(12) don't feel　(13) can't　(14) is visiting
B 1 attractive　2 explain　3 nervous　4 souvenir
　5 relatives　6 spend　7 darker　8 relaxed
　9 delayed　10 disgusting　11 gorgeous
　12 sunbathing　13 good-looking　14 guess
C　(1) the biggest/the largest　(2) taller
　(3) heavier　(4) bigger/larger
　(5) the most important　(6) more accurate
　(7) ancient　(8) tall　(9) long
D 1
　pleased/disappointed; stay up late/go to bed early; clean/polluted; excited/bored; go to work/have the day off; tanned/pale; fashionable/old-fashioned; correct yourself/make a mistake; visit relatives/entertain friends
E　(1) you'd like to lose　(2) you'll see
　(3) are planning to go　(4) you won't need
　(5) will be　(6) you'd prefer to stay
　(7) you'll get　(8) will turn
F 2
　see face; feel ashamed; look like you; turn the corner; call out your name; bring back memories
3 1 look like you　2 turn the corner
　3 call out your name　4 feel ashamed
　5 see face　6 bring back memories
4　(1) saw　(2) looked　(3) walked　(4) thought
　(5) was　(6) turned　(7) called out　(8) felt
　(9) wasn't　(10) can　(11) see　(12) Brings
　(13) can't　(14) they're not

module 7

Vocabulary and speaking (PAGE 56)

Ambitions and dreams

See *Teacher's tips: working with lexical phrases* on pages 12–13.

1 a) Focus students on the pictures and the examples in the speech balloons. Elicit one or two more examples of ambitions. To personalise the topic, tell students about your ambitions when you were young.

b) Put students in pairs or small groups to discuss the questions. Ask one or two students to feed back from their pair or group.

2 Do an example with the class. Give students a few minutes individually to put the ambitions into the categories. Encourage students to use their mini-dictionaries here. Check any new words and practise by repetition drilling. Pronunciation to check: *business* /ˈbɪznəs/, *degree* /dɪˈɡriː/, *abroad* /əˈbrɔːd/, *millionaire* /ˌmɪljəˈneə/, *orchestra* /ˈɔːkəstrə/.

Put students in pairs or small groups to compare and explain their answers.

3 Give students a minute or two individually to think about their answers to these questions, and to ask you for any language they need. Feed back briefly on some of the most interesting ideas and unusual ambitions.

4 Remind students of the importance of remembering word combinations, and of how to record them systematically, for example via word locusts (Module 1). Direct students to the phrases in Exercise 2 and elicit an example, *learn (how) to drive/speak a foreign language*. Give students a few minutes individually to underline more examples, before checking in pairs and with the whole class. If students made posters for the combinations in Module 1, they can add those with *go* and *play* from this exercise, and make new posters for *have, get* and *become*. Students can then test their partners like this: A: *married* B: *get married*

> **ANSWERS**
> **learn** (how) to drive
> **become** famous/a millionaire/really good at …
> **start** your own business
> **go** to university/abroad
> **have** a (large) family/a child
> **write** a novel or a poem
> **play** in a band or an orchestra
> **get** a degree/married/a job
> **buy** your own home
> **travel** around the world
> **appear** on TV or in a film

ADDITIONAL PRACTICE

Workbook: Vocabulary (Ambitions and dreams), page 45
[RB] **Resource bank:** 7A *Ambition dominoes* (Verb/noun collocations), page 142

Reading (PAGE 57)

1 Students discuss as a class which people they have seen in films/on TV, and what they know about them (where they are from, what films they have been in, information about their private lives, etc).

2 Check briefly that students understand what all the jobs are, and what people do in those jobs. Then ask them, as a class or in pairs, to guess which person did which job.

Tell students to read the text and see if their guesses were correct. Words to check: *make a living, support a family, argue with someone*.

> **ANSWERS**
> Dustin Hoffman – waiter; Harrison Ford – carpenter; Antonio Banderas – model; Roseanne Barr – assistant chef; Ewan McGregor – street musician; Tom Hanks – bellman; Michael Caine – soldier

3 Establish that the questions may relate to more than one of the people in the text. Put students in pairs to discuss the questions before checking with the whole class.

> **ANSWERS**
> **a** Dustin Hoffman 'a nervous-looking waiter spilled coffee'
> **b** Harrison Ford 'supporting his young family'
> **c** Roseanne Barr 'quit after arguing with her boss'
> **d** Tom Hanks 'play the role of bellman'
> Michael Caine 'his experience of military service helped him' 'heroes weren't all tall, with perfect teeth … but ordinary guys … that's the way I always try to play them.'
> **e** Tom Hanks 'You make good tips and a nice wage, working three, four days a week.'
> **f** Tom Hanks 'a nice wage'. Possibly Ewan McGregor, if students think that £20 a day is good for a street musician.
> **g** Michael Caine 'he hated life as a soldier'. Possibly Dustin Hoffman, and Roseanne Barr because she had a bad relationship with her boss.

4 Students work in pairs to discuss the questions. Feed back briefly on any interesting points.

> **Exercise 4: alternative suggestion**
>
> In pairs, students think of other jobs which would provide useful experience for someone becoming an actor (or newsreader, TV presenter, news reporter, etc.). They then justify their choices to the rest of the class.

Language focus 1 (PAGE 58)

Present Perfect and Past Simple with *for*

> **Language focus 1: notes on the approach to the Present Perfect**
>
> Rather than dividing the Present Perfect into several different uses, as is customary in many teaching materials, our approach is to show that the Present Perfect has essentially one meaning: it connects the past to the present. The past action or state is still part of the present in some way. Therefore, in both Language focus 1 and 2 students are shown that the Present Perfect refers to 'a period of time that continues from the past to the present', which we believe is more useful for students than distinguishing different uses.

1 Students look at the pictures. See if they remember that Antonio Banderas was a model before he was an actor. Direct students to the two sentences and give them a minute or two, individually or in pairs, to consider questions a and b before checking with the whole class.

> **ANSWERS**
> a *became famous* is finished   *has been a famous actor* continues up to the present
> b the first sentence uses the Present Perfect, the second sentence uses the Past Simple

2 Establish that students will find the information they need in the text, but they may need to make the sentences themselves, for example *Tom Hanks has won several Academy Awards. Before he was famous, he worked as a bellman in the Hilton Hotel.* Put students in pairs to make their sentences, before checking with the whole class.

> **POSSIBLE ANSWERS**
> a Tom Hanks has appeared in many films/has won several Academy Awards. Before he was famous, he worked as a bellman in the Hilton hotel.
> b Roseanne Barr has been a comedienne/has appeared on TV for many years. Before she became famous, she was an assistant chef in an expensive restaurant.
> c Michael Caine has appeared in over ninety films/has been a film actor for over forty years. Before he was famous, he spent two years in the army.

> **Language focus 1: alternative suggestion**
>
> If you do not have time or do not wish to use the reading text in class:
>
> *Either:* give students the reading text for homework, then ask them to tell you or a partner as much as they can remember about it. Ask them what job Antonio Banderas did before he was famous, then move on to the Language focus.
>
> *Or:* use the famous people on page 57 of the *Students' Book* for discussion as suggested. Ask students to guess which jobs the people did before they were famous. Tell them the answers yourself, then focus on the pictures of Antonio Banderas and proceed with the Language focus.
>
> In both cases you will need to omit Language focus 1, Exercise 2 and move straight from Exercise 1 to the *Analysis*.

Grammar analysis

1 Give students time to match the sentences with the timelines. Copy the timelines onto the board, to help you clarify the following points in feedback.

  a refers to a finished period of time in the past

  b refers to a period of time which began in the past and continues to the present

  c refers to a period of time starting in the present and continuing into the future

> **ANSWERS**
> a – timeline 2   b – timeline 3   c – timeline 1

2 Elicit the Past Simple and Present Perfect forms of the verbs onto the board. Then elicit the question and negative forms for both tenses. Highlight:

- *have* and *has* are often shortened to *'ve* and *'s*.
- negatives are formed with *haven't* and *hasn't*.
- in questions *have/has* and the pronoun are inverted.
- the form of the past participle. For regular verbs, this is verb + *ed*; irregular past participles have to be learnt individually. Refer students to the list on page 148 of the *Students' Book*.

3 Point out that we can add *for* to the end of the questions, for example *How long has he been famous for?* Elicit the question forms for sentences a–c in question 1 above:

a *How long were you in New York (for)?*

b *How long have you been in New York (for)?*

c *How long are you in New York (for)?*

ADDITIONAL PRACTICE

RB **Resource bank:** *Learner-training worksheet E* (Using the *Mini-dictionary*: irregular verbs – part 2), page 146

PRACTICE

Note

You may wish to do the *Pronunciation* box at this point, if your students would benefit from hearing some examples before the Practice activities.

1 Focus students on the examples. Establish that they can complete the sentences with either the Past Simple or the Present Perfect, depending on what is true for them. As students write their sentences, circulate to help with vocabulary.

....

Exercise 1: alternative suggestion

For stronger classes, students do the exercise orally, without writing out their sentences first. This also gives more opportunity for student–student correction.

....

Pronunciation

See *Teacher's tips: helping students with pronunciation* on pages 10–11.

1 [7.1] Do an example of your own with the students first, for example *I had my first car for eight years*. Show them how to count the words on their fingers, and point out that contractions count as two words. Play the recording twice if necessary, to allow students to get used to this type of exercise.

ANSWERS

a 9 b 8 c 9 d 7 e 8 f 8 g 9 h 10 i 8 j 9

2 Play the sentences again, stopping after each one to give students time to write.

ANSWERS

See tapescript Module 7, recording 1 on page 162 of the *Students' Book*.

Focus students on the example sentence. Point out that *for* is weak because it is not stressed. Show students that the *r* in *for* links to the next word if it begins with a vowel, for example *for/about*.

3 Before students practise saying the sentences, ask them to look for more examples of weak forms as highlighted above. Then play the recording or say the sentences yourself, for students to repeat.

ADDITIONAL PRACTICE

RB **Resource bank:** 7B *Life circles* (Present Perfect and Past Simple), page 143

2 Put students into pairs and do this exercise as a race: the first pair to tell you which of the verbs are regular/irregular, then the first pair to complete all the Past Simple and past participle forms. Refer students to the list of irregular verbs on page 148 of the *Students' Book*.

ADDITIONAL PRACTICE

RB **Resource bank:** 7C *Happy verb families* (Irregular past tenses and past participles), page 144

3 Give students a minute or two to look at the ideas and comment on them with a partner.

a Students look at the verbs in the left hand column of the list on page 148 of the *Students' Book* (five verbs are enough to remember in one go) for about a minute. They then cover the column and write as many as they can remember on a separate piece of paper. They uncover the column to check.

c Students choose two of the verbs from the list and write sentences with them. If possible, the sentences should have some personal relevance, for example *I left home at 7.30 this morning*, as this will be more memorable.

d Students repeat the verbs in the right hand column to themselves several times, then

e test each other on those verbs.

Discuss briefly which method(s) different students preferred. Set students the task of trying the ideas for the next week/two weeks. Ask them to be ready to report back at the end of that time.

ADDITIONAL PRACTICE

Workbook: Present Perfect (Exercises 1, 2, 3), pages 41–42

Language focus 2 (PAGE 59)

Present Perfect and Past Simple with other time words

1 Students look at the picture. Ask them briefly what they think each of Robbie's friends is like, from their appearance. Students complete the sentences individually or in pairs, before checking with the whole class.

> **ANSWERS**
> 1 had   2 was   3 went   4 wanted   5 didn't go
> 6 spent   7 studied   8 decided   9 didn't enjoy
> 10 liked

2 Encourage students to predict what has happened to each of Robbie's friends before they read the text to see if their predictions were correct. To make this stage more structured, write the predictions on the board and ask students to underline any information in the text which is the same. Then check answers as a class.

3 Put students in pairs or small groups to discuss the questions.

> **ANSWERS**
> a   Ameet **has** had ten different jobs, **has** started his own company, **hasn't** made a million pounds. Edward **has** moved to the United States, **has** made a lot of money, **hasn't** had a girlfriend. Lucy **has** appeared in plays and commercials, **hasn't** been to Hollywood. Kate **has** worked for Greenpeace, **has** had a baby. Hannah **has** been married three times, **has** lived in four different countries.
> b   Depends on students' ideas. For example they might find it surprising that Edward is the one who has made a lot of money.

Grammar analysis

1 Give students a few minutes, either individually or in pairs, to answer a and b and underline the verbs.

> **ANSWERS**
> a   Exercise 1 is about a past time that is finished. Exercise 2 is about a period of time that continues from the past to the present.[1]
> b   Exercise 1 uses the Past Simple. Exercise 2 uses the Present Perfect.
> [1] See note on page 50 about the approach to the Present Perfect.

2 a Elicit more examples of time phrases from students, for example *in 1999, in March, last week, on Saturday, two weeks ago, when he left school.* Demonstrate how these cannot be used with the Present Perfect by writing one or two sentences on the board, for example ~~I've seen him last week. We've been to France two years ago.~~ Ask students to correct them.

b Start by asking students to find more examples of the Present Perfect with no time phrase in Exercise 2, for example *He has worked in the import-export business. He has been an estate agent. Edward has moved to the United States. Kate has worked for Greenpeace. Hannah has been married three times.*
Check that students understand the meaning of the time words. Ask questions like: *Which one means 'not at any time'? Which one means 'a short time before now'? Which one means 'before now, maybe sooner than you expected'?* Direct students to the *Language summary* on page 153 of the *Students' Book* for further examples.

PRACTICE

1 a) If necessary, highlight the difference between *been* and *gone* before starting this exercise. Put two examples on the board **1** *He's been to the hospital.* **2** *He's gone to the hospital.* Ask students in each case: Where is he now? **1** He's not at the hospital: he's either at home again, or somewhere else. **2** He's either at the hospital or on his way there.

Go through the example in the book with the class. Emphasise that students need to put the words in the correct order and put the verbs into the Present Perfect.

> **ANSWERS**
> 1   I haven't finished school yet.
> 2   I've just had lunch.
> 3   I've already been on holiday this year.
> 4   I've never broken an arm or a leg.
> 5   I haven't been to the dentist's yet this year.
> 6   I haven't done anything exciting this week.
> 7   I've never met anyone famous.
> 8   I haven't travelled on a plane this year.
> 9   I haven't done any sport this week.
> 10   I've never stolen anything.

b) Demonstrate what students have to do, either with the example or by doing one of the sentences yourself. Students discuss answers in pairs or small groups.

2 If necessary, give students time to think about their answers to these questions and ask you for any vocabulary they need, before discussing their answers with a partner. After the discussion, feed back on any interesting points that you overheard.

Exercise 2: alternative suggestion

Set up the exercise as a survey. In groups of four to six, students find out who has visited the most foreign cities, changed school/job the most times, etc. Groups then compare their findings.

3 Give students time to think of three or four people that they knew and to make some notes about them. They could also tell a partner about the people, to help them clarify what they are going to write. Refer students back to Exercise 2 on pages 59–60 of the *Students' Book* before they start writing.

ADDITIONAL PRACTICE

Workbook: Present Perfect (Exercises 4–8), pages 42–44

Wordspot (PAGE 61)

know

See *Teacher's tips: working with lexical phrases* on pages 12–13.

1 Do the first one with the class. Students then work individually or in pairs before checking with the whole class.

ANSWERS
a   I was at school with her.
b   I'm not sure. I'll let you know tomorrow.
c   You know, the one you borrowed last week.
d   I'm sorry, I didn't know about it.
e   Yes, first press VCR on the remote control, then …
f   I know. What about some perfume?
g   he knows a lot about cars.
h   You know the way to Marta's house, don't you?
i   Yes … I wrote it down somewhere …

2 Give students a few minutes to look at the diagram and discuss their ideas with a partner. Check the answers with the class.

ANSWERS
section a: I'm sorry, I didn't know about it. Do you know Sylvia's new phone number?
section b: Do you know how to programme this video? … he knows a lot about cars. You know the way to Marta's house …
section c: Yes, I know Ally.
section d: You know, the one you borrowed … I know. What about some perfume?
section e: I'm not sure. I'll let you know tomorrow.

3 Put students in pairs. Refer A to page 140 and B to page 144 in the *Students' Book*. Feed back on any interesting or amusing answers.

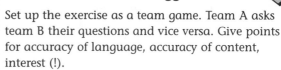

Exercise 3: alternative suggestion

Set up the exercise as a team game. Team A asks team B their questions and vice versa. Give points for accuracy of language, accuracy of content, interest (!).

Prepare an interview

See *Teacher's tips: making speaking Tasks work* on pages 6–7 and *responding to learners' individual language needs* on pages 8–9.

Preparation for task (PAGE 62)

1 Put students in pairs or small groups to discuss the people in the pictures and find out from each other as much as they can about them. If any of the pairs or groups know nothing about any of the people, feed back with the whole class, eliciting information from those who do know.

POSSIBLE ANSWERS
Gwyneth Paltrow: film star. In 1999, won an Oscar for Best Actress for her part in the film *Shakespeare in Love*. Has recently appeared in films such as *A Perfect Murder* and *The Talented Mr Ripley*.
Tony Blair: elected Prime Minister of Great Britain in 1997.
Venus Williams: 20-year-old American tennis star. Often plays doubles with her sister Serena.
Edgar Davids: Dutch footballer. Played for AC Milan, bought by Juventus in 1997. Chosen for FIFA's all-star World Cup squad.
Steven Spielberg: film director and one of America's most successful film makers. Has made films such as *Jaws*, *Raiders of the Lost Ark* and *ET*. In 1993, won an Oscar for the film *Schindler's List*. In the same year, *Jurassic Park* became the most successful film of all time.
Madonna: pop and film star. Has starred in films such as *Evita* and *The Next Best Thing*.

2 Set the scene for an interview with a journalist. Refer students to well-known magazines or news programmes which feature interviews with celebrities. Give students about five to ten minutes to choose the best questions for each person. Limit this to two or three questions per person, to keep the pace moving. Encourage students to use their mini-dictionaries to look up any unfamiliar vocabulary. Conduct a brief feedback if necessary.

Preparation for task: alternative suggestion

If you feel that the people in the pictures will be of limited interest to your students, bring in pictures of people (from magazines and newspapers) that you know will be of more interest. Alternatively, ask students to bring in pictures of famous people that they are interested in.

Task (PAGE 63)

1 Before putting students in pairs to choose their famous person, go through the list and elicit an example for each choice. If possible, to make this more authentic, bring in relevant pictures and articles, for example about someone in the news at the moment, or someone visiting the country. Students who really cannot think of someone for themselves can choose one of these people. Emphasise, however, that both students in the pair should know something about the person.

2 Give students ten to fifteen minutes to prepare their questions. *Either*: focus explicitly on the *Useful language* box at this point and elicit some examples of the different questions. *Or*: simply draw students' attention to it. Circulate and help with vocabulary and formation of the questions, encouraging students to be ambitious in their language where possible.

3 While students are practising their interviews in pairs, circulate and help them to think of convincing answers. This is important so that the interview does not break down when they perform it. Suggest ways of opening and closing the interview, for example *Thank you very much for joining us today. I'd like to start with a question about ...* and *Thank you for answering my questions. Good luck with your next film/match,* (etc).

4 *Either:* pairs take turns to act out their interview for the class. The other students guess who the person is. During the interviews, make notes of examples of good language use and errors for analysis and correction later. Focus specifically on students' use of the Present Perfect, and praise interesting/ambitious questions, good use of vocabulary, good use of intonation in the questions, etc.

Or: record the interviews on audio or video cassette. This will take more time to set up, and some students may initially be shy of being recorded, but it should ultimately be more motivating and rewarding for the students. To give the interviews more focus, suggest that students make some kind of talk show with several different celebrity guests. Choose a more confident student to be the main presenter, who links all the interviews. Provide some useful language, for example *Welcome to another edition of 'Talkabout'./ We're very pleased to have with us today .../Many of you will know our next guest from .../Our next guest is new to the world of ... but she is already famous in ...*

After making the recording, replay it for students to hear/see themselves and comment briefly on the performances. Then, as an alternative to conducting language feedback on the spot, take the recording away and prepare the analysis and corrections for the next lesson. Alternatively, if you are able to record each interview on a separate cassette, students take the recordings away to a language laboratory or study centre, if they have access to one, and listen/comment.

Task: alternative suggestions

a *If you have short lessons:* spread the Task over two lessons. Do the Preparation for task, get students to choose the famous person and prepare questions, in the first lesson. Students practise their interviews, act out the interviews and have feedback in the second lesson.

b *If you have a large class:* put students into groups of eight to ten to act out the interviews. It is too time consuming to act out all the interviews in front of the whole class.

Optional writing

If possible, bring in one or two interviews from well-known magazines. Discuss briefly with students the format that they use: it is really an interview written down, rather than a summary involving reported speech. Students work individually or in pairs on the article. They can write up their own interview or choose another one that interested them to write up. When the articles are finished, make them into posters with pictures and coloured headlines, etc.

ADDITIONAL PRACTICE

Workbook: Improve your writing (A mini-biography), page 46

Real life (PAGE 63)

Checking that you understand

1 🔲 [7.2] Students look at the pictures accompanying the three conversations. Elicit ideas about possible problems with understanding in each situation, for example in a, you don't understand the technical language the salesman uses. Put students in pairs to discuss where the phrases in the box go. Suggest that students write them in pencil, so they can make any changes necessary when they listen to the recording.

Play the recording, stopping after each conversation for students to write in any changes. Check briefly with the whole class.

ANSWERS
See tapescript Module 7, recording 2 on page 162 of the *Students' Book*.

Pronunciation

1 [7.2] Play the conversations again. Students follow in their books. Stop after each key phrase (those from the box) and ask students which were the stressed words (those which had more emphasis and which carried the main information in the phrase).

ANSWERS

Could you say that again, please?

What exactly is a warranty agreement?

I'm sorry, I don't understand.

What does 'or Dover' mean?

Can you explain what 'Bay Yin Tar Vey Zee' is?

Sorry, what was that?

How do you spell it?

What do you mean exactly?

2 Put students in pairs to practise the conversations. Remind them to sound polite in their questions, especially in the situations where the speakers do not know each other.

2 Students either write out their conversations in full or just make notes from which to act out the conversations in groups or for the whole class. While students are preparing their conversations, circulate to help with the wording of the explanations in a and b.

ADDITIONAL PRACTICE

RB **Resource bank:** *Learner-training worksheet F* (Spelling with double letters), page 146

Do you remember? (PAGE 64)

ANSWERS
1 a) get b) become c) get d) had e) became
  f) have g) became h) got
2 **a)** spoken/broken rung/sung chosen/frozen bought/thought caught/taught driven/given flown/known
  b) 1 got 2 said 3 put 4 gone 5 found
3 a) Have you been to the cinema this week?
  b) We've just moved to this area.
  c) I think we've already seen this film.
  d) I'm sorry, I haven't phoned the bank yet.
  e) That book's wonderful: I've read it three times.
  f) He's never been abroad.
  g) Have you finished in the bathroom yet?
4 a) I lived b) have you been c) She's lived
  d) I had, I sold e) They moved

module 8

Language focus 1 (PAGE 65)

Using articles

1 Students look at the pictures and discuss briefly what they can see. Use the pictures to check the meaning of *bowler hat, foggy* and *kilt*. Put students in pairs or small groups to discuss the statements. Feed back briefly on some of their ideas. If you have a multi-nationality class, ask students from the countries mentioned to comment on the statements relating to them.

2 [8.1] Ask students to listen and note whether the speaker says the statement is true or a myth, and why. Put students in the same pairs or groups as before to compare their answers. If students from one of the countries mentioned disagree with the speaker, the discussion will be more lively!

> **ANSWERS**
> 1 false   2 true in the south   3 true
> 4 more likely to be true in Paris   5 false   6 true
> 7 false   8 false – only some areas are dangerous
> 9 true for older people   10 false   11 false   12 true

3 Put students in pairs or groups to discuss this question. Make it clear that students should talk about what other people think of their countries, rather than their ideas about other countries, in order to avoid comments being misinterpreted.

Grammar analysis

1 Give students a few minutes individually or in pairs to look back at the text and think about the rules. If students are struggling, prompt them.
Ask them to find all the names of cities and countries in the text and elicit the fact that there is no article. Then write statement 1 on the board with articles in front of the nouns, and ask students to correct the mistakes, for example *The English businessmen carry the umbrellas and wear the bowler hats*. Finally, ask students to find more examples of 'talking about things or people in general', for example *Italian families, Japanese tourists, photos, French women, Scottish men, kilts*, etc. Point out that the nouns are all in the plural form.

> **ANSWERS**
> a   we do not normally use *the*
> b   we do not normally use *the*

2 Go through the list of exceptions with the students. Ask them to think of more examples, preferably from their own country, as this will be more memorable.

Ask students what kinds of country take *the*, then refer them to the *Language summary* on page 153 of the *Students' Book* to check.

Note
The *Language summary* covers more uses of articles: *a/an* and *the* for first and second mention; using *the* when something is seen as unique; using *the* with superlative forms. Some of these uses may be familiar or straightforward for students with a similar article system to English. If your students do not use articles in their first language, you may prefer not to overload them with all these uses at this stage.

PRACTICE

1 **a)** Go through the example with the class. Demonstrate that students need phrases from b, c and e to make complete sentences, and that phrases from a and d are optional. Check that students understand *general statements* (talking in general about a group of things or people) as in rule 1a of the *Analysis* box.

b) Put pairs together into groups of four or six to read out their sentences and agree/disagree. Encourage them to give reasons if they disagree, to introduce an element of discussion.

2 **a)** Do the first sentence as an example with the class. Point out that students have to put in *the* where necessary, and decide if the content of the statements is true or not. Students work in pairs or small groups to help each other with the answers. Check for the correct use of *the* **before** playing the recording.

> **ANSWERS**
> 1   France, Italy, the United Kingdom, the European Union
> 2   The river Nile, Asia
> 3   San José, San Diego, California
> 4   the Andes, South America
> 5   Hawaii, Tahiti, Madagascar, the Pacific Ocean
> 6   Lake Superior, Canada, the United States
> 7   The river Rhine, Switzerland, Germany, Europe

b) [8.2] Students listen and check. You can run this as a competition, pausing the recording before each answer to ask what different pairs/groups think. Then play the correct answer and award points accordingly.

> **ANSWERS**
> See tapescript Module 8, recording 2 on page 162 of the *Students' Book*.

In order for students to change the sentences, play the recording again and stop after each sentence. Students can help each other in pairs before checking with the whole class.

ANSWERS
2   The river Nile is the longest river in Africa. The river Yangtze is the longest river in Asia.
5   Hawaii and Tahiti are both islands in the Pacific Ocean. Madagascar is in the Indian Ocean.
6   Lake Superior is the second largest lake in the world. The Caspian Sea, in Central Asia, is the largest lake in the world.
7   The river Danube, which flows through many countries including Germany, Austria, Hungary and Yugoslavia, is the longest river in Europe.

Exercise 2: additional suggestion

Students work in small groups to make posters with maps and pictures to illustrate some of the facts in Exercise 2. They can label them, for example *the river Nile: the longest river in Africa*. This helps to make some of the rules about the use and non-use of *the* more memorable.

ADDITIONAL PRACTICE

Workbook: Articles (Exercises 1–3), pages 47–48

Vocabulary (PAGE 66)

Geographical features

See *Teacher's tips: working with lexical phrases* on pages 12–13, and *making the most of the Mini-dictionary* on page 14.

1 a) Students work individually or in pairs to check the words in bold in their mini-dictionary. Each person in the pair agrees to look up different words. They then teach each other. The pronunciation of several of these words will be difficult for students to anticipate. Either do the *Pronunciation* box at this point, or drill the following words and come back to the *Pronunciation* box after the Practice, as consolidation: *coast* /kəʊst/, *island* /ˈaɪlənd/, *canal* /kəˈnæl/, *desert* /ˈdezət/, *cathedral* /kəˈθiːdrəl/, *climate* /ˈklaɪmət/, *volcano* /ˌvɒlˈkeɪnəʊ/, *scenery* /ˈsiːnəri/.

b) *Either*: do this as a race, with students working on the list in teams of three to six until they have found all the answers. *Or*: do this as a quiz game. Call out a number at random and the first team to find the answer gets a point.

ANSWERS
See page 143 of the *Students' Book*.

Pronunciation

See *Teacher's tips: helping students with pronunciation* on pages 10–11.

 [8.3] Demonstrate that the *e* in *forest* is pronounced /ə/. Point out that the other words in this list have a sound which is pronounced differently to how it is spelt. Give students a minute or two in pairs to try saying the words.

Play the recording for students to check their answers. Play it again for students to repeat.

ANSWERS

/ə/	/aɪ/	/eɪ/	/aɪ/	/ə/
forest	climate	volcano	island	mountain
/iː/	/iː/	/əʊ/	/ə/	/ə/
scenery	beach	coast	canal	desert

2 Students work individually or in pairs before checking with the whole class.

ANSWERS
a Lake Como   **b** Crete

Exercise 2: alternative suggestions

Use the material for listening practice. Students focus on the map and cover the sentences. You read the descriptions, stopping after each one to see which pair can find the answer first.

3 Direct students to the map in the book or bring in a map of the country you are teaching in. While students work in pairs, circulate to help with the descriptions.

Students either read out their descriptions to the whole class or join up with other pairs to work in groups of six.

ADDITIONAL PRACTICE

Workbook: Vocabulary (Geographical features), page 49; Vocabulary booster: things you find in cities, page 50

Language focus 2 (PAGE 67)

Phrases with and without *the*

1 Check that students understand the three types of text that they need to identify. Encourage them to skim the passages quickly, without worrying about unfamiliar vocabulary for the moment.

ANSWERS
a = guidebook for tourists   **b** = a letter to a friend
c = an encyclopedia

2 **a)** Before students look at the texts again in more detail, pre-teach the following: *destination, skyline, coincidence, coal mining, border*. Then give students time to find the three phrases identified from passage a.

b) Establish that students need to look for the preposition that comes **before** the nouns listed, and to note whether *the* is used or not. Students work individually or in pairs before checking with the whole class. Alternatively, students work in two groups. Each student works on a different extract, and they then exchange their answers.

ANSWERS
b: at school, on holiday, on the coast
c: in the south, on the border

Grammar analysis

1 Ask students to look through the lists they have just written and the phrases here. Elicit the fact that *at university* does not need *the* because it is a place like home, work or school. Establish that most of the other phrases describe geographical location or the exact position of something, and stress that students should try to learn these phrases in groups, for example *on the coast, on the border, in the south, in the north*.

2 Draw students' attention to the pattern *in the* with parts of the day, and point out the exception.

PRACTICE

1 Make sure that students write these sentences on a separate piece of paper, so that they can hand them to you later. Stress that they can use their own ideas as long as they also use one of the phrases with/without *the*.

....
: **Exercise 1: alternative suggestion**
:
: Students write five sentences about other students in
: the class. They then take turns to read them out, for
: example *I think Natasha prefers to study in the evening*.
: The student referred to says if they are true or not. If
: a student gets more than two of their sentences
: wrong, they are out. Points can be awarded for the
: sentences they get right.
....

2 Take in the pieces of paper, then shuffle and redistribute them. Students take turns to read out the sentences without saying who wrote them.

ADDITIONAL PRACTICE
Workbook: Articles (Exercises 4–6), pages 48–49
[RB] **Resource bank:** 8A *Snakes and Ladders* (Use and non-use of articles), page 147

Complete a map of New Zealand

See *Teacher's tips: making speaking Tasks work* on pages 6–7 and *responding to learners' individual language needs* on pages 8–9.

Preparation for task (PAGE 68)

1 Students look at the map of New Zealand and discuss briefly what they know about the country. Put students in pairs and give them a few minutes to look at the quiz. Encourage them to guess the answers if they are not sure, and to use their mini-dictionaries for unfamiliar vocabulary. If your students really know nothing about New Zealand, do not spend long on predicting the answers. Check the following words and move quickly on to the listening: *farmland, fjord, glacier, lamb, wool*.

2 [8.4] Play the recording and ask students to circle the correct answer. Students compare answers in pairs before checking with the whole class, and comment on anything they found surprising/interesting.

ANSWERS
1 b   2 a   3 b   4 c   5 c   6 all of them   7 a

3 **a)** [8.5] Give students a minute or two to familiarise themselves with the map and the names of the places they need to listen for. Play the recording once and give students time to compare answers with a partner. If students found this difficult, play the recording again.

ANSWERS
Auckland: 4
The Cook Straits: 2
Northland: 5
Stewart Island: 1
Wellington: 3
The Southern Alps: 6

b) Ask students to make very brief notes, just one or two words, about each feature as they listen again. Students then look at the tapescript on page 163 of the *Students' Book* to check their answers and underline any information which they missed.

ANSWERS
Stewart Island: smaller than North and South Islands
The Cook Straits: small sea between North and South Island
Wellington: capital city, beautiful harbour
Auckland: biggest city, one million people, on the coast, called 'city of sails' because of all the sailing boats
Northland: region north of Auckland, hottest part, lots of beaches

The Southern Alps: very beautiful, has lakes and fjords in the south, people ski and do adventure sports

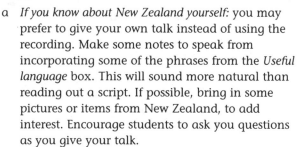

Preparation for task: alternative suggestions

a *If you know about New Zealand yourself:* you may prefer to give your own talk instead of using the recording. Make some notes to speak from incorporating some of the phrases from the *Useful language* box. This will sound more natural than reading out a script. If possible, bring in some pictures or items from New Zealand, to add interest. Encourage students to ask you questions as you give your talk.

b *If you have a multi-nationality class, who will be using the second set of instructions for the Task itself:* they will not need to have prior information about New Zealand. Give a talk about another country, one that you know well, and that your students know very little about. Arouse students' interest with a short quiz about the country, and provide a map for your talk. Give students place names to match to numbers on the map as they listen.

Task (PAGE 69)

Direct the class to the appropriate instruction card: mono-nationality groups find out more about New Zealand; multi-nationality groups prepare maps of their own countries.

Mono-nationality groups:

1 Direct students to pages 141 and 144 in the *Students' Book* and make it clear that they should not look at their partner's map. Establish that they will be finding out about places on each other's maps. Group all the As and the Bs together to prepare what to say. Then pair up one A with one B for Exercise 3.

2 Give students individually or in A/B groups five to ten minutes to think about their explanations, making notes if necessary. Draw their attention to the *Useful language* box. Circulate and help with vocabulary and the wording of the explanations.

3 Make sure that both A and B know which places they have to ask about before they start. If possible, arrange the seating so that students cannot easily see each other's maps. Students add the new information to the map on page 69 in the *Students' Book* as they listen to each other. As students exchange information, make a note of any examples of good language use and/or errors for analysis and correction later.

When they have finished, students compare maps and check how many places they marked correctly. Encourage them to work out why they marked any places inaccurately, and to review what they should have said to be more accurate.

4 Students can stay in the same pairs as before to plan the tour. Give them a length of time for the tour, for example four days, a week, or ask them to limit the tour to four to five places. If there is time, ask one or two of the pairs to present their tours to the rest of the class. Alternatively, students present the tours to each other in groups of six to eight. Provide feedback for the students on the language used during the Task.

Multi-nationality groups:

1 Have some plain paper for students to draw on and an atlas to hand. If you have some students from the same country, give them the option of working together for this stage. Make sure that students draw their maps on two separate pieces of paper, and that they do not show their detailed map to other students. Circulate and help students to choose places to mark.

2 Give students ten minutes to think about how to describe the places and make notes as necessary. Circulate and help with vocabulary and the wording of the explanations. Pair students from different countries and make sure that they do not show their partner the detailed map. As students exchange information, make a note of examples of good language use and/or errors for analysis and correction later.

3 Students compare their partner's map with their original and review any inaccuracies.

4 Give students a few minutes to tell each other which of the places mentioned they would most like to see. Then feed back on one or two points of interest. Provide feedback for the students on the language used during the Task.

Writing (PAGE 70)

Formal and informal letters

The aim of this section is to enable students to recognise the layout and language of a formal letter. They do not have to produce a formal letter at this level.

1 **a)–b)** Start by asking students what kinds of people/places they receive formal letters from, for example the bank, a telephone company. Then give students a few minutes to look at the questions and briefly scan the letters. Students discuss their answers in pairs before checking with the whole class.

ANSWERS

a A clerk is writing to Mr J. Williams to confirm a hotel booking. It is a formal letter: the layout, the headed paper, the fact that it is typed and the language tell you this.

b Andi is writing to his friend Sam to say that he can come and stay with him in New Zealand. It is an informal letter: the fact that it is handwritten, the language, underlining and the exclamation marks tell you this.

2 **a)–c)** Students discuss these questions in pairs or as a whole class.

ANSWERS

a Letter **a** has the sender's full address in the top right corner, and the addressee's name and address set below it, on the left hand side. The full date is given.
Letter **b** has just the sender's city (although the complete address could also be written, or no address at all) and the date is written without the year. The key thing to point out is that the address and date are much less important for informal letters.

b The informal letter has contractions. These are not acceptable in a formal letter.

c 1 Dear Sir – Yours faithfully
2 Dear Mrs Kemble – Yours sincerely
3 Dear Kate – Love
4 My darling Joanna – With all my love

3 Give students a few minutes individually to find the formal phrases, before checking in pairs and/or as a class.

ANSWERS

It's fine for you to stay here – I am pleased to confirm your reservation
about – approximately
I'll make sure there's somewhere for you to park – I will reserve a parking space
I'm sending you – I enclose
I'm sure you'll have a great time – hope that you will have a pleasant stay
get in touch if you've got any questions – Please do not hesitate to contact me if you have any further queries.
I can't wait to see you again – I look forward to welcoming you

4 Encourage students to make notes, before they start writing. They then tell a partner their ideas, and ask them to comment/make suggestions. Students write up the letter for homework. Alternatively, they can write a first draft in class, then a second draft for homework.

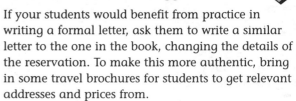

Exercise 4: alternative suggestion

If your students would benefit from practice in writing a formal letter, ask them to write a similar letter to the one in the book, changing the details of the reservation. To make this more authentic, bring in some travel brochures for students to get relevant addresses and prices from.

Do you remember? (PAGE 71)

ANSWERS

2 a) the Atlantic – it is an ocean, the others are mountain ranges
b) the Nile – it is a river, the others are seas/oceans
c) the Suez – it is a canal, the others are rivers
d) the Earth – because the Sun and Moon are in the sky

3 a) at night
b) on the left
c) at university
d) at the bottom
e) in the south
f) on the wall
g) on the north-east coast
h) in the middle

ADDITIONAL PRACTICE

Workbook: Improve your writing (Formal letters and informal notes), page 52

[RB] **Resource bank:** *Learner-training worksheet G* (Noticing and remembering prepositions and articles in phrases), page 150

module 9

Vocabulary and speaking (PAGE 72)

Modern and traditional

See *Teacher's tips: working with lexical phrases* on pages 12–13, and *making the most of the Mini-dictionary* on pages 13–14.

1 Ask students to name some of the objects/places they can see in the pictures. Then direct them to boxes A and B and give them a few minutes, individually or in pairs, to match the items, using their mini-dictionaries where necessary.

ANSWERS
a fast food restaurant/a traditional restaurant
e-mail/letters and telegrams
a personal computer/a typewriter
a rock concert/a circus
a shopping mall/a corner shop
a CD player/a cassette player
an electronic organiser/a diary and an address book
a CD-ROM/an encyclopedia
a computer game/a board game
a microwave/a cooker
a hypermarket/a market
a theme park/a fair

2 Put students in pairs to discuss which box the items should go in. Students may not agree on which items are modern/traditional and this should generate plenty of discussion.

POSSIBLE ANSWERS
Box A: a mobile phone, the Internet, air conditioning, a photocopier, a fax machine, a motorway, a skyscraper (many of these could arguably be seen as traditional by younger students)
Box B: a library, a bicycle

3 Go through the example with the class. Then give students a few moments individually to choose the three pairs of items and think about the advantages/ disadvantages, before putting them in pairs or small groups to compare their ideas. If necessary, give a personal example of an item which you have problems with. The question can then be discussed in groups or as a class.

ADDITIONAL PRACTICE

Workbook: Vocabulary (Modern and traditional), page 57; Vocabulary booster: technology, page 58

Reading and vocabulary (PAGE 73)

1 Put students in small groups to discuss the question and ask them to report back on the most popular type of shop within the group.

2 **a)** Ask students to look at the pictures and predict what kind of shop each person runs, and what the advantages of each type of shop might be. Then ask them to read the text very quickly and match the pictures to the paragraphs. Give them a time limit and point out that they only need to read the first sentences of each paragraph in order to do the exercise.

ANSWERS
a paragraph 3   b paragraph 2   c paragraph 1

b) Give students time to read through the text carefully and make a note of their answers, before comparing answers in pairs and/or as a class.

ANSWERS
Differences: Dilip and Andrija's shop sells only stationery, whereas Nicole's shop is a hypermarket and sells everything. Dave Stirling sells only CDs, but he sells through the Internet, not from a shop.
Advantages: 1 Dilip and Andrija offer personal contact with their customers. **2** In Nicole's hypermarket people can do all their shopping in one place, and it has a restaurant and entertainment for children. **3** CDs cost much less and people can buy them without leaving home.

3 These questions can be discussed in small groups or as a whole class.

Language focus 1 (PAGE 74)

May, might, will, definitely, etc.

It is not necessary for students to have read the text on page 73 in order to do Language focus 1. The context of future changes links back equally well to Vocabulary and speaking on page 72.

1 Establish the context of changes in the future, perhaps by referring back to the hypermarket and the Internet 'shop' in the reading text on page 73 of the *Students' Book*. Check that students understand *replace,* then put them in small groups to discuss their opinions.

2 **a)** [9.1] Students look at the pictures of the three people. Tell students to write the letter a, b or c next to the appropriate person/picture as they listen. Ask them to comment on whether the people's opinions are the same as theirs.

ANSWERS
Lucy: b   Mary: a   Stefan: c

b) Give students a minute or two to read through the texts, and to predict the kind of language that goes in the gaps. Play the recording again for students to complete the gaps. If you think your students will have difficulty hearing the words, or need help with spelling, write the following prompts on the board first: *probably, definitely, will, won't, may, might.* Avoid spending time on *may, might,* etc. when checking answers as this is covered in the *Analysis* box.

ANSWERS
2 probably buy
3 might stop
4 definitely be
5 may not disappear
6 probably won't replace
7 will probably use

Grammar analysis

Students discuss their answers to questions 1 and 2 in pairs before checking with the whole class. As you check the answers, highlight:

- *may* and *might* show uncertainty: it's possible that this will happen, but also possible that it won't. There is not a significant difference in the degree of probability between the two: intonation is more important in showing how certain you are.
- the use of the infinitive without *to* in all the forms.
- the pronunciation of *may* /meɪ/ and *might* /maɪt/.
- the pronunciation of *definitely* /ˈdefɪnətli/ and *probably* /ˈprɒbəbli/.
- *probably* and *definitely* come **after** *will* and **before** *won't*.
- the negative forms: *may not* and *might not* (these are not usually contracted).

ANSWERS
1 1 will definitely use   2 'll probably use
   3 may/might use   4 probably won't use
   5 definitely won't use
2 **a** *probably* and *definitely* come after *will* (positive sentences) and before *won't* (negative sentences)
   b *may not/might not (mightn't)* + infinitive without *to*

PRACTICE

1 **a)** Go through the example with the class. Show students that they need to give a reason for their opinion. Give students a few minutes to prepare their sentences.

b) Demonstrate with a student. Then put students in pairs to compare answers.

Exercise 1: alternative suggestion

To challenge stronger students: ask students to spend a few minutes thinking about their opinions rather than writing. They then pair up and ask each other about their ideas: 'What do you think about number 4?' etc.

Note
You may wish to do the *Pronunciation* box at this point, especially if students have had problems pronouncing *won't*.

2 Students work individually on their predictions, adding a reason wherever possible. They then compare answers in pairs or small groups. Feed back briefly to the class on any surprising answers.

Pronunciation

See *Teacher's tips: helping students with pronunciation* on pages 10–11.

1 [9.2] Ask students to listen to the phrases and decide which sounds different: *won't, want* or *don't.*

2 [9.3] Play the sentences for students to hear *won't* in context, and get them to repeat.

ADDITIONAL PRACTICE

Workbook: *may, might, will, definitely,* etc. (Exercises 1–4), pages 53–55

RB **Resource bank:** 9A *In the 2020s (will, won't, may* and *might* for future possibility), page 151

Wordspot (PAGE 75)
change

See *Teacher's tips: working with lexical phrases* on pages 12–13.

1 Students work on the diagram individually or in pairs before checking answers with the whole class. Students then copy the complete diagram into their notebooks, into the separate Wordspot section, if they have started one.

ANSWERS

section a: c	section c: b	section e: e
section b: a	section d: f	section f: d

2 **a)–b)** Put students in pairs to discuss their answers to a and b. Point out that they need to use *change* in their answers to b. Feed back briefly with the whole class.

POSSIBLE ANSWERS

a **change colour:** the sky, leaves on trees, a person's skin (in the sun)
change appearance: dye/cut hair, lose/gain weight, wear a different style of clothes, grow a beard/moustache
need some change: for a drinks machine, for a car park, for a bus fare, to leave a tip in a restaurant, at a motorway toll
b you change your address; you change money; you get £38 change; it changes into a prince (!)

3 Before starting the activity, check that students know how to ask the necessary questions by eliciting one or two examples, *Have you changed your phone number recently? Have you got a lot of change in your pocket?* Students then move round the class, writing down the name of anyone who answers *yes* to a question. Encourage students to ask follow-up questions, for example *Why did you change it? What name would you change it to?* etc. Get one or two students to report back to the class on interesting answers.

Exercise 3: alternative suggestion

If it is not possible for the whole class to stand up and move around, put students in groups of six to eight to ask each other the questions across the group.

Language focus 2 (PAGE 76)

Present tense after *if, when, before* and other time words

1 Students discuss briefly what they can find in leisure centres, why they would/wouldn't go to one, if there is one in or near their town, do they use it and how often, etc. Direct students to the descriptions and pictures of the two proposed sites. Give them a few minutes, in pairs, to discuss the good/bad points of each. Feed back briefly. Be careful to avoid overlap with Exercise 2.

POSSIBLE ANSWERS

Site A: good for public transport but could cause parking and traffic problems; existing cafés and restaurants could lose business because of the cafés and restaurants in the complex.
Site B: room for a car park, and would bring entertainment facilities to the area, but would spoil the beauty of the area, and cause traffic problems.

2 Do the first sentence with the class as an example. Then put students in pairs to discuss the rest. Feed back with the whole class, encouraging students to justify their answers.

ANSWERS

a both **b** site B **c** both **d** both **e** site B
f site A **g** both

Grammar analysis

Direct students back to sentences a–g and give them a few minutes, individually or in pairs, to think about questions 1 and 2. As you check the answers, highlight:

- the fact that although the sentences are talking about the **future**, we use a **present verb form** after *if, when, before, as soon as.* This may well be different in the students' own language. Point out that, for example, *If they will build the complex on this site, more people will use it.* is wrong, and invite students to correct it.
- the fact that the two clauses can be reversed, as in sentence f, and that there is no comma between the clauses in this case.
- the difference in meaning between *if, when,* and *as soon as* (see *Language summary* on page 154 of the *Students' Book*).
- the fact that *will* and *won't* are most commonly used in the main clause, but that other verb forms are also possible, for example *may* (sentence c) and *should* (sentence g). The *Language summary* covers other future verb forms and other modals. Point these out if you feel it will not overload your students.

ANSWERS

1 b **2** a the present **b** *will, won't, may, should*

PRACTICE

1 **a)** Students work individually and/or in pairs before checking with the whole class.

ANSWERS

2 is, will complain	6 will lose, put
3 opens, will create	7 find out, make
4 don't have, will need	8 build, won't be able
5 be, don't build	to park

b) Give students a few minutes to write their sentences before putting them in pairs or small groups to compare their ideas and discuss the questions. If you wish, you can extend this into a whole class discussion/debate and finish with students voting for their preferred site.

2 When students have completed the conversations, encourage them to practise reading them aloud a few times in their pair. They can then act them out for the class without referring to their books too much, and will therefore sound more natural.

3 [9.4] As students listen, they decide which conversations were most similar to the recorded examples.

Exercise 3: additional suggestion

The recorded conversations can be used as models for work on intonation. Students listen and repeat, trying to copy the intonation. They then act out the conversations in their pairs.

ADDITIONAL PRACTICE

Workbook: Present tense after *if, when, before* and other time words (Exercises 5 and 6), page 56

RB **Resource bank:** 9B *Worried parents* (Present tense after *if, when, as soon as* and other time words), page 152

Decide on five improvements to your school or office

See *Teacher's tips: making speaking Tasks work* on pages 6–7 and *responding to learners' individual language needs* on pages 8–9.

Preparation for task (PAGE 78)

1 Introduce the topic of magazine/newspaper competitions. You could bring in some authentic examples to pass round. These do not have to be in English, as they are simply to provide a prompt for discussion. Put students in pairs or small groups to discuss the questions. If any of your students or someone they know has won a competition, ask them to tell the class what they had to do, what they won, etc.

2 Students scan the entry form very quickly, so that they can tell you it's about making improvements to a workplace. Explain *facelift* if necessary.
Then ask students to read the entry form again more carefully, to answer questions 1–4. Words to check: *basic equipment, luxuries, redecoration, study/sports facilities, your environment, new features.* Students discuss answers in pairs or groups before checking with the whole class.

ANSWERS
a Three prizes of between £10,000 and £50,000. You have to spend it on improving your workplace.
b You can spend it on the appearance of the place, study facilities, the outside area, sports facilities, a more comfortable environment.

---

c Five ways of improving your workplace, exactly what you want to include, where, and why, and how the features will make your workplace better.
d No (the magazine will do this).

Task (PAGE 78)

1 Students need to decide as a class whether they are going to enter for their school or workplace (if they all work for the same company, for example). Then give students time individually to think and make notes about their ideas. Circulate and help with vocabulary and wording of ideas.

Task: additional suggestion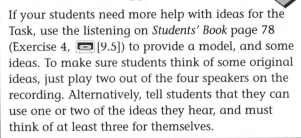

If your students need more help with ideas for the Task, use the listening on *Students' Book* page 78 (Exercise 4, [9.5]) to provide a model, and some ideas. To make sure students think of some original ideas, just play two out of the four speakers on the recording. Alternatively, tell students that they can use one or two of the ideas they hear, and must think of at least three for themselves.

---

2 Before putting students in pairs or small groups to compare their ideas, direct them to the *Useful language* box. *Either:* go through the *Useful language* box with the class. Point out the use of the modal verbs *should, will, might* and check the meaning. *Or:* simply let students refer to the *Useful language* box as necessary. While students are discussing their ideas, make a note of examples of good language use and/or errors for analysis and correction later.

3 **a)** Write up students' ideas as you elicit them from the groups, or get a confident student to do this.

b) Students decide which they think are the five best improvements from the list. Make sure students understand they can only vote three times each. Go through the list, asking for votes (a show of hands) for each idea, and write the totals next to them. The five improvements with the highest number of votes win.

4 [9.5] Direct students to the table and establish that they need only make notes. After listening, students compare answers in pairs before checking with the whole class, or in the tapescript on *Students' Book* page 163. Using the tapescript, focus specifically on the language the people use to express the reasons for their improvements, for example *so (that) ... to ...*, to help students with the Optional writing.

ANSWERS

	Where?	Improvements?	Why?
a	office	put in air conditioning	so we don't have to open windows – it's noisy
		get comfortable chairs	because our chairs are really uncomfortable
		put in lifts	because we're on the fifth and sixth floors – to make our lives easier!
b	school	have a cafeteria	so people don't have to stand in the corridor/street
c	school	have a computer room	so students can learn whenever they have time
		put a video in every classroom	because videos are more interesting for language learning
d	office	have a gym	because it would be good for the company – people would probably work harder

Task: alternative suggestions

a *If you have short lessons:* leave out the voting and the listening stages of the Task. Once students have discussed their ideas in pairs/groups (Exercise 2), ask them to write their entries for homework, so there is still a clear outcome for the Task.

b *If you have a large class, and think the voting stage is too time-consuming:* regroup students after Exercise 2. This way they have new partners to explain their ideas to. Ask them to agree on the best five, as a group.

Optional writing

Students write their entry in their notebooks. Take in the completed entries and redistribute them, asking students to comment on how persuasive they are.

Real life (PAGE 80)

Shopping in a department store

1 Introduce the topic with a brief discussion of department stores that students know, what kinds of things you can buy there, etc. Focus students on sentences a–i and check that they understand the three choices of place. Put them in pairs to decide where they might hear the sentences, before checking with the whole class.

ANSWERS
cash desk: c, h
clothes department: d, e, g
anywhere in the store: a, b, f, i

2 🔊 [9.6] Play the recording, stopping after each conversation for students to write their answers. You will probably need to play the recording twice. Check answers with the whole class. Students can then practise the conversations in pairs. They can also test each other: one reads the first line of the conversation, the other has their book closed and tries to remember the second line.

ANSWERS
a I'm just looking, thanks.
b On the ground floor, near the entrance.
c Sorry madam, we don't accept credit cards: cheques or cash.
d We only have what's there, I'm afraid.
e Just over there, on the right. Can you see them?
f Certainly, if you keep the receipt.
g Sorry, we haven't got any left.
h Thank you.
i Yes sir, just next to the restaurant on the fourth floor.

3 🔊 [9.7] To avoid students calling out all their answers together to the situations, put them in pairs. Tell them to confer in their pairs when you pause the recording. Then nominate different pairs to give you their ideas before playing the recorded version. Make it clear to students whether their version is acceptable English, even if it is not the same as the recording.

Do you remember? (PAGE 80)

ANSWERS
1 c) I'll be a princess and **I'll live** in a castle.
    d) We **might not** have telephones.
2 a) I might watch TV when I get home tonight.
    b) I might buy some CDs if I go shopping tomorrow / If I go shopping tomorrow, I might buy some CDs.
    c) I'll study English if I have time this weekend / If I have time this weekend, I'll study English.
    d) I'm going to work in the USA when I can speak English well / When I can speak English well, I'm going to work in the USA.
    e) I'll wash my hair as soon as I get up.
3 a) pay by cheque   b) expand your business
    c) keep your receipt   d) deliver some letters
    e) chat about the weather
4 a) in   b) for   c) back   d) into   e) on   f) of

ADDITIONAL PRACTICE

RB **Resource bank:** *Learner-training worksheet H*
(Deducing meaning from context – part 1), page 153

65

module 10

Reading, listening and vocabulary (PAGE 81)

See *Teacher's tips: working with lexical phrases* on pages 12–13, and *making the most of the Mini-dictionary* on pages 13–14.

1 **a)** Elicit one or two examples, then put students in pairs to make their lists.

Exercise 1a: alternative suggestions

- Make this activity a race. Give students, in pairs, one minute to write down as many health problems as they can. Alternatively, without setting a time limit, see which pair is the first to write down ten problems.

- Mime a sequence of health problems yourself, for example *a cold, a cough, a headache, backache, cut yourself, burn yourself, hay fever, stress.* Then ask students to write down as many as they can remember and compare with a partner.

b) Give students a time limit to scan the quiz (for example thirty seconds) so that they only look at the problems, not the choices. Feed back briefly on the problems mentioned, answering any questions about vocabulary.

2 Establish that none, one, two or all the answers to each question may be correct. Put students in pairs to work through the quiz together. Students use their mini-dictionaries to check unfamiliar vocabulary. Give them a limit of three words each to look up, to encourage them to use the dictionary only for those words which they cannot guess from context.

3 [10.1] Tell students to circle the correct answer(s) as they listen, and to make brief notes on other information the doctor gives. If students find the listening challenging, play it again, stopping after each question to check the answers. Students discuss the question in pairs or as a class.

ANSWERS
1 c (twenty minutes under the tap)
2 c (open windows, get in a bath of cool water)
3 c (have hot drinks)
4 b and c (potatoes, etc. are OK if they are not fried)
5 b (a little alcohol is OK)
6 b (you need to move to help the muscles in your back)

Exercise 3: alternative suggestion

Do the listening as a jigsaw. One group listens to questions 1–3, the other group (if possible in another room) listens to questions 4–6. Then students from the two groups pair up and exchange information.

4 Go through the examples with the class. Refer students back to the quiz to find more word combinations. Students work individually or in pairs before checking with the whole class.

ANSWERS
I've got: a temperature/backache/a pain in my chest
to take: aspirin/regular exercise/antibiotics
to put: a plaster/water/butter or oil on it

Pronunciation

See *Teacher's tips: helping students with pronunciation* on pages 10–11.

1 Put students in pairs to say the words to each other and mark where the stress falls.
2 [10.2] Play the recording for students to check. As you go through the answers, point out:
- in *medicine* ●●, *aspirin* ●●, and *temperature* ●●●, one of the syllables is not pronounced.
- *ache* is pronounced /eɪk/.
- the second *a* in *bandage* is pronounced /ə/.

ANSWERS

● ●	● ●	● ● ● ● ●	● ● ●
plaster	aspirin	antibiotics	exercise

● ●	● ●	● ● ●	● ● ●
headache	healthy	prescription	temperature

5 **a)** Go through the example, or get three students to demonstrate it. Then put students in groups of three (and some groups of four if necessary – the fourth person is D, and also gives advice) to prepare their conversations. Encourage students to do the exercise orally, rather than writing out a script. Get them to practise the conversations in their groups before acting them out for the class.

b) While students act out their conversations, make a note of good language use and/or errors, for analysis and correction at the end of the activity.

ADDITIONAL PRACTICE

RB Resource bank: 10A *What can I do for you?*
(Vocabulary relating to health problems), page 154

Language focus 1 (PAGE 82)

Used to

1 Introduce the idea of life two or three hundred years ago. Either elicit ideas from the whole class, or put students in small groups to discuss their ideas first.

2 Words to check: *average, cure, diseases, methods, hygiene.* Focus students on the pictures. Ask them what they show about life in those times, for example very large families, more people died young, etc. Students read the paragraphs quickly and match them to the pictures.

> **ANSWERS**
> **para. 1:** picture c   **para. 3:** picture d
> **para. 2:** picture a   **para. 4:** picture b

Grammar analysis

1 Direct students to the first example of *used to* in paragraph 1: *a lot of babies used to die.* Give them time to find five more examples in the other paragraphs, and to decide which explanation is wrong. Students discuss answers in pairs before checking with the class.

> **ANSWERS**
> **Examples:**
> para. 2 *Families often used to have ten or twelve children …*
> para. 3 *Many people didn't use to have enough to eat./They used to believe that …*
> para. 4 *Even rich people didn't use to wash very often/they used to cook with a lot of strong spices …*
> **Explanation c is wrong.**

2 Students should be able to tell you the negative form, from the examples in paragraphs 3 and 4. They may be able to work out the question form. If not, write a couple of examples on the board: *Did people use to have enough to eat? Did people use to wash a lot?* Highlight the use of the auxiliary *did* and the word order, as in any other Past Simple question form.

PRACTICE

1 Words to check: *pigeons, electricity, witches.* Go through the example and point out that most of the beginnings in A have two possible endings in B. Students work individually or in pairs before checking with the whole class.

> **Exercise 1: alternative suggestion**
>
> To make this a speaking activity, students work in pairs. They look at either at box A or box B and cover up the other box. A reads out a beginning and B responds with a suitable ending. They then change over.

> **Pronunciation**
>
> See *Teacher's tips: helping students with pronunciation* on pages 10–11.
>
> [10.3] Play the recording once for students to listen to the rhythm of the of the phrases. Highlight the fact that *to* is weak /tə/ and that the *s* in *use* is pronounced /s/, not /z/ as in the verb *to use.* Play the recording again for students to repeat after each part.

2 Give students a few minutes individually to complete the sentences. Put students in pairs to compare sentences, encouraging them to ask follow-up questions if appropriate, for example *Why?/Why not?*

> **Exercise 2: alternative suggestion**
>
> Students move around the class comparing their sentences, and see how many people have similar answers.

ADDITIONAL PRACTICE

Workbook: *Used to/didn't use to* (Exercises 4 and 5), pages 60–61

RB Resource bank: 10B *The Ghost* (*used to* and Past Simple), page 155

Vocabulary (PAGE 83)

Accidents

See *Teacher's tips: working with lexical phrases* on pages 12–13, and *making the most of the Mini-dictionary* on page 14.

1 Focus students on the pictures. Give them a minute or two, individually or in pairs, to find the words in bold that they illustrate. Encourage students to use their mini-dictionaries to check unfamiliar words. Check the meaning of any other new vocabulary, for example *slip, bump into, slightly* and check the pronunciation of: *bruise* /bru:z/, *hurt* /hɜ:t/, *burn* /bɜ:n/.

> **ANSWERS**
> **The words illustrated are:** cut yourself, drop, bump into, get a bruise, bleed, fall over, break an arm/leg.

2 Go through the example. Emphasise that there are several possible answers in many cases. Students work in pairs before reporting back to the class.

POSSIBLE ANSWERS

a If you bump into the corner of a table, you'll probably get a bruise/you will probably only hurt yourself slightly.
b If you fall over in the street, you'll probably get a bruise/you might cut yourself/you might break an arm or a leg.
c If you slip on some ice, you'll probably get a bruise/you might hurt yourself badly/you might break an arm or a leg.
d If you cut yourself with a sharp knife, you will probably bleed/you might hurt yourself badly.
e If you drop a glass on the floor, you might cut yourself /you will probably only hurt yourself slightly.
f If you touch a hot pan, you will probably burn yourself.

3 Put students in pairs or small groups to discuss the situations. Ask one or two pairs to report back to the class at the end.

ADDITIONAL PRACTICE

Workbook: Vocabulary (Accidents, Other health words), page 61

Language focus 2 (PAGE 84)
Past Continuous

1 Use the pictures to check the following vocabulary: *to knock someone over, to crash into something, a traffic jam, a cyclist, a country lane.*

Elicit the story of what happened in the first cartoon from the whole class. Then put students in pairs to explain the other three stories. Feed back briefly on their ideas, but do not correct any mistakes with the Past Continuous at this stage.

2 Check that students understand the idea of filling in a claim form to send to the insurance company, and check the following vocabulary: *to admit that it's your fault, accidentally, unfortunately, half-witted.* Then ask students to match the extracts to the pictures.

ANSWERS
1 d   2 b   3 c   4 a

Grammar analysis

Past Simple and Past Continuous

1 Give students a minute or two, individually or in pairs, to look at the example and answer the questions. Copy the example and timeline onto the board to highlight the different verb forms while checking the answers.
2 Students work individually or in pairs to find other examples of the Past Simple and Past Continuous. Check answers with the class.

ANSWERS

1 The Past Simple describes the main event, the Past Continuous describes the situation at the time it happened.
The Past Continuous actions started first. (The timeline highlights the fact that these actions were *already in progress* when he knocked over the man).

2 **Examples of Past Simple:** he admitted/I turned into/crashed/I bumped into/who passed/a cow walked into/I learnt afterwards
Examples of Past Continuous: As I was coming home from work/While I was waiting in a traffic jam/I was looking/I was driving carefully

3 If necessary, elicit the table for Past Continuous, positive, negative and question forms onto the board. Alternatively, refer students to the *Language summary* on page 154 of the *Students' Book*. Highlight: the contractions *wasn't/weren't* in the negative; the inversion of the subject and *was/were* in the question form.

Time words
Other time words in the claim forms: *as, when.*

PRACTICE

1 Direct students back to the cartoon for accident c to remind them what happened. Then refer them to page 142 in the *Students' Book*. Establish that the picture shows the scene just before the accident. Tell students that they need to explain what happened, from the picture. Words to check: *to repair the road, to argue, to fight, a helmet, to laugh.*

a) Give students one minute to study the picture. Then tell them to turn back to page 85.

b) Put students in pairs, A and B, and direct them to their question prompts. Demonstrate that students need to make the prompts into questions. Drill the example question to help students with the intonation. Students take turns to ask each other their questions and make a note of their partner's answers. While they are doing this, make a note of any problems with the question forms for correction after the activity.

c) Students discuss whose fault the accident was in pairs, before reporting back to the whole class.

Pronunciation

See *Teacher's tips: helping students with pronunciation* on pages 10–11.

1 ▭ [10.4] Play the example sentences. Highlight the fact that the weak forms *was* /wəz/ and *were* /wə/ occur in positive sentences, but not in negative sentences. Play the sentences again or say them yourself at natural speed, for students to repeat.

2 ▭ [10.5] Play the six sentences once through for students to listen to before attempting to write. Play them again, stopping after each one for students to write.

ANSWERS
See tapescript Module 10, recording 5 on page 164 of the *Students' Book*.

Drill the sentences. Help students to make *was* and *were* weak by stressing the present participle: was *listening*, were *looking*.

2 Before students complete the story, check the following vocabulary: *furious, brake, to cause damage.* Ask students to read the story through once, to familiarise themselves with it before attempting to fill in the gaps. They could answer a comprehension question like: *Why did the bus crash into the shop window?* Students work individually before checking answers in pairs and/or with the whole class.

ANSWERS
1 went	9 saw
2 left	10 was waiting
3 was snowing	11 jumped
4 walked	12 hit
5 were standing	13 took
6 drove	14 was standing
7 stopped	15 moved
8 told	16 crashed

3 a) Give students a few minutes to finish the sentences, then put them in pairs to compare answers.

b) Students test each other by asking about the sentences at random, for example *What was I doing at seven o'clock this morning? – You were ...* etc.

ADDITIONAL PRACTICE

Workbook: Past Continuous (Exercises 1–3), pages 59–60

RB **Resource bank:** 10C *Bob's night out* (Past Continuous and Past Simple), page 156

Describe a rescue and decide who is Hero of the Year

See *Teacher's tips: making speaking Tasks work* on pages 6–7 and *responding to learners' individual language needs* on pages 8–9.

Preparation for task (PAGE 86)

1 a) Set the scene. If there have been any stories of heroic rescues in the news recently, you could refer to them to help you. Check students understand each person is a hero because they rescued someone. Establish that these three people are finalists and the newspaper will give the winner £10,000. Put students in pairs to look at the pictures and guess what the three people did.

b) Direct students to the table. They should be able to answer the first three questions.

ANSWERS
		Kathy	Shirley	Simon
1	Age	32	67	10
2	Where?	at a bus stop	on a ship at sea	by the sea
3	Who?	an old lady	passengers from the ship	a man

2 a) Put students in pairs to put the pictures in order. They should tell the story to each other as they do so. Circulate and supply vocabulary as necessary, for example *cigarette lighter, to threaten, to tie up.* Then ask students to read the story to check their answers (order = d, b, a, c). Words to check: *to set fire to, a shoelace.*

b) Students work individually or in pairs to complete the first column of the table. They then check with the whole class. Ask students to comment briefly on Kathy's story: how brave she was, etc.

ANSWERS
4 The old lady needed help because a mugger was threatening her with a knife.
5 She was lighting a cigarette.
6 She set fire to his trousers with her lighter, then she knocked him down and tied him up with a shoelace.
7 Yes, she is much shorter than the mugger.

Task (PAGE 87)

1 a) Tell students that they are going to find out about another finalist. Divide the class in half, As an Bs. Direct the two groups to pages 141 and 145 in the *Students' Book*.

b) Put students into pairs or groups of three within their big A or B group. Tell them to help each other to complete the relevant column of the table, using the pictures and words provided. Give students ten to fifteen minutes to do this. Circulate, helping with vocabulary and making sure that weaker students manage to fill in all the information.

2 Establish clearly that groups A and B have been working on different stories. Tell students to pair up with someone from the other group. Students ask each other the questions from the table to find out about the third finalist, and fill in the column. While students are doing this (and in Exercise 3), collect any examples of good language use, especially of the Past Continuous and any new vocabulary, and/or errors for analysis and correction later.

3 Put pairs of students together into groups of four to decide on the prizes. Draw their attention to the *Useful language* box. Tell students to be prepared to explain their decisions to the rest of the class. Nominate one confident student in each group to do this.

Task: alternative suggestions

a *If you have short lessons:* do the Preparation for task in the first lesson, then the Task itself in the second lesson. Divide students into As and Bs at the end of the first lesson, and give them the relevant story at the back of the book to look at for the next lesson.

b *If your students enjoy role-playing:* in Exercise 2, students take on the role of the person in their story, and their partner interviews them about their experience, for example *Who did you rescue? Why were you there and what were you doing?* etc. Students fill in the relevant column in the table.

Writing (PAGE 87)

Using adverbs in narrative

1 Give students a few minutes to look up the adverbs in their mini-dictionaries. To check their understanding before working on the story, give some simple sentences, which they complete with the correct adverb, for example

We were driving along when .... the car in front stopped. .... we couldn't stop in time and we hit it. .... nobody was hurt. I got out of the car .... and saw that it was damaged. I went to talk to the other driver, and .... after a long discussion, he agreed that it was his fault. I was .... glad to get home that day!

2 Tell students to read the story through once before attempting to complete the sentences. Students work individually or in pairs before checking with the whole class.

ANSWERS
The adverbs can be added to the story in the following order: certainly, suddenly, Immediately, Unfortunately, Eventually, fortunately.

3 Direct students to the circled *and* in the text, and point out how it joins the two parts of the sentence. Ask students to count how many more times *and* is used in the text (5). Tell them to look for other words that join sentences or parts of a sentence together. Elicit these from the class, or put students in pairs to look for them first.

ANSWERS
but   when   then   soon   so   but   later   but

4 a) Tell students to choose an option and to spend five to ten minutes writing the main facts of the story. Tell them not to worry about adverbs and linking words for the moment. Circulate and help with vocabulary, use of past tenses, etc.

b) If students work in pairs, they can read each other's stories and suggest places where adverbs/linking words can be added. Students then write a final draft for homework.

Exercise 4: alternative suggestion for weaker classes

Using the pictures and vocabulary for the story of Simon Rowland, elicit the story from the class and write it on the board. Guide students to use adverbs, linking words and past tenses accurately. Rub out some phrases or words from the story, and ask students to write the story in their notebooks, supplying the missing phrases/words as they do so.

Do you remember?
(PAGE 88)

ANSWERS
1 a) *medicine/antibiotics* instead of *headache*
  b) *backache/a cold/a headache/a temperature* instead of *exercise*
  c) *cream/oil* instead of *a prescription*
  d) *cool/drinking lots of water* instead of *to bed*
2 We can use *used to* in b, c, e.
4 a) He went off the road and crashed **into** a tree.
  b) Be careful – you'll cut **yourself** with that knife!
  c) I've dropped a contact lens **on** the floor and I can't find it.
  d) Grandma couldn't see in the dark and she bumped **into** the door.
  e) She hurt **herself** while she was playing in the garden, doctor.
  f) I think I slipped **on** some oil on the kitchen floor.
  g) He's too old to drive now – I'm worried that he'll knock someone **over**.
  h) Can you see where I burnt **myself** on the iron?
5 a) Eventually   b) slightly   c) Fortunately
  d) accidentally   e) suddenly

module 11

Reading and vocabulary (PAGE 89)

See *Teacher's tips: working with lexical phrases* on pages 12–13, and *making the most of the Mini-dictionary* on pages 13–14.

1 You could start by telling students about a hobby or interest of your own. If possible, bring in pictures/objects to illustrate it. Then put students in small groups to discuss questions a and b. Feed back.

2 a) Focus students on the box. Elicit that the more usual things to collect are coins, stamps and dolls. Students brainstorm other things people collect in groups.

b) Ask students to read the article quickly. They should underline any of the hobbies or types of collection mentioned, and identify them in the pictures.

> **ANSWERS**
> **The text mentions:** football; shopping; collecting dolls, light bulbs, aeroplane sick bags, plastic figures from cereal packets.

3 Go through the example in the table. Words to check: *honeymoon, to comb hair, to break into somewhere.* Give students a couple of minutes to complete the first column of the table. Students then check their answers in the text. Allow students five minutes to read the text and complete the second column of the table. Encourage students to give reasons in their own words. Put students in pairs to compare answers and discuss which obsession is the strangest.

> **ANSWERS**
> **Beverley Bloom:** shopping/she writes in the newspaper about it, she spends more than £50,000 a year
> **Imelda Marcos:** shopping/she had a huge number of shoes, bras and tights in her palace
> **Tony Mattia:** collecting Barbie dolls/he has thousands of dolls, he combs their hair for hours every day
> **Hugh Hicks:** collecting light bulbs/he has 60,000 light bulbs
> **Nick Vermeulen:** collecting aeroplane sick bags/he has more than 2,000 sick bags
> **John Weintraub:** collecting figures from cereal packets/he tried to steal one

4 Focus students on the example in the puzzle, pointing out that they need to look back at the text and that the words are not in the same order as they appear in the text. Students work individually before checking with the class.

> **ANSWERS**
> **b** obsessed   **f** interested
> **c** unusual   **g** collection
> **d** shopper   **h** favourite
> **e** desperate   **i** champion
> **Hidden word:** obsession.

Language focus 1 (PAGE 90)

Gerunds (*-ing* forms), verbs of liking and disliking

1 Students discuss which of the things they like/dislike. Encourage them to give reasons.

Note
If students ask about the difference between *like* and *enjoy*, explain that *like* (= think X is nice) can be used to talk about any of the things a–e. *Enjoy* is used to talk about things that you do/experience, for example *enjoy the walk/shopping*.

2 [11.1] Ask students to listen and write each item from Exercise 1 next to one of the photos. All the answers can be seen as unusual in some way. Put students in pairs to discuss why they are unusual and if they or anyone they know has similar feelings.

> **ANSWERS**
> Helena – ice cream (hates)
> Oliver – spiders (likes)
> David – birthday with his family (doesn't like)
> Melissa – washing-up (likes)
> Julia – chocolate (doesn't like)

3 Check students understand all the words in the box. Play the recording again for students to write the name of the person next to the word(s) they use.

> **ANSWERS**
> Helena – cold and horrible
> Oliver – sweet, lovely and furry
> David – boring
> Melissa – relaxing
> Julia – disgusting

Grammar analysis

1 As you go through the examples, point out the gerund and the noun/pronoun in each case. Elicit some other examples to add to the tables, for example:
  a Spending holidays with my family *is wonderful.*
    Being on my own on holiday isn't my idea of fun.
  b I find washing up *boring.*
    I find *having a bath* really relaxing.

c She's crazy about *opera, George Clooney.*
  She's interested in shopping, football.

Note
Students may ask about present participles, which are also referred to as *-ing* forms. If so, show them that present participles are verb forms, and are often used to make verbs continuous, for example *She's travelling in Europe./He was staying with his friends./We've been working for hours, etc.*

2 Put students in pairs to decide where the examples go on the line. Point out that d is in the middle because *I don't mind* doesn't express a preference. Copy the line onto the board so that you can put the answers on it in feedback. Pronunciation to check: *loathe* /ləʊð/, *can't stand* /kɑːntstænd/, *don't mind* /dəʊntmaɪnd/.

> **ANSWERS**
> The difference between some of these verbs, for example *can't stand and loathe, be crazy about* and *love,* is a matter of style (*can't stand* is more informal than *loathe*). The order below is a suggestion:
>
> least likes _____ most likes
>   g f i j **d** e c b h a

PRACTICE

1 a) Go through the example with the class, or do one of your own. Emphasise that students need to think of unusual likes/dislikes, like the people on the recording. Give students a minute or two individually to think about their answers, before putting them in pairs to discuss them. Remind students to get their partner to justify their answers, by asking *Why?/Why not?* etc.

b) Tell students to look at column B for examples of more usual likes/dislikes. Students then compare opinions with their partner and see what they have in common. Feed back briefly on any interesting/amusing answers.

2 Students can use ideas from Exercise 1, column B to complete the sentences. Alternatively, give them these prompts on the board: *playing computer games, smoking, going to the gym, cooking, walking, politics.* Students can also use their own ideas. Put students in pairs or small groups to compare answers.

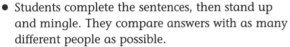

::::
Exercise 2: alternative suggestions

• Students complete the sentences, then stand up and mingle. They compare answers with as many different people as possible.

• Students write out their sentences on a piece of paper. Then, working in groups of four to six, they shuffle the pieces of paper so that they each have someone else's sentences. They take turns to read out the sentences. The rest of the group guesses who wrote them.
::::

ADDITIONAL PRACTICE

Workbook: Gerunds (*-ing* forms), page 64; Verbs of liking and disliking, page 65; Vocabulary booster: *-ed* and *-ing* adjectives, page 67–68

RB **Resource bank:** 11A *The Lovebug Dating Agency* (Gerunds; expressions for liking and disliking), page 158

Language focus 2 (PAGE 92)

Like doing and *would like to do* (gerunds and infinitives)

Elicit briefly some ideas as to what the pictures show. Each pair of pictures shows a person doing something they like and dreaming/thinking about something they want. Give students a few minutes, individually or in pairs, to match the sentences to the pictures, before checking with the whole class.

> **ANSWERS**
> 1 c   2 h   3 e   4 d   5 f   6 a   7 b   8 g

Grammar analysis

1 Do an example with the class. Then give students a few minutes, individually or in pairs, to underline the gerunds and infinitives.

2 Students look at rules a and b. As you go through the answers, highlight:

• *plan* and *hope* are always followed by an infinitive.

• *like* and *love* are followed by a gerund, and describe a general feeling (*love* is more emphatic than *like*).

• *would like* and *would love* are followed by an infinitive, and describe something you want to do ('*d love to* = want to very much).

• the question forms are *Would you like to ...?* and *Do you like ... ing? (Would/Do you love ...?* is not so common.)

> **ANSWERS**
> 1 Sentences with a gerund: 3, 6, 8
>   Sentences with an infinitive: 2, 4, 5, 7
> 2 a *Like/love* + verb + *-ing* means *enjoys.*
>   b *Would like/love* + *to* + verb means *wants to.*

PRACTICE

1 a) Before directing students to pages 141 and 144 in the *Students' Book,* do an example on the board, *Do/Would you like (learn) English?* Establish that the full question should be *Do you like learning English?* because it is asking about a general feeling. Elicit some possible answers *Yes, I do./Yes, very much./No I don't./No, not at all.*

b) Give students time to prepare their questions. Then put students into A and B pairs to ask and answer their questions. Ask students to report back on one or two of their partner's answers.

2 [11.2] Put students in pairs to think of possible endings for the conversations. Ask for some of their ideas before playing the recording. As they listen, students note which pair's answers came closest to the recording.

ANSWERS
a 'd love to   **b** 'd like to   **c** want to   **d** hope to
Point out that it is not necessary to repeat the verb (*Thanks, I'd love to stay.*) in short answers like this.

Pronunciation

See *Teacher's tips: helping students with pronunciation* on pages 10–11.

1 Say the two sentences for students. Point out that in the first *to* is weak because it is squashed in the middle of the question. In the second *to* is held for longer and is therefore not a weak sound. Ask students to look for more examples of the weak *to* in conversations a and b (*Would you like to stay …? Have you been to the …?*), and for more examples of the stronger *to* in a, b and d (*love to, like to, hope to*).
2 Play the conversations again, stopping after each line for students to repeat. Put students into pairs to practise.

ADDITIONAL PRACTICE

Workbook: Gerunds and infinitives (Exercises 4 and 5), pages 65–66

Wordspot (PAGE 93)

like

See *Teacher's tips: working with lexical phrases* on pages 12–13.

1 Check the meaning of the words in the box. Ask students to give you a word or phrase to describe one or two of them, for example *silk – very soft, cats fighting – make a horrible noise*. Elicit ideas for a, then put students in pairs to do the rest. Students discuss their ideas in pairs then feed back to the class. Point out/elicit that in all the sentences, *like* is used to make comparisons.

ANSWERS
a an angel, a model   **e** washing-up water
b a bird, cats fighting   **f** a bird, an angel, cats
c silk   fighting
d a bird

2 Establish that this exercise deals with different uses of *like* and that the word is missing from each phrase. Do the first one with the class. Students work individually or in pairs before checking with the class.

ANSWERS
a He's so young. He doesn't look **like** a doctor.
b Which do you **like** best – chocolate or ice cream?
c Would you **like** something to eat?
d What does that cake taste **like**?
e Open it at the top, **like** this.
f Your eyes are **like** your brother's.
g I'll come and meet you at the airport if you **like**.
h What was the concert **like**?

In b, c and g *like* is a verb. In all the others it is a preposition, and the meaning is quite different.

3 Give students a few minutes to put the phrases in the correct section. Check answers with the whole class.

ANSWERS
section a: b   **section c:** d, h   **section e:** e, g
section b: a, f   **section d:** c

4 [11.3] Put students in pairs and tell them to be ready to discuss their answers after each question/instruction. They do not need to write their answers.

Exercise 4: additional suggestion

To give students practice in forming questions with *like*, ask them, with their partners, to write down as many of the questions from the recording as they can remember. They then take turns to ask **you** the questions.

Make a list of the most important things in life

See *Teacher's tips: making speaking Tasks work* on pages 6–7 and *responding to learners' individual language needs* on pages 8–9

Preparation for task (PAGE 94)

1 Elicit some things that students think are important in life, and/or give some ideas of your own. Students look at the table and see which things were mentioned by the class. Students read statements a–d and decide whether they are true or false before discussing answers.

ANSWERS
a false   **b** true   **c** false   **d** false

2 Give students a minute or two to think about the question(s), then put them in pairs or small groups to discuss their answers. *If you have a mono-nationality class:* all the students should answer the same question, according to whether their country is represented or not. *If you have a multi-nationality class:* students answer different questions, which should generate some interesting cross-cultural comparison.

3 Focus students on the pictures and discuss briefly what the people are doing. Then ask students to find the activities illustrated in the list of important things in life. Give students time to check unfamiliar vocabulary in their mini-dictionary and/or with a partner.

Pronunciation to check: *religion* /rɪˈlɪdʒən/, *a successful career* /əsəkˈsesfəlkəˈrɪə/, *salary* /ˈsæləri/, *healthy* /ˈhelθi/, *a busy social life* /əbɪziˈsəʊʃəlaɪf/.

> **Preparation for task: alternative suggestion**
>
> If you have short lessons, start by eliciting some ideas for important things in life. Leave out Exercises 1 and 2, and move straight to the pictures and list of important things in Exercise 3. This should enable you to complete the Task in one lesson.

Task (PAGE 95)

1 **a)** Establish that students have to choose between the things in each pair. Do a brief model yourself, explaining your choices for three or four of the pairs in the list, and incorporating some of the phrases from the *Useful language* box, part a. Give students about ten minutes to think about their choices and how to express their ideas.

b) Circulate and help with vocabulary. Encourage any students who finish early to practise explaining their choices to you.

2 Put students in small groups to compare their answers. Point out that they can say if they would prefer not to talk about a particular subject, and direct them to the *Useful language* box part b. Either go through the language in the box explicitly at this point, or simply let students refer to it as necessary. While students are discussing their answers, note down any examples of good language use and/or errors for analysis and correction later. *Me too!/Me neither!* and *That's the same for me!* are covered in the Real life section which follows the Task.

3 Students stay in the same groups to write their list of the eight most important things (including their own ideas). They then compare and discuss them. Ask students to be ready to report back on how many of the eight things were the same in their group. For feedback, ask a spokesperson from each group to report back to the class.

4 The first question here is aimed at older students, the second at younger ones. Students discuss their answers as a class, or in pairs/groups.

> **Task: additional suggestions**
>
> a *If your students enjoy role-playing:* they can act out the interviews. One person takes the role of a famous person answering questions, and the other is the interviewer.
>
> b *For extra listening practice:* make a tape of you and another English speaker discussing your choices for the most important things in life. Students listen and note which things they found predictable/surprising, and/or note the language used to explain and compare choices.

Real life (PAGE 96)

Finding things in common

1 **a)** Point out that all the phrases in the box are ways of showing that you agree. Students work individually or in pairs to complete the conversations.

b) [11.4] Play the recording, stopping after each conversation for students to make any changes necessary.

> **ANSWERS**
> b   So do I!   c   Me neither.   d   Me neither.
> e   So am I!   f   It's the same for me.

> ## Grammar analysis
>
> Tell students to look back at the conversations to answer the two questions. As you check the answers, elicit an example for *so* and *neither* and write them on the board, for example *I go to an aerobics class. – So do I; I didn't understand. – Neither did I.* Highlight the fact that the auxiliary must match the tense of the original statement, and emphasise that *so* and *neither* are used only when the second speaker agrees with the first. It may help to show students how to **dis**agree: *I don't like whisky. – Oh, I do; I'm really hungry. – I'm not.* (with the stress on the pronoun).
>
> > **ANSWERS**
> > a   If you agree with positive sentences you use *so*.
> > b   If you agree with negative sentences you use *neither*.

2 Students work individually or in pairs before checking with the whole class.

ANSWERS

a I'm feeling really tired tonight. – Yes, so am I!

b I'm not very hungry, actually. – No, neither am I.

c I absolutely hate whisky. – So do I. It's disgusting, isn't it?

d My boyfriend doesn't like dancing very much. – Really? Neither do I, I must say.

e I was really ill last week! – That's funny – so was I!

f Actually, I wasn't here last lesson. – No, neither was I, unfortunately.

g We went to Istanbul for our holidays last year. – What a coincidence, so did we!

h We didn't enjoy the film much. – No, neither did we.

Pronunciation

See *Teacher's tips: helping students with pronunciation* on pages 10–11.

1 Drill the two examples. Get students to mumble them first, as shown, to feel the rhythm.

2 [11.5] Play the conversations, stopping after each one for students to practise in pairs.
We can pronounce *neither* /ˈnaɪðə/ or /ˈniːðə/.
In this book we pronounce it /ˈnaɪðə/.

3 [11.6] Play the recording, stopping after each beep for students to respond. Either ask individuals to answer, or invite all the students to call out.

Real life: additional suggestion

First, show students how to disagree, for example *I didn't like the film. – Oh really, I did.* Then give them some sentence beginnings. These can be dictated or handed out on slips of paper. For example:

When I was little, I wanted to be a … Last night I was … My last holiday was in … I really don't like …

Students complete the sentences so that they are true for them. They then read the sentences to a partner, who agrees or disagrees.

ADDITIONAL PRACTICE

Workbook: *Me too, so do I*, etc., page 66

RB **Resource bank:** 11B *Neither do I (So do I, Me too, Me neither, Neither do I*, etc.), page 160

Consolidation modules 7–11

ANSWERS

A

(2) saw   (3) was sitting   (4) the   (5) was crying
(6) asked   (7) stopped   (8) said   (9) gave   (10) Ø
(11) Ø   (12) Ø   (13) said   (14) Ø   (15) Ø   (16) Ø
(17) were you crying

B

1 **you can play:** an instrument, a board game, a role
2 **you can accidentally:** hurt yourself, drop something, spill something
3 **with a business, people:** start it, improve it, expand it
4 **your doctor might tell you to:** take antibiotics, stay in bed, keep warm
5 **with a computer, people might:** deliver it, replace it, chat on it

C

Eliza: enjoys going to parties/has been married four times/used to be a film star/might travel round the world next year

Philip: used to earn more than he does now/loves cooking/hasn't had a holiday for three years/spends a lot of time thinking about food

Carla: would love to have a big family one day/has made over £1 million/will probably retire in a few years/doesn't like shopping

D
Key:

s	k	y	s	c	r	a	p	e	r	
			l							i
	e	q	u	i	p	m	e	n	t	s
b			m					o	i	l
r	e	p	l	a	c	e		y		a
u			t					s		n
i		b	l	e	e	d		d		d
s		u				e		h		
e		m		r			g	r	o	w
s	u	p	p	o	r	t	e	r		b
			w				e		b	
t	i	p		s	c	e	n	e	r	y

E
There are six situations for this activity on page 145 of the *Students' Book*.

module 12

Listening and vocabulary (PAGE 99)

Designer goods

See *Teacher's tips: working with lexical phrases* on pages 12–13, and *making the most of the Mini-dictionary* on pages 13–14.

1 Establish that designer goods are those made by well-known and fashionable designers. Elicit some names for the products listed, for example Lee jeans, BMW cars, Gucci accessories, Lancôme cosmetics. You could bring in magazine advertisements for some of the products, to pass round or put on the classroom walls. Briefly discuss where the products are made and if any of them are made in students' countries.

2 Give students a few minutes to decide which statements they agree with. Encourage students to use their mini-dictionaries where necessary. Put them in pairs or groups to compare answers. Feed back briefly on some of their opinions. Pronunciation to check: *afford* /əˈfɔːd/, *advertising* /ˈædvətaɪzɪŋ/, *waste* /weɪst/, *possessions* /pəˈzeʃənz/.

Note

Point out that 'designer labels' means 'designer products'.

3 [12.1] Focus students on the pictures of the three people. Get them to predict what the people will say about designer goods, for example the grandmother will probably think they are a waste of money, whereas the son will probably say they are better than non-designer products, etc. Play the recording and ask students to make brief notes about what each person says.

> **ANSWERS**
> **Valerie:** has mixed feelings
> **Nicola:** is against designer goods
> **Rory:** has mixed feelings

4 Check the meaning of *cool* in this context (=fashionable). Give students time to read statements a–f. Play the recording again.

> **ANSWERS**
> **a** F (she was poor when she was young, and when she was first married) **b** F (not perfume and cosmetics) **c** T **d** T **e** T **f** F (only the designer trainers and jeans look cool)

> **Exercise 4: alternative suggestion**
>
> If you have a strong class, instead of doing Exercise 4, ask students to listen and decide which of the statements in Exercise 2 the speakers agree with.

ADDITIONAL PRACTICE

Workbook: Vocabulary (Designer goods), page 73

Language focus 1 (PAGE 100)

Passive forms

Ask students to comment briefly on what they think of the products shown in the pictures. Students then match the sentences individually or in pairs, before checking with the whole class.

> **ANSWERS**
> **Porsche sports car: c** They were first built in Germany in the 1940s. **e** They are often driven in Formula 1 races.
> **Swatch watch: b** The design is changed every year. **f** They were first made in Switzerland in the 1980s.
> **Ray-Ban sunglasses: g** They were worn by Will Smith in the film *Men in Black*. **h** They are often seen in Hollywood films.
> **Chanel No. 5 perfume: a** More than 10 million bottles are sold every year. **d** It was created by clothes designer Coco Chanel in 1925.

Grammar analysis

1 Go through the example with the class. Highlight the fact that the passive is used when the person who does the action is not important or not known. Put the sentence *More than 10 million bottles are sold every year.* on the board and ask students why the passive is used, (because we are more interested in the number of bottles than who actually sells them).

2 Give students a few minutes to answer the questions. To check the form of the passive (Past Simple, Present Simple and with *will*), elicit a table onto the board. Alternatively, refer students to the *Language summary* on page 155 of the *Students' Book*. As you check answers, highlight:

76

- the form of *be* which changes according to whether the subject is singular/plural, and whether the time is past, present or future.
- the future formed with *will be* and the past participle.
- the verb *be* which can be contracted, for example *It's made ...*
- the question form made by inverting the subject and *be*, for example *Is it made ...?*

ANSWERS

a **Present Simple passive:** *More than 10 million bottles are sold ... The design is changed ... They are often driven ... They are often seen ...*
Past Simple passive: *They were first built ... It was created by ... They were first made ... They were worn by ...*

b **Singular:** *is changed, was created*
Plural: *are sold, were first built, are often driven, were first made, were worn*

c *will be* + past participle

3 Point out that if it is necessary or important to mention who did the action, the agent can be included, using *by*. Ask students for another sentence which includes the agent, for example *They were worn by Will Smith.*

PRACTICE

1 **a)** Ask students which company is featured in the pictures, what they make, and what students think the connection between the pictures is. Then ask them to read the text through quickly (without attempting to complete the gaps) to see if their predictions were correct. Words to check: *manufacturer, to sponsor someone, to sign a contract, to associate someone with something, to recognise something.*

b) Establish that all the verbs need to be in the passive and do the first one with the class.

c) [12.2] Play the recording through. Stop if necessary, for students to check their answers.

ANSWERS

1 will be made	7 was signed
2 is named	8 will be associated
3 was started	9 is recognised
4 is known	10 was created
5 was sponsored	11 was paid
6 was asked	

Pronunciation

See Teacher's tips: helping students with pronunciation on pages 10–11.

1 [12.3] Play the recording once for students to listen to the stress and weak forms in the sentences. Then play the sentences again for students to repeat. Help students

by suggesting that they start with the stressed participle, then add the rest of the sentence to it, for example *started > it was started > it was started in the 1970s.*

2 Put students in pairs to practise reading the paragraph. To help them with the rhythm, play the relevant part of [12.2] or read the paragraph yourself. Ask students to 'shadow read': to read at the same time as you/the recording, copying the rhythm and speed.

2 Ask students to read sentences a–j through quickly and say which facts they found most surprising. Then do the first one as an example. Emphasise that students should first decide if the sentence is active or passive. Students do the rest individually or in pairs.

ANSWERS

a	are stolen	f	was sold
b	will be manufactured	g	eat
c	designed	h	will be sold
d	is read	i	started
e	produces	j	were made

ADDITIONAL PRACTICE

Workbook: Passive forms (Exercises 1–3), pages 69–70; Listen and read, page 73: Active or passive?, page 74

RB **Resource bank:** 12A *The Handbag Gang* (Past Simple passive), page 162

Language focus 2 (PAGE 102)

Sentences joined with *that*, *which* and *who*

1 [12.4] Give students time to read the rules and check that they understand them. Ask *How long do you have to discuss the answer? How many points do you get if you know the words in English?* Pre-teach *stuff*, a general word for *substance* or *material*. Play the recording, stopping after each definition.

Alternative suggestions for game rules

If you have a multi-nationality class and it is difficult to check if students know the word in their own language:

a allow students to look up the word in bilingual dictionaries, for 2 points.

b give teams 2 points if anyone can *draw* the item.

c have the words jumbled up on the board, masked with a large piece of paper. If none of the teams knows the word from the definition, reveal the words on the board for ten seconds. The first team to choose and call out the correct one gets a point. Alternatively, have the words on an overhead projector transparency, and turn the projector on for ten seconds.

ANSWERS

a	a sunhat	g	lipstick
b	a designer	h	sandals
c	soap	i	a butcher
d	a florist	j	earrings
e	a belt		
f	an answering machine/answerphone		

2 This stage is diagnostic. If your students have difficulty deciding on the pronoun, move onto the recording quite quickly. If students have some ideas about when to use the pronouns, encourage them to work together and help each other. There may be uncertainty about when to use *that*. If so, tell students just to use *who* and *which* for the moment, and deal with *that* after they have listened to the recording again. Play the recording once through for students to check their answers.

ANSWERS

a which   b who   c that   d who   e that   f which
g that   h which   i who   j which

Grammar analysis

1 Go through the examples with the class. Copy them onto the board if it helps to clarify them. As you do so, highlight:

- the relative pronouns *who, which* and *that* replace the pronouns *it, they, he,* etc. in the middle of the sentence. It is not necessary to use both, for example not *It's a hat which ~~it~~ protects* ...

- no comma is necessary in the middle of the sentence.

- *that* is often used instead of *which*.

- *that* can be used instead of *who,* but this is not so common. (At this level, you may want students to concentrate on using *who,* as they can sound unnatural if they **over**use *that*).

2 Give students a few minutes, individually or in pairs, to join the sentences.

ANSWERS

a A plumber is a person **who (that)** mends pipes.
b A calculator is a small machine **which/that** does arithmetic for you.
c A kettle is a machine **which/that** heats water.
d A scarf is a thing **which/that** you wear round your neck.
e Sun cream is stuff **which/that** you put on your skin when it's very sunny.

PRACTICE

1 **a)** Students work individually to match the people to the definitions, without using dictionaries. They have to guess any words they don't know, from the definition.

ANSWERS

1 car dealer   2 jeweller   3 antique dealer
4 newsagent   5 chef   6 estate agent   7 carpenter
8 greengrocer

b) Go through the example. Give students a few minutes to write the sentences, then compare answers in pairs/small groups.

Exercise 1b: alternative suggestion

After writing their sentences, students work in pairs. A closes his/her book and B reads out the sentences, but with some wrong answers for A to correct.

B: A person who cooks meals in a restaurant is a cooker.
A: No, a person who cooks meals in a restaurant is a chef!

ANSWERS

2 A person who makes and sells rings and necklaces is called a jeweller.
3 A person who buys and sells old furniture is called an antique dealer.
4 A person who sells newspapers, cigarettes, etc. is called a newsagent.
5 A person who cooks meals in a restaurant or hotel is called a chef.
6 A person who sells houses and flats is called an estate agent.
7 A person who makes things from wood is called a carpenter.
8 A person who sells fruit and vegetables is called a greengrocer.

2 **a)** Put students in pairs, A and B. Direct them to the appropriate box and give them time to prepare their questions. Make it clear that they do **not** need to think of the answer to the questions.

b) Direct students to pages 139 and 145 in the *Students' Book.* Go through the example or get a strong pair of students to demonstrate. Drill the example question, to remind students to use questioning intonation. As students ask and answer the questions, note down any problems with pronunciation (words like *scissors, toothpaste, gloves*) to work on at the end of the activity.

> **Exercise 2b: alternative suggestion**

Students work in pairs. Give them a few minutes to look at the fourteen definitions in boxes A and B. Explain that there are seven pairs (swimming trunks – swimsuit). Students close their books and try to remember the other six pairs of words. This can be done as a race. Students try to write down all the pairs as quickly as they can. Alternatively, do the exercise orally, with students calling out answers round the class.

> **ANSWERS**
> swimming trunks – swimsuit
> teapot – coffee maker
> washing-up liquid – washing powder
> backpack – sleeping bag
> toothpaste – toothbrush
> gloves – socks
> scissors – ruler

ADDITIONAL PRACTICE

Workbook: Relative clauses with *which, who* and *that*, page 72

Vocabulary (PAGE 103)

Objects

See *Teacher's tips: working with lexical phrases* on pages 12–13, and *making the most of the Mini-dictionary* on pages 13–14.

1 **a)** Students work individually, marking the objects without looking in their mini-dictionaries.

b) Students work in pairs, pooling their knowledge and checking in their *Mini-dictionaries*. At this stage, encourage students to see which objects they have with them, and which they can see around them in the classroom. Bring in pictures/realia for the items students are not likely to have with them, so that you can use these for checking pronunciation. Drill unfamiliar/difficult words, in particular: *wallet* /ˈwɒlɪt/, *purse* /pɜːs/, *corkscrew* /ˈkɔːkskruː/, *identity card* /aɪˈdentətikɑːd/, *mobile phone* /ˈməʊbaɪlfəʊn/, *tissues* /ˈtɪʃuːz/, *driving licence* /ˈdraɪvɪŋlaɪsɪns/, *comb* /kəʊm/.

2 Give students a few minutes to put the words on the diagram. Then ask them to compare answers in pairs or small groups. There are no correct answers here, the idea is to show students a way of organising their vocabulary, so that they can refer back to it easily. Students work individually and in pairs, to find words to add to each list. They then discuss where to put them, for example *swimsuit, swimming costume, gloves, socks = things that you wear.*

3 Elicit a few ideas for the first question. Then give students a few minutes to answer the others. Put students in pairs to find five things in common. Ask one or two pairs to report back to the class on their findings.

ADDITIONAL PRACTICE

Workbook: Vocabulary (Everyday objects), page 73

RB **Resource bank:** 12B *What's this?* (Relative clauses with *that, which* and *who*), page 164

Decide what you need for a trip

See *Teacher's tips: making speaking Tasks work* on pages 6–7 and *responding to learners' individual language needs* on pages 8–9.

Preparation for task (PAGE 104)

1 [12.5] Introduce the idea of going away for a day or two, or for longer. Discuss with students what they always take with them, how organised they are about packing, what things they forget to take, etc. Then focus students on the items in the box and make it clear that as they listen, they just have to cross out the two things that Neil and Lucy are **not** taking.

> **ANSWERS**
> They are not taking driving licences or sun cream.

2 Put students in pairs to compare answers and discuss their ideas for questions a–f.

3 Play the recording again. Give students time to confirm/change their answers in pairs before discussing them as a class.

> **ANSWERS**
> **a** a city (they mention walking around sightseeing)
> **b** They are going to go sightseeing and to the theatre.
> **c** They think it will be hot.
> **d** They are going abroad. They mention passports, travellers' cheques and a phrasebook.
> **e** No.
> **f** by plane (they are going to meet at the check-in desk)

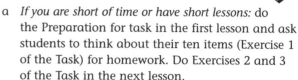

> **Preparation for task:**
> **alternative suggestions**
>
> If you want to provide a model yourself:
>
> *Either:* talk about a recent trip you went on, telling students what you took with you and why, and whether all the items were necessary. If possible, bring in photos, postcards, etc. to illustrate your talk.
>
> *Or:* tell students about a trip you are planning, and some of the things you are planning to take with you. Invite suggestions about what to take/not to take, with reasons why.

Task (PAGE 105)

1 **a)** Set the scene. Students are going away on a short trip, and need to decide what to take with them. Put them into pairs: As, Bs and Cs. Direct them to pages 142, 145 and 146 in the *Students' Book*. It does not matter if you do not have equal numbers of A, B, C pairs.

b) Give students a minute or two to read the description of the trip, then circulate and check that they understand key factors, such as the method of transport, the weather forecast, etc. Students then prepare their lists of ten items to take individually, asking you for any vocabulary they need.

c) Give students time to prepare their reasons for taking their chosen items. Draw their attention to the *Useful language* box, part a. Either do this explicitly, going through the use of *could/should* for making suggestions, and *might/if* clauses for prediction, or simply refer to the box and leave any explicit language work until after the Task. Language for making suggestions is dealt with in the Real life section after the Task.

2 Students work in their pairs, discussing their ideas until they agree on the same ten items. As you monitor the pairs, make sure they are thinking of reasons for taking each item. Note down any examples of good language use and/or errors, for analysis and correction later.

3 How you group students for this stage will depend on how many pairs you have. Students either stay in their pairs and join up with another pair, for example As and Bs, Bs and Cs, As and Cs, or they make groups of three: one A, one B and one C. Students then take turns to go through their lists, explaining why they are taking the items.
a) Their partners note down their answers to the questions.
b) Once it has been established where they are going and what kind of trip it is, their partners then suggest items students have forgotten. Refer students to the *Useful language* box, part b. Note down language for analysis and/or correction afterwards. Invite one or two groups to report back on some of the items chosen and how sensible/strange, etc. they were.

> **Task: alternative suggestions**
>
> a *If you are short of time or have short lessons:* do the Preparation for task in the first lesson and ask students to think about their ten items (Exercise 1 of the Task) for homework. Do Exercises 2 and 3 of the Task in the next lesson.
>
> b *If you want to provide more of a challenge:* introduce some unexpected factors to the discussion in Exercise 2 of the Task. While the pairs are trying to agree on their ten items, go round with slips of paper with information such as:
>
> ● for As – a news flash saying that thunderstorms are predicted.
>
> ● for Bs – a news flash warning of train strikes/delays, or saying that parts of the science museum are closed.
>
> ● for Cs – a note saying that they have been offered the use of a car.
>
> Students then have to take account of this information and see if it affects any decisions they have made.

Real life (PAGE 105)

Making suggestions

1 Give students a minute or two in pairs to name all the objects in the pictures. Circulate and help pairs with any words they are not sure of.

2 [12.6] Check that students understand the three questions, then play the recording. Give students time to compare answers in pairs before checking with the class.

> **ANSWERS**
> a a couple/on the phone/pasta and ice cream – deciding what to have for dinner
> b a shop assistant and customer/in a shop/perfume and lipstick – customer is deciding what to buy for his mother
> c two young male friends/visiting another country/ashtray and purse – deciding what to take back for a girlfriend
> d mother and son/in a shop (department store)/trainers and backpack – if he has the cheaper trainers, he can have the backpack as well

3 **a)** [12.7] Establish that in all the conversations, people are making and responding to suggestions. Focus students on the gapped sentences, and give them a minute or two to predict any of the missing language, before playing the recording.

ANSWERS

a	shall I get	g	do that
b	don't we have	h	I should
c	Let's have	i	about getting
d	How about	j	idea
e	think so	k	we ask
f	could buy	l	suppose

b) Once students have completed the extracts, put them in pairs to discuss which phrases are used for asking for/ making/responding to (accepting or rejecting) a suggestion.

ANSWERS

ask for a suggestion: a, h
make a suggestion: b, c, d, f, i, k
respond to a suggestion: e (rejecting);
g, j (accepting); l (accepting reluctantly)

Pronunciation

See *Teacher's tips: helping students with pronunciation* on pages 10–11.

[12.8] Play the phrases on the cassette, or say them naturally yourself. Point out how the intonation helps the speaker sound interested/polite. Play or say the phrases again, for students to repeat.

Pronunciation: additional suggestion

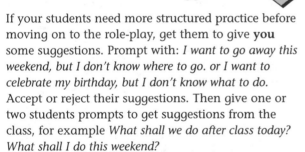

If your students need more structured practice before moving on to the role-play, get them to give **you** some suggestions. Prompt with: *I want to go away this weekend, but I don't know where to go.* or *I want to celebrate my birthday, but I don't know what to do.* Accept or reject their suggestions. Then give one or two students prompts to get suggestions from the class, for example *What shall we do after class today? What shall I do this weekend?*

4 Give students five to ten minutes in pairs to prepare their conversations. Suggest that they make notes, rather than writing out the conversation word for word, so that it sounds more natural. If you have a large class, and it would be too time-consuming for all the conversations to be acted out, put students into groups of six (three pairs) to act them out. Make a note of any examples of good language use and/or errors for analysis or correction afterwards.

Do you remember? (PAGE 106)

ANSWERS

2 a) Yoghurt is made from milk.
  b) Nelson Mandela was freed from prison in 1990.
  c) The Internet is used by millions of people every day.
  d) In the future, letters will be replaced by e-mails.
  e) The Berlin Wall was pulled down in 1989.
  f) Spanish is spoken by more than 250 million people.
3 a) The people who live in Holland speak Dutch, don't they?
  c) That's the actor who was in *Die Hard*.
  d) Have you got that book which/that I lent you last week?
4 • a baker – bread
  • a greengrocer – fruit and vegetables
  • a newsagent – newspapers, sweets, cigarettes
  • an estate agent – houses, flats
  • a jeweller – jewellery
  • an antique dealer – antiques
5 a) Let's go out for a meal
  b) How about a game of football?
  c) We could go and see a film.
  d) Why don't we stay in and watch TV?

module 13

Vocabulary and speaking
(PAGE 107)

Jobs and personal characteristics

See *Teacher's tips: working with lexical phrases* on pages 12–13, and *making the most of the Mini-dictionary* on pages 13–14.

1 Check that students understand the jobs given in the diagram. Ask, for example *What does (an architect) do?* Check the pronunciation of *accountant* /əˈkaʊntənt/, *architect* /ˈɑːkɪtekt/ and *lawyer* /ˈlɔːjə/. Put students in pairs and set the time limit of three minutes for them to add as many jobs as they can. Put pairs together into groups of four to compare answers. This enables you to circulate and to check spelling and pronunciation of the words. Feedback as a class may not be necessary, or can be kept brief with discussion only of the less common/familiar jobs.

> **POSSIBLE ANSWERS**
> **money:** bank manager, cashier
> **the arts and media:** artist, film director, TV producer/presenter, singer, journalist, editor, musician
> **other:** engineer, soldier, farmer, gardener, politician
> **transport:** bus/train driver, pilot, ticket collector, mechanic, driving instructor
> **hotels and restaurants:** receptionist, porter, chef
> **building/houses:** builder, plumber, carpenter, estate agent, interior designer
> **medicine:** nurse, pharmacist, surgeon
> **learning:** a secondary school teacher, a university lecturer, a professor

2 You could demonstrate how to divide the jobs into the different categories by giving a personal example. Highlight the meaning of *wouldn't mind…*). Then give students a minute or two to think about their answers. They should be able to give a reason for each one. Encourage students to think of ways of describing the qualities needed for the different jobs, in preparation for Exercise 3, for example *I'd hate to be an accountant, because I'm not good at maths.* Put students in pairs to discuss their answers.

3 **a)** Give students a few minutes, individually or in pairs, to check the meaning of the vocabulary and decide which jobs are being described. The answers will depend on which jobs students thought of for Exercise 1. Pronunciation to check: *patient* /ˈpeɪʃənt/, *experience* /ɪkˈspɪəriəns/, *careful* /ˈkeəfəl/, *sympathetic* /ˌsɪmpəˈθetɪk/, *honest* /ˈɒnəst/.

> **POSSIBLE ANSWERS**
> **patient, experience:** teacher, nurse
> **well-qualified, careful:** architect, accountant
> **good with people, smart, well-mannered:** waiter/waitress, receptionist (and other jobs dealing with the public)
> **sympathetic, latest methods:** doctor, nurse
> **imagination:** actor/actress (and other creative, media jobs)
> **good with money and numbers, honest:** accountant, cashier

b) Establish that students can use any of the words/phrases from Exercise 3a and any other vocabulary they can think of, to describe the qualities. Then put them in pairs to practise.

ADDITIONAL PRACTICE

Workbook: Vocabulary (Jobs and personal characteristics), page 77; Vocabulary booster: jobs, page 77

Language focus 1 (PAGE 108)

Present Perfect Simple and Continuous with the 'unfinished past'

1 Check that students know what is involved in the three jobs and put them in pairs or groups to discuss the qualities needed. Feed back briefly.

2 Ask students to read the texts and answer the questions in their pairs/groups. Ask one or two students to tell the class their answers and encourage a brief class discussion. Words to check: *charge (money), strict.*

> ### Grammar analysis
>
> **1** Focus students on the examples and give them a minute or two to consider the question. While they do this, copy the examples onto the board so that you can refer to them more easily in feedback.
>
> > **ANSWER**
> > The person is still a driving instructor/doctor.
>
> **2 a** Remind students that the Present Perfect always indicates a connection between the past and present, as shown already in Module 7. Demonstrate, using the

timeline, that the Present Perfect Simple and Continuous are used in the same way, for actions which started in the past and continue to the present.

b Point out that with many verbs, the speaker **chooses** to use the continuous form if he/she wants emphasise **how long** the action has continued. Other possible examples:

I've waited for an hour./I've been waiting for an hour.

I've studied English for three years./I've been studying English for three years.

c Remind students that state verbs cannot be used in the continuous form. Elicit one or two example sentences, *She's had that car for ten years.* (not ~~been having~~); *I've known my teacher for six months*. (not ~~been knowing~~)

Elicit/Write the table for the form of the Present Perfect Continuous on the board. See page 155 of the *Language summary* for a complete table. Remind students of the following:

- the contraction of the subject and verb *have*.
- the inversion of the subject and verb *have* in the question form.
- the spelling of the present participle (see page 151 of the *Language summary* for rules).

PRACTICE

1 Establish that students should use the Present Perfect Continuous wherever possible. Do the first one as an example. Students work individually before checking in pairs.

ANSWERS
a have been waiting
b have you had
c haven't been working
d has been raining
e haven't known
f Have your parents been living
g has been travelling
h has Chris been

2 [13.1] Play the recording. Stop after each conversation for students to confirm/change their answers. Highlight the contractions used.

ANSWERS
a 've been waiting
b have you had
c **haven't** been working
d 's been raining
e **haven't** known
f Have your parents been living
g 's been travelling
h 's Chris been

Practice: additional suggestion

Students rewrite the conversations, changing one or two pieces of information in each. For example *You look pleased! – Yes, I've been talking to Richard on the phone, and he asked me to go out to the theatre with him.* Students then act out their conversations for the class, or in groups of six if you have a large class.

ADDITIONAL PRACTICE

Workbook: Present Perfect Continuous, page 75

RB Resource bank: 13A *Century People* (Present Perfect Simple and Continuous for unfinished past), page 165

Language focus 2 (PAGE 110)

How long ...?, for, since and *all*

Do the first question with the class. Then put students in pairs to do the other three.

ANSWERS
1 How long has he been travelling?
2 How long has she been working with children?
3 How long has she been working as a driving instructor?
4 How long have you had your car?

Grammar analysis

1 Give students a minute or two to answer a and b, referring them back to the sentences above. As you check the answers, elicit one or two examples of a **period** of time (*for twelve years, two weeks, a few days*) and of a **point** in time (*since seven o'clock, yesterday, Saturday, two weeks ago*).

2 Elicit the answers from students as a whole class. (The answers will depend on what time/day/year it is!)

3 Point out that using *all* in front of the time emphasises the duration of the activity.

POSSIBLE ANSWERS
all morning/afternoon/evening, all week, all weekend, all year, all month, all winter

PRACTICE

1 [13.2] Use the example to demonstrate the exercise. Play the recording through, twice if necessary, for students to complete the rest of the phrases.

ANSWERS

b	since your last birthday	f	since last summer
		g	for ages
c	all week	h	since the weekend
d	since nine o'clock this morning	i	all winter
		j	for a long time
e	for months and months	k	since he was born
		l	all his life

Exercise 1: additional suggestion

Use the recording for controlled oral practice. Stop after each time phrase for students to respond with *for/since/all* and the time phrase.

Pronunciation

See Teacher's tips: helping students with pronunciation on pages 10–11.

1 [13.3] Play the recording, pointing out that the stress in each example is on the main verb and/or the time phrase. The other unstressed parts of the sentence are squashed in between.

2 To help students to produce the contractions and weak forms, drill them in the stressed parts first, then add the unstressed parts afterwards, for example *waiting > I've been waiting; known … long > I haven't known her for long; How long … had your car? > How long've you had your car?*

2 Demonstrate what students have to do using the examples in section 1 of the table. Give students a few minutes to think about their questions – if you have a reasonably strong class, tell students not to write out their questions, but just to practise saying them to themselves. Circulate and help with the wording and pronunciation of the questions.

3 **a)** Go through the example with the class. Tell students they should ask five of the questions (if you are short of time, reduce this to three or four). Students stand up and interview three people that they do not normally work with in class. Make sure that all students are involved, and that everyone has someone to interview.

b) Invite a strong student to read out some information, beginning *This person…* The other students guess who it is. Then ask a few other students to do the same, depending on how much time you have available.

Exercise 3: alternative suggestion

If it is impractical for your students to stand up and move around the class, put students into groups of four to interview each other.

ADDITIONAL PRACTICE

Workbook: Time phrases with *for* and *since* (Exercises 2–5), pages 75–76

RB **Resource bank:** 13B *Old friends* (Present Perfect Simple and Continuous for unfinished past), page 166

Wordspot (PAGE 111)

how

1 Students work individually or in pairs before checking with the whole class. Give students a few minutes to add the phrases to the diagram before checking with the whole class.

ANSWERS

b	How about	f	How fast
c	How much	g	How are
d	How do	h	How about
e	How long	i	How do

ANSWERS

section a: question d
section b: questions a, c, e, f
section c: question g
section d: questions b, h (*How about …?* can be followed by a noun or verb + *-ing*)
section e: question i

2 **a)** Put students into A and B pairs and direct them to pages 143 and 147 in the *Students' Book*. Give them a few minutes individually to complete the questions with the correct *how* phrase.

ANSWERS

Student A
1 How far   2 How many   3 How about (a walk, a drink, etc.)   4 How tall   5 How old   6 How big
Student B
1 How do you spell   2 How much   3 How about
4 How long   5 How do   6 How fast

b) Demonstrate that students should read the question and the choice of answers to their partner, who has to choose the correct one. Students score a point for each correct answer.

Exercise 2: additional suggestion

Students write two or three multiple-choice questions of their own in pairs, using phrases with *How*. They then read them out for the rest of the class to guess.

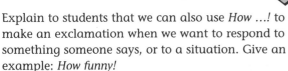

Exercise 2: additional activity

Explain to students that we can also use *How …!* to make an exclamation when we want to respond to something someone says, or to a situation. Give an example: *How funny!*

Write the list of adjectives and the situations a–e below on the board or on an overhead projector transparency. Students work in pairs. Give the pairs a minute or two to match the adjectives with the appropriate situations and form suitable exclamations.

> awful   kind   stupid   rude
> nice   strange   lovely

a   My boss didn't say hello to me this morning.

b   Dave's had a terrible accident on his motorbike.

c   Mrs Woods has offered to look after the children this evening.

d   We're going to the Bahamas for our holiday this year.

e   I can't find my wallet anywhere – but I had it two minutes ago.

Feed back with the whole class.

Students can act out the conversations, trying to remember the appropriate adjective to use in the response.

ANSWERS
a   How rude/strange!   b   How awful!   c   How kind!
d   How lovely/nice!   e   How strange!

Select a new mayor for Queenstown

See *Teacher's tips: making speaking Tasks work* on pages 6–7, *responding to learners' individual language needs* on pages 8–9.

Preparation for task (PAGE 112)

1 a) Before discussing the questions about a mayor, use the pictures to elicit as much as possible about Queenstown, for example that it is a city on the coast and has a large tourist industry, that it has a warm climate, that peanut farming is its other main industry. Then discuss the questions with students. Ask them to think particularly about what the duties of the mayor of Queenstown are, for example attending events to publicise and raise the profile of the city as a tourist place, attending meetings with peanut farmers and finding ways to make the farming industry more successful, etc. Ask students about the advantages and disadvantages of the job, and whether they would like to be mayor or not.

b) Direct students to the text, to confirm the points about the city and set the scene for the election.

2 [13.4] Tell students that they are going to find out about two of the four candidates for the job of mayor. Ask students to look at the pictures of Zelda and Max, and to give you their first impressions. Which one do they think has the appropriate kind of image for a mayor? Give students a minute or two to read through the two texts and predict the kind of information that is missing, for example a number, a verb form, etc. Play the recording once through, for students to complete the gaps. Then ask students to compare answers in pairs and with the whole class. Words to check: *game show, fame, slogan, deputy mayor, local economy.*

ANSWERS
Zelda 1 three   **2** has been working   **3** two years ago   **4** no experience
Max 1 fifty   **2** all his life   **3** forty   **4** seventy-six

3 Put students in pairs or small groups to discuss the candidates. Encourage them to make notes about the positive and negative points, to refer back to later. If they have trouble thinking of points, give prompts to consider such as age, experience in politics, relevant work experience, promises, image.

Task (PAGE 113)

1 First check the following vocabulary from the information on pages 142 and 146 of the *Students' Book*: *a police investigation, a newspaper editor, corruption, to reduce taxes, to be better off, voluntary work.* Put students in pairs. Give them ten minutes to complete their fact file. Circulate and, if necessary, help students with summarising their opinion about the good and bad points of their candidate.

2 Give students a minute or two to think about the questions they need to ask to complete the fourth fact file. Get one pair to demonstrate: A asks the first question and B writes the answer, in note form, in the fact file. Then give students time to exchange all the information about the other two candidates. Collect examples of good language use and/or errors for analysis and correction later.

3 Give students time individually to prioritise the candidates from 1–4. Direct them to the *Useful language* box, parts a and b, to help them explain their choice. *Either:* highlight the language explicitly now, pointing out the use of prepositions: *do (a lot, more)* **for** *someone/prefer X* **to** *Y/experience* **of***/knows more* **about***. Or:* leave it until after the Task, so as not to distract students. Circulate and help students with the language they need to explain the reasons for their choices.

4 Put students into small groups to explain and compare their choices. Direct them to part c of the *Useful language* box. Elicit one or two more phrases for agreeing and disagreeing, for example *That's true…/Exactly!/I see what you mean, but …* While students are doing this, note down examples of good language use and/or errors for analysis and correction later. If you have time, and students seem motivated, ask each group to report back on their opinions, and widen the discussion to the whole class. You can also have a class vote for the new mayor.

Task: alternative suggestion

If you have short lessons, do the Preparation for task in the first lesson. Divide the class into As and Bs and direct them to the appropriate fact file (Jack Novak or Cristina Scarlatti) and ask them to complete it with the relevant information for homework. Then, in the second lesson, students can exchange their information and do the rest of the Task.

Task: additional suggestions for role-plays

One of the following role-plays can be done between Exercises 2 and 3 of the Task.

1 Set the scene for a public meeting, where all four candidates for mayor will be present to speak to the people of Queenstown and answer questions. Allocate the roles of the four candidates to strong students who will have the confidence to make a short speech introducing themselves and their ideas, and give them time to prepare what they will say. Give all the other students in the class different roles as people from Queenstown such as hotel owners, peanut farmers, shopkeepers, young people, retired people, conservationists, etc. Ask these people to prepare questions they want to ask at the meeting. Also choose someone to chair the meeting. Circulate and help with language/prompt with ideas. Arrange the seating so that the four candidates and the 'chair' are at the front, then start the meeting. It is probably best not to participate yourself, so that you can give students feedback on their performance afterwards.

2 Set up interviews between news reporters and the four candidates. Ask half the class to be reporters, and the other half to be one of the candidates (it does not matter if there are more of one particular candidate than others). Give students time to prepare what they will say. Reporters think about their questions and make notes to refer to. Candidates try to anticipate the questions and think of convincing answers, and make notes to refer to. Put students in pairs to conduct the interviews, then have a brief feedback session where the reporters tell the rest of the class what they found out.

Writing and Real life (PAGE 114)

An application for a job

1 Students look at the photos and information about *Work Canada*. Discuss with them what the different jobs involve and which of the jobs they would like to do, or whether any of them have done jobs like this in an English-speaking country. Establish that *Work Canada* is an organisation which helps young people find temporary jobs in Canada.

2 Ask students to read Iris's letter and to answer two or three straightforward questions, for example *Which of the jobs is she interested in? What is she doing at the moment? What experience does she have?* Students discuss their answers in pairs and/or with the whole class. Then direct students to the application form and give them time to complete it with the relevant information from the letter.

Circulate so that you can check for accuracy and help students to make corrections if necessary. Check answers with the whole class for any sections which students found difficult.

ANSWERS

First name <u>Iris</u>   Last name <u>HAUPTMANN</u>
male ☐   female ☑   (tick)
Address <u>Borgfelder Strasse 11</u>   Postcode <u>20537</u>
City/Country <u>Hamburg, Germany</u>
Tel (include town & country code)
(home) <u>00 49 40 – 33 23 09</u>
Tel (work) ___ – ___   Fax ___ – ___   e-mail ___ – ___
Best time to reach me is <u>after 6 pm</u>
Date of birth <u>12.07.79</u>
Earliest travel date (year/month) <u>mid–June</u>
Driving licence yes ☑   no ☐   learning ☐
Languages spoken <u>German, English, Spanish</u>
Present occupation or studies <u>studying for degree in</u>
<u>languages</u>
Which of these work areas interests you?
(tick at least one box)
hotel ☐   restaurant ☑   child care ☐
sports instructor ☑   activity leader ☐
tour guide ☑
Describe any relevant experience you have.
<u>restaurant work, 3 years as a tennis coach for teenagers,</u>
<u>member of university tennis team</u>
How did you hear about *Work Canada*?
newspaper ☐   website ☐
personal recommendation ☑
other ___

3 **a)** Students work in pairs and prepare questions and answers. For stronger students, suggest they write hypothetical questions, such as *What would you do if ... (one of the tourists in your group got ill)?* etc.

b) Students take turns to interview each other. They then decide whether they are suited to the job(s) they have applied for. During the interviews, collect examples of good language use and/or errors for feedback afterwards.

Writing: additional suggestions

a   *If you want to give students letter writing practice:* ask them to write a letter like the one from Iris in Exercise 1, applying to *Work Canada*. Ask students to look at the layout and content of the letter, noting where the writer's address and the date are, what information is contained in each of the three paragraphs, and how the letter begins and ends. The letter can then be written for homework.

b   *If the* Work Canada *jobs will not appeal to your students:* bring in some authentic job adverts for Exercise 2. Ask students to write a letter applying for one of the jobs. In Exercise 3, students exchange letters, prepare questions based on the relevant job advertisement, and interview their partner.

Do you remember?

(PAGE 115)

ANSWERS
2   (1) has been playing/has played
     (2) has never played
     (3) has been staying/has stayed
     (4) has been practising/has practised
     (5) have been eating/have eaten
     (6) have only left
     (7) have been waiting/have waited
     (8) has not had
4   1 tour guide
     2 TV presenter
     3 taxi driver
     4 newspaper editor
     5 sports instructor
5   If necessary demonstrate the activity first (using *teacher* as your example). Remind students that the answer can only be *Yes* or *No.*

ADDITIONAL PRACTICE

RB **Resource bank:** *Learner-training worksheet J*
(Deducing meaning from context – part 2), page 168

module 14

Language focus 1 (PAGE 116)

Some, any and quantifiers

1 Give students a minute or two in pairs to think about their answers to the questions. Provide prompts if necessary, for example size/location/age/rooms/decoration to help students think about why they would/would not like to change where they live.

2 **a)** [14.1] Elicit some predictions about extracts a–g. Then do the first extract as an example with the class. Play the rest of the extracts through once.

> **ANSWERS**
> 1 V/? 2 C 3 C 4 V 5 C 6 C/? 7 V

b) Make it clear that students should decide if the **opinion** is positive or negative, not the grammar of the sentence. Then play the extracts again.

> **ANSWERS**
> a negative   d negative   g positive
> b negative   e negative
> c positive   f negative

Grammar analysis

Some of this should be revision for students at this level, so give them time to discuss their answers to the questions in pairs, before going through the answers with the class.

> **ANSWERS**
> 1 *Some* is used in affirmative sentences, *any* is used in negative sentences. *Any* is usually used in questions, for example *Are there any nice pubs near here?*
> 2 c is wrong – it should be *There **are no/aren't any** clothes shops here.*
> 3 *a lot of* is used in a positive sentence; *many* is used in a negative sentence
> 4 *many* is used with countable nouns; *much* is used with uncountable nouns
> 5 The speaker is unhappy in b and c. The words ***too** many* and ***aren't** enough* tell us this.
> 6 *a few* means 'a small number of'; *some* means 'an indefinite number of'

Pronunciation

See *Teacher's tips: helping students with pronunciation* on pages 10–11.

[14.2] Play the recording or say the phrases yourself, once or twice. Isolate the links and get students to repeat them, for example /zə/, before drilling the complete phrases. Students then practise saying other examples from the *Grammar analysis* box which contain similar linking.

PRACTICE

1 If necessary do the first one with the class, getting students to explain why two of the three quantifiers are not correct. Students then work individually or in pairs before checking with the whole class.

> **ANSWERS**
> a a lot of   d no   g any
> b enough   e some   h a few
> c many   f a lot of

> **Exercise 1: additional suggestion**
>
> For further practice, students make true sentences about their home town, using some of the ideas in the exercise. To structure their work, ask them for three positive and three negative points.

2 **a)** Tell students to think of a place where they would like to visit/go on holiday. It should either be somewhere that they know something about and have always wanted to go to, or that they have been to perhaps once before and would like to go again. Direct students to the prompts in the box and give them a few minutes to prepare their reasons for going to the place of their choice.

b) Go through the example with the class. Emphasise that students should try to persuade their partners to change their minds, and if possible to agree on a place to go. After the activity, ask one or two students to report back on how successful they were.

ADDITIONAL PRACTICE

Workbook: *some, any* and quantifiers (Exercises 1–4), pages 81–82

RB **Resource bank:** 14A *The Hungry Hippo café* (*some, any, much, not enough,* etc.), page 169

Vocabulary (PAGE 118)

Describing houses and apartments

See *Teacher's tips: working with lexical phrases* on pages 12–13, and *making the most of the Mini-dictionary* on pages 13–14.

1 Check that students understand the choice of text type in the question, then give them a few minutes to read the extracts. Encourage students to read quickly and not worry about unfamiliar vocabulary, as this is dealt with in Exercise 2. Students discuss and justify their answers in pairs before going through them with the class.

ANSWERS
a a letter (it is informal in tone and contains adjectives which express an opinion: *lovely, spacious, wonderful*)
b a brochure for holiday homes (it is more formal in tone – *situated in, set in* – and gives a more factual description: number of rooms, distance from village)
c a story (it is written in the past, and describes the actions of a character from the story)

a describes an apartment (more common in US English, British English = *flat*), b and c describe houses

2 Students work in pairs so they can help each other with any vocabulary they already know. As you check the answers, drill any unfamiliar or problematic vocabulary, for example *spacious* /ˈspeɪʃəs/, *private* /ˈpraɪvət/, *suburbs* /ˈsʌbɜːbz/, *old-fashioned furniture* /əʊldfæʃəndfɜːnɪtʃə/, *rug* /rʌg/, *sunny courtyard* /sʌnɪˈkɔːtjɑːd/.

ANSWERS
a **where things are:** right in the city centre; in a small village; in the suburbs, at the end of a quiet street
b **types of building:** a three-storey house
c **phrases to describe buildings and places:** there's lots of light, rather dark
d **things buildings have:** a wonderful view; a charming balcony; a private garden; a swimming pool
   3 bathrooms; an attractive living room; a modern kitchen; a path; a sunny courtyard
e **things rooms have:** a fireplace, colourful rugs, a wooden floor

3 You could demonstrate the activity by getting students to ask **you** the questions first. Check their intonation – that they sound interested – and give them time to ask the questions. Ask them to make brief notes on their partner's answers. One or two students report back about their partner's flat/house, or make groups of four to exchange information about each other's partners.

ADDITIONAL PRACTICE

Workbook: Vocabulary (Exercises 6–7), page 84; Vocabulary booster: things in a house, page 85

Language focus 2 (PAGE 118)

Describing where things are

Students work individually then compare answers in pairs, in order to pool their knowledge about these prepositions and phrases describing position. As you check the answers, you may need to deal with the following areas of confusion:

● *opposite* means that the two things are facing each other, whereas *in front of* does not.

● *above* means 'in a higher position' and may be confused with *over*, which can have a similar meaning. However *over* can also be used with movement or to suggest that one thing is touching the other, for example *She jumped over the wall./He put a cloth over the food.*

● *inside* means that the thing is completely surrounded. Students may confuse it with *into*, which implies movement, for example *He walked into the room. Put the food into those bags.*

Pronunciation to check: *between* /brˈtwiːn/, *opposite* /ˈɒpəzɪt/, *above* /əˈbʌv/, *next to* /nekstə/.

ANSWERS
b in front of   h outside
c opposite   i above
d between   j below
e next to   k under
f near   l on top of
g inside

Language focus: alternative suggestion

Use children's building blocks or any other small wooden/plastic blocks to demonstrate the prepositions and phrases. Then, if you have enough, give students three blocks each and instruct them to put them in different positions, for example *Put one on top of the other.* Students then complete the sentences in the book to consolidate.

Grammar analysis

Students work in pairs to answer questions 1 and 2. Check answers with the whole class.

ANSWERS
1
● in front of
● on top of

2
- next to
- in front of, on top of

PRACTICE

1 Students work individually or in pairs. To make the activity more competitive, set a time limit, for example ninety seconds. Ask students to write their answers in their notebooks in random order, then close their books and try to remember the question in each case, for example *My keys. – Oh yes. What is at the bottom of your bag?*

2 Put students into A/B pairs and direct them to pages 143 and 147 in the *Students' Book*. Make it clear that they should **not** show their picture to their partner. If possible, ask students to turn to face each other, so that it is more difficult to see each other's books. Check the following items of vocabulary, which are in both pictures: *first/second floor, curtains, sign, post box, balcony, newspaper seller, a man shaving*. Tell students that they need to find out:
- if there are the same things in their partner's picture as their own, and
- if the things are in the same place. Suggest that they put a circle in pencil around the differences, or that they make a brief note of each difference. Students continue until at least one pair has found all ten differences.

> **ANSWERS**
> 1A – sign says 'Metro', B – sign says 'Bus Stop'
> 2A – woman has three children, B – woman has four children
> 3A – man is standing in the main entrance, B – man is standing at the right of the entrance
> 4A – man is not smoking, B – man is smoking
> 5A – cat is on the ground, B – cat is lying on top of post box
> 6B – cat is asleep
> 7A – woman is behind curtains, B – woman is on the balcony
> 8A – man is shaving on second floor, B – man is shaving on first floor
> 9A – sign between second and third window says 'Rooms £25 with shower', B – sign says 'Rooms £25 with bath'
> 10A – bird on top of balcony on second floor, B – no bird

ADDITIONAL PRACTICE

Workbook: Prepositions (Describing where things are), page 83

Real life and Writing (PAGE 119)

Giving directions

1 Check that students understand why Mark/Lola have written the directions. Give them a few minutes to read through the directions and complete the gaps. Students compare answers in pairs before checking with the whole class. As you check the answers you may need to highlight the following:
- the difference between *take the train/bus* (meaning *catch*) and *it takes … minutes* (for the length of the journey).
- the meaning of *along, past* and *towards*. Demonstrate these prepositions of movement via drawings on the board, or by using suitable objects (pen, ruler, book, etc.) to represent streets and buildings.
- the difference between *turn right* (showing movement) and *is on the right/left* (showing position).

> **ANSWERS**
> 1 the train   2 Get off   3 it takes   4 cross   5 turn
> 6 along   7 towards   8 past   9 on the left
> 10 opposite   11 take   12 about

2 a) 🔲 [14.3] Direct students to the map and give them a minute or two to familiarise themselves with it, particularly the position of the bridge and the names of the station and the roads. Play the recording through once for students to mark Jeff's house. You may need to play it again if students have difficulty marking the house on the first listening.

> **ANSWER**
> The house is in Venetia Road, the second house on the right as you go into the road.

b) Give students time to read through the instructions before playing the recording. Students compare answers in pairs, then check with the whole class.

> **ANSWERS**
> 1 When you **come out of** Manor House station, take the Finsbury Park **exit** and **turn left**. Then go up Green Lanes with Finsbury Park on your **left**.
> 2 You go **past** the park and there's a bridge **in front of** you. Keep going towards the bridge and **take** the road on the left just **before** you get to the bridge.
> 3 Then my road's the **second** turning on the **left**.
> 4 My house is at the **beginning** of the road. It's number four, the second house on your **right**.
> 5 It takes about **ten** minutes.

f Graceland
g Aaron Spelling's house
h Bill Gates' house

3 Refer students to paragraph 2 of the text to answer the first question. Elicit what the possible advantages of such a house would be, etc. Then refer students to paragraph 3 to do the second question. Let them draw their sketch in pairs. Students could then compare in groups and decide which sketch is the best.

ANSWERS
a It is a revolving house.

4 a) Students can work individually or in pairs to answer this question, before feed back in groups or with the whole class.

b) Students work individually on their dream home, referring back to the text for ideas if necessary. Students can then compare their descriptions in small groups or as a class.

ADDITIONAL PRACTICE

RB **Resource bank:** 14C *Building your dream* (Vocabulary extension – word building, dependent propositions and collocations), page 172

Describe a favourite room

See *Teacher's tips: making speaking Tasks work* on pages 6–7 and *responding to learners' individual language needs* on pages 8–9.

Preparation for task (PAGE 122)

1 Focus students on the pictures of rooms and discuss which ones they like/don't like and why. If necessary, use the pictures to check the names of items of furniture and other relevant vocabulary, for example *view, cushions, ornaments*. Then ask students to consider the most/least important aspects of a room from the list, and tell their partner. Alternatively, ask students to put the points in order from 1–5, from most to least important. Demonstrate this by showing how **you** would order the five points.

2 🔲 [14.4] Make sure that students understand what kind of information is required in each section of the table. Point out that the speaker may talk about a room they like now, or about one they remember from earlier in their life. Remind students that while they listen, they should write notes, not full sentences, for example *parents' house, country* NOT *It is in her parents' house in the country.* After listening to the recording once, encourage students to compare answers. Play the recording again if necessary.

Exercise 2: additional suggestion

Use the completed directions in 2b for pronunciation practice, getting students to repeat the phrases after you. Then ask students to look back at the map and try to remember the complete directions to Jeff's house.

3 a) You could demonstrate this by drawing a rough map of your area (**not** marking your house) on the board. Tell students how to get to your house from the station/bus stop. Ask one or two volunteers to come and mark where they think your house is on the map. Students then draw their own rough maps and think about how to give directions to their houses, using relevant phrases from Exercises 1 and 2.

b) Put students in pairs. Ask them to exchange maps, then take turns to direct each other to their houses.

Exercise 3: alternative suggestion

If students have difficulty drawing a map of their local area, suggest that they direct their partner to somewhere from the school, if possible using a map of the town.

4 First ask students to think of a reason for having a party at their house. Then give them some ideas for how to start the note, for example *Dear ...; I'm/We're having a party to celebrate ...; It's on ...; at ...; Please bring ...; Hope you can come!* Refer students back to Exercise 1 and direct them to the language in the box. Students can address their note to someone else in the class, who then telephones to accept/decline the invitation, or to check the directions, for example if they come by car instead of bus/train.

ADDITIONAL PRACTICE

Workbook: Improve your writing (Notes giving directions), page 86

RB **Resource bank:** 14B *Where's the nearest bank?* (Language for giving directions), page 171

Reading (PAGE 120)

1 Words to check: *metal, cathedral, tower, pyramid, observatory, lake, gold.* Focus students on the pictures and elicit one or two initial reactions from the class. Put students in pairs or groups of three or four to discuss and justify their answers. Ask a student from one or two groups to report back to the class.

2 Students read the text individually, then discuss answers in pairs before checking with the whole class.

ANSWERS
a the cathedral in Majorada del Campo
b Bill Gates' house
c Aaron Spelling's house
d the cathedral in Majorada del Campo
e Graceland

ANSWERS

	Where it is/ was and what he/she does/did there	Description of the room: furniture, view, etc.	Why he/she likes/liked the room
Sandra	grandmother's living room; drink tea, talk, play with old toys	small, lots of old-fashioned wooden furniture; fireplace; big armchairs; full of ornaments, books	because of old-fashioned toys and ornaments – really interesting
Tom	café in quiet street; has lunch or coffee, reads the newspaper	big window with view of street; not very big; wooden floors; second-hand wooden furniture; colours – blue and yellow; paintings on walls	because he feels relaxed; friendly atmosphere; jazz or soul music

Preparation for task: alternative suggestion

If you want to provide a model yourself, prepare a short talk about a favourite room, or two favourite rooms, one from your childhood and one from the present. Incorporate some of the useful language, for example *I spend a lot of time -ing there./It's got a view of …* While they listen, students complete a grid or draw a plan of the room. Also encourage them to ask questions as you give the talk.

Task (PAGE 123)

1 First discuss with students what kinds of place qualify as rooms, for example rooms in a private house, including attic, basement, conservatory (even a garden shed); rooms in public places like cafés, restaurants, libraries, waiting rooms (for example at a station). Give students time to choose and start making notes about their room, and direct them to the *Useful language* box. Point out that there is a choice of present or past for each phrase in the box, depending on whether the room is one they like now, or one from earlier in their life. Either focus on language here, eliciting ways of completing some of the phrases, for example *I spend a lot of time reading/relaxing/chatting to friends there. It's got a friendly/relaxed/lively* atmosphere. or leave the language analysis until after the Task. Circulate, helping with vocabulary and if necessary prompting with questions, for example *Why do you like the view/atmosphere? What else was there apart from the furniture/paintings/plants?*

Students can rehearse parts of their talk with you, or with a partner, to check that what they plan to say is comprehensible/interesting/detailed enough.

2 **a)** Put students in groups of four or five to give their talks. Those listening make notes under the three headings from the table on page 122, or draw a rough plan/sketch of the room. They should also be encouraged to ask questions about the room.

b) After all the talks, give the groups time to discuss which of the listed activities (or any others not listed) each room would be suitable for. Note down examples of good language use and/or errors for analysis and correction later.

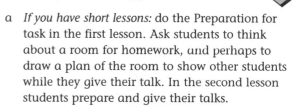

Task: alternative suggestions

a *If you have short lessons:* do the Preparation for task in the first lesson. Ask students to think about a room for homework, and perhaps to draw a plan of the room to show other students while they give their talk. In the second lesson students prepare and give their talks.

b *Role-play:* students prepare and act out an interview between a journalist and a writer/designer/artist, talking about a favourite room and how it inspired them. They can base this on one of the rooms in the pictures, or you can bring in pictures of interesting-looking rooms from magazines for them to choose from.

Do you remember?
(PAGE 123)

ANSWERS
1 • **places to live**: suburbs, village, building, apartment
• **things in a house**: balcony, furniture, fireplace, courtyard
• **words to describe a room**: modern, attractive, spacious, elegant, wonderful, private
3 c) Oh dear, I think I put **too** much salt …
d) The taxi will be here in **a** few minutes.
e) There's a lot **of** noise next door …
4 a) The cat is sitting **on** the table, behind the fish bowl.
There's a mouse **under** the table.
b) There's a bone **in front of** the dog.
The cat is **outside** the house.
There's a mouse **near** the window.

module 15

Vocabulary (PAGE 124)

Verb phrases to do with money

See *Teacher's tips: working with lexical phrases* on pages 12–13, and *making the most of the Mini-dictionary* on pages 13–14.

1 **a)–b)** Put students in pairs to check the meanings of the words in the box, using their *Mini-dictionary*. Elicit some ideas about what is happening in one or two of the pictures. Students discuss the rest of the pictures and match them to the verbs/phrases in the box. As you check the answers, elicit full sentences to describe each picture, so that you can highlight the following points:

- you borrow (money) **from** someone, and you lend (money) **to** someone.
- you bet (money) on **something**, for example a horse/ a number.
- you waste money **on** things when you spend more than you should in a way that is not sensible.
- you owe money **to** another person/a bank.

Pronunciation to check: *can't afford* /kɑːntəˈfɔːd/, *waste* /weɪst/, *earn* /ɜːn/, *owe* /əʊ/.

> **POSSIBLE ANSWERS**
> Stock Exchange: invest
> Shopping: can't afford, spend
> Factory: invest, earn
> Bank: save, borrow, lend, pay back
> Racetrack: waste, lose, win, bet, owe

NOTE:
The Stock Exchange is a place where stocks and shares are bought and sold.

> **Exercise 1: additional suggestion**
> Students cover the words in the box and use the pictures to test each other on the vocabulary.

2 You could demonstrate the activity by doing an example about yourself. Then give students a few minutes to complete the statements. Before students compare answers, remind them of how to agree with/show interest in their partner's answers, for example *Yes, that's the same for me. I agree. Me too. So do I. Really? Why do you think that? Oh dear. Why?/Why not?* Students either work in pairs or stand up and mingle, choosing different statements to discuss with each person they talk to. Ask one or two students to report back to the whole class on some of the main differences they found.

ADDITIONAL PRACTICE

Workbook: Vocabulary (Verb phrases to do with money), page 89

Language focus 1 (PAGE 125)

The Past Perfect

Focus students on the pictures. Elicit some ideas about what happened and check students understand the meaning of *rubbish tip*. Give students a few minutes to read the text and discuss in pairs what Ilona's mistake was.

> **ANSWER**
> Ilona threw away a pair of her husband's shoes, not knowing that they had £15,000 inside them.

Grammar analysis

1 Copy the example and timeline onto the board. Go through a–c with the class and highlight:

- the Past Perfect is used when it is necessary to show that one action happened before another in the past.
- the form is *had* + past participle for all persons. If necessary, elicit a table for the Past Perfect, positive/negative and question forms onto the board. Alternatively refer students to the *Language summary* on page 157 of the *Students' Book* to check.
- *had* and the subject are inverted in the question form.
- the negative form is *had not*, often contracted to *hadn't*.
- the contracted form *'d: I'd, he'd*, etc.

2 Refer students back to the text to underline two more examples of the Past Perfect.

> **ANSWERS**
> 1 **a** there are two past actions
> **b** hiding the money was the first action
> **c** *threw* is Past Simple, *had hidden* is Past Perfect
> 2 Two other examples of the Past Perfect: *what had happened, they had burned*

PRACTICE

1 Students work individually or in pairs to match the beginnings and endings, and complete the gaps. Check answers with the whole class.

> **ANSWERS**
> **a** She couldn't afford the shoes because she **had spent** all her money on lottery tickets.
> **b** By the time George retired he **had earned (earnt)** enough money to buy a holiday home.
> **c** Hilda and Jerry bought a new car with the money they **had won** on the lottery.

d Kate needed some advice because she **had never invested** money before.

e When Grandma died, nobody knew that she **had saved** thousands of pounds in a box.

Exercise 1: additional suggestions

a Students cover the endings in B and, working in pairs, try to remember the endings.

b Students think of different endings for the sentence beginnings in A, for example *She couldn't afford the shoes because she had spent a lot of money on a holiday.*

---

2 **a)** Students read the story quickly to answer the question. Check the meaning of: *a will.*

b) Students work individually to complete the gaps, before checking answers in pairs and/or with the class.

ANSWERS
1 died   2 came   3 had remembered   4 got
5 had lived   6 had not seen   7 were   8 heard
9 had left   10 was*   11 received
* *had been* is also possible, because the article is reporting what she said in the will, *'the plant has been my best friend'*

---

c) Give students a few minutes in pairs to think of reasons why Justine gave Willi so much money, then discuss all their ideas as a class, encouraging them to use the Past Perfect to explain why. Direct students to page 141 of the *Students' Book* to check the real reason (Willi was the owner of the shop where Justine had bought the plant).

ADDITIONAL PRACTICE

Workbook: Past Perfect (Exercises 1 and 2), page 87

Language focus 2 (PAGE 126)

Reported speech

1 Focus students on the picture story. Check they know the verbs *smile* and *wave.* Put students in pairs to work out what happened in the story. They can make brief notes about each picture, but it is not necessary for them to write out the whole story. Ask one or two pairs to tell the class their version.

2 [15.1] Play the recording, asking students to see how near their stories were to the real one. They can make a note of any differences next to the relevant pictures.

ANSWER
See tapescript Module 15, recording 1 on page 167 of the *Students' Book.*

Exercise 2: additional suggestion

Students act out one of the following situations related to the story, using reported speech where appropriate:

● the conversation between the couple and the waiter/restaurant manager when they receive the bill.

● the interview between the old lady and a police officer when she is later arrested.

Grammar analysis

1 Make clear to students:
direct speech = the person's actual words
reported speech = those words reported by another
    person.
Point out that, apart from the verb changes, subject pronouns and possessive adjectives can also change, for example *you > she, my daughter > her daughter.* Give students a minute or two to answer the questions. Check answers with the whole class.

2 Refer students to the alternatives and give them a minute or two to answer the question.

ANSWERS
1   Present Simple > Past Simple
    Past Simple > Past Perfect
    will > would
2   *She said me that her name was Mary.* is wrong.

PRACTICE

1 Remind students that some sentences should be false. Then give students a few minutes to complete the sentences.

2 Put students in pairs. Demonstrate that they should take turns to read out their sentences and make a note of their partner's answers.

3 Go through the examples with the class. Show how reported speech is used when challenging the sentences you think are false. When students have finished, ask them to report back on which of their partner's true sentences they challenged wrongly.

ADDITIONAL PRACTICE

Workbook: Reported speech (Exercises 4 and 5), page 88

RB Resource bank: 15A *Lottery winners* (Reported speech), page 173

Wordspot (PAGE 127)

make

See *Teacher's tips: working with lexical phrases* on pages 12–13.

1 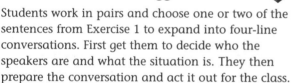 [15.2] Students work individually to complete the gaps. They then compare ideas in pairs before listening to the recording.

ANSWERS

a	a phone call	f	a cup of tea
b	profit	g	cry
c	dinner	h	angry
d	friends	i	a mess
e	noise	j	feel

2 Do the first one with the class. Then give students time, individually or in pairs, to add the phrases to the diagram.

ANSWERS

section a: sentences c, e, f, i
section b: sentence b
section c: (*make* + adjective) sentence h, (*make* + verb) sentences g and j
section d: sentences a and d

Exercise 2: additional suggestion

Students work in pairs and choose one or two of the sentences from Exercise 1 to expand into four-line conversations. First get them to decide who the speakers are and what the situation is. They then prepare the conversation and act it out for the class.

---

3 Give students a few minutes to think about their answers. Then put them in pairs to discuss. Ask one or two pairs to report back on which answers were the same.

POSSIBLE ANSWERS

things that make you angry: traffic jams, people who are rude, people who are late, problems on public transport
things that make a lot of noise: babies crying, men repairing the road, thunder, planes flying over your house
reasons why people make speeches: at a wedding, at a political meeting, to say goodbye to someone who is leaving a company
things that are made in Scotland: whisky, tartan, kilts, shortbread (a kind of biscuit)
things that you can make with eggs: cakes, omelettes, sauces
mistakes that you often make in English: forget the 3rd person -s, forget the article

---

Exercise 3: additional activity

Write the following up on the board or on an overhead projector transparency.

Find someone who:

- is going to make dinner tonight.
- makes more than five phone calls a day.
- has made a difficult decision recently.
- is wearing something made of wool.
- likes making beds.
- has made someone laugh today.
- would like to make a lot of money.
- never makes a mess.

Before you start, remind students of the different question forms they need, for example *Are you going to …?/Do you …?/Have you …?/Are you …?/Would you like to …?* Encourage students to ask follow-up questions, for example *Do you make more than five phone calls a day? Really? Who do you phone?*

Students then walk around and if possible find someone who says yes to each question. Students make a list of the names.

If it is not possible for students to walk around the classroom, put them in groups of four to ask each other the questions and see how many of them answer the same.

As a round up, ask students if they found out anything unusual/surprising.

Find the differences between two stories

See *Teacher's tips: making speaking Tasks work* on pages 6–7 and *responding to learners' individual language needs* on pages 8–9.

Preparation for task (PAGE 128)

1 Before students read the first paragraph of the article, write the headline on the board and ask them to think of ways in which a criminal could be unlucky. Then students read and answer questions a–c.

ANSWERS

a He was a local businessman. People <u>thought</u> he was honest (but the implication is that he is not).
b He had made some bad investments and lost all his money.
c **Possible answers:** He decided to rob a bank./He decided to leave the country.

2 Students read the rest of the article. They then compare their answers to the questions in pairs or small groups, before checking with the whole class.

> **ANSWERS**
> **three ways in which he tried to make money:** by playing roulette, by betting on a horse, by investing in a travel company
> **three ways in which he was unlucky:** the casino didn't accept his bets, his horse came last in the race, the travel company collapsed (being stopped for speeding wasn't unlucky, since it stopped him from killing himself)

Task (PAGE 129)

1 [15.3] Students should have the article in front of them as they listen to the interview with Carson, so they can note down differences as they listen. After listening, give students a few minutes individually to count the differences they have, and think about how to explain them in English. Circulate and help with vocabulary queries while they do this.

2 Put students in groups and refer them to the *Useful language* box. If necessary, point out that they need to use reported speech to compare what the article said and what Carson said. Make it clear that students need to produce a list of at least ten differences agreed on by the group, which they can refer back to later. As you monitor this stage, collect examples of good language use and/or errors for analysis and correction later.

3 [15.4] Students listen to the recording, then check in their groups that they identified all the differences.

> **ANSWERS**
> See tapescript Module 15, recording 4 on page 167 of the *Students' Book*.

Task: additional suggestions

a If you are short of time: do the Preparation for task and Task as a jigsaw reading/listening. Start with the whole class reading the headline and first paragraph of the article. Then explain that students are going to find out about two versions of Carson's story. Divide them into two groups. Keep one group in the classroom to listen to the interview, send the other group somewhere quiet to read the article and answer the questions. Put less confident/weaker students into the group who are reading, as they will have plenty of time to read the article carefully while the other group are listening. Provide the group who are listening with some comprehension questions to guide them, for example:

- Did Carson steal £60,000?
- Why did he go to Monte Carlo and what happened there?
- What happened at the horse race?
- What did he invest in, after that?
- Why did he drive to the cliffs, and whose car was he driving?
- Why did the policeman stop him?
- How long did he spend in prison?

Give both groups time to check their answers together, then bring back the group who were reading. Pair students up, one from the reading group, one from the listening group, and tell them to find the ten differences between the stories. Get one or two pairs to report back to the class about the differences they found. Play the recording [15.3] for the class to check.

b *Role-plays:* when they have finished the Task, students work in pairs and act out one of the following situations:

- the conversation between Carson and the police officer when he was arrested.
- another interview where Carson is asked to explain the differences between the two stories.

Real life (PAGE 129)

Dealing with money

1 Focus students on the pictures. Elicit where the people are in each case: at a hotel reception, near a drinks machine, in a market, in a bank, in a café. Students then discuss, as a class or in pairs, what the people need to do.

> **ANSWERS**
> **Picture a:** change money, ask about the exchange rate
> **Picture b:** ask for change, find some pound coins
> **Picture c:** ask the price of something, ask if they can pay by credit card, pay in cash
> **Picture d:** open a bank account, ask about the exchange rate
> **Picture e:** ask if they can pay by credit card, ask if service is included, leave a tip, find some pound coins

2 [15.5] Tell students to write the number of the conversation next to the correct picture as they listen.

> **ANSWERS**
> **Picture a:** conversation c   **Picture d:** conversation e
> **Picture b:** conversation a   **Picture e:** conversation d
> **Picture c:** conversation b

3 Give students a few minutes to read the sentences. See if they can predict any of the answers. Play the conversations again, stopping after each one for students to write their answers. Students then compare answers in pairs before checking with the whole class.

> **ANSWERS**
> a The person wants to change **$200** into pesos. The exchange rate is **1 peso** to the dollar. She receives **200 pesos**.
> b The person needs **£1.50** for the machine. Her friend gives her **4** pound coins and **2** fifty pence coins.
> c The girl would like to buy some earrings. The larger ones cost **£20** , and the smaller ones cost **£12**. She decides to buy **the smaller ones**. She pays **in cash**.
> d He needs his **passport**, and a **letter from his employer or place of study**.
> e They had **a glass of white wine**, **a mineral water** and **a club sandwich**. They cost **£9.50**. They pay **£10** in total.

4 Go through the example with the class. Point out that in each case, students have to cross out a word. They do not **change** any of the words. Students work individually or in pairs before checking with the whole class.

> **ANSWERS**
> Unnecessary words: **b** of   **c** any   **d** cost   **e** be
> **f** my   **g** the   **h** to   **i** the   **j** to

Pronunciation

See *Teacher's tips: helping students with pronunciation* on pages 10–11.

🔲 [15.6] Play the recording, stopping after each sentence for students to repeat. Make sure that their intonation sounds polite.

---

5 Put students into pairs and give them time to invent three situations (one or two if you are short of time). Circulate and help with language queries as they prepare their conversations. If you have time, the pairs can choose one of the conversations to act out for the class.

ADDITIONAL PRACTICE

RB Resource bank: 15B *Get Rich Quick!* (Vocabulary: money), page 174

Do you remember?

(PAGE 130)

> **ANSWERS**
> 1 **Clever Clare** invested some money/saved some money. (b)
> **Unfortunate Fred** lost some money/lent some money. (a and d)
> **Lucky Luke** spent some money/bet some money. (c and e)
> 2 a) You **earn** money from a job, you **win** money in a competition/game.
> b) You **borrow** money **from** another person/a bank. You **lend** money **to** another person.
> c) You **spend** money when you buy or pay for things. You **waste** money if you buy too many things that are not useful/sensible.
> 4 **Possible order:** c), b), e), g), a), d), f)
> a) 'I'll never leave you.'
> b) 'My name's Rita.'
> d) 'I love another man.'
> e) 'You've got/You have a nice smile.'
> g) 'I love you.'

ADDITIONAL PRACTICE

RB Resource bank: *Learner-training worksheet K* (Using the *Mini-dictionary* to find dependent prepositions), page 176

module 16

Reading and vocabulary (PAGE 131)

See *Teacher's tips: working with lexical phrases* on pages 12–13, and *making the most of the Mini-dictionary* on pages 13–14.

1 Focus students on the pictures and elicit some ideas about why the 1960s were important, for example the assassination of J.F. Kennedy; the Vietnam war; peace protests; demonstrations against nuclear weapons; the civil rights movement; hippies, 'flower power' and the 'summer of love'; the sexual revolution; the music and fashion of the period, etc. Then direct students to the photos of John Lennon and Martin Luther King, and put them in pairs to discuss the questions. Even if students know very little or nothing about the two people, they should be able to answer some of the questions by looking at the photos and captions, and to guess the others.

> **ANSWERS**
> **John Lennon:** was a pop star; was married to a Japanese woman; received an award from the British Queen
> **Martin Luther King:** was a civil rights leader; won a Nobel Prize; was a Christian minister

2 Divide the class into As and Bs and direct them to the appropriate texts and questions. Encourage students to guess the meaning of unfamiliar vocabulary as they read, and to use their mini-dictionaries for any items which they cannot guess. Students then discuss answers to their questions with people who have read the same text.

> **ANSWERS**
> **A**
> a They sat in bed in their hotel.
> b *All you need is love* and *Give peace a chance.*
> c To protest about Britain's part in the Vietnam war and the war in Nigeria. He returned it in 1968.
> d In 1971. It was about his idea of the perfect world.
> e He was shot.
> f Outside his apartment in New York. Mark Chapman (a crazy fan) killed him.
> **B**
> a There was a demonstration for civil rights.
> b Martin Luther King was speaking. His famous words were, 'I have a dream ...'
> c 200,000 people
> d It was peaceful.
> e Black people got civil rights, and Martin Luther King won the Nobel Prize for Peace.
> f He was assassinated in 1968.

3 Put students into A/B pairs. Direct them to the set of questions referring to the text they have **not** read. Tell students to be ready to answer their partner's questions without looking back at the text, so that they sound more natural and use their own words to relate the facts.

4 Give students a minute or two to think about the questions. Then put them in groups of three or four to discuss their ideas. For the last question, prompt students to think of other famous singers/writers/politicians, from any time in history or from the present, and tell each other about them.

5 Go through the example with the class. Remind students that adverbs are usually formed by adding *-ly* to the adjective (so if the adjective ends in *-l*, it needs to be doubled). The only exception in the exercise is *tragic*. Adjectives ending in *-ic* add *-ally* to form the adverb (other examples: *dramatically, democratically*).

> **ANSWERS**
> | b | violence | violent | violently |
> | c | power | powerful | powerfully |
> | d | freedom | free | freely |
> | e | religion | religious | – * |
> | f | tragedy | tragic | tragically |
> | g | strength ** | strong | strongly |
>
> * avoid *religiously*, since its most common meaning is not connected to religion in the literal sense, for example *He followed the instructions religiously.*
> ** compare: *long > length*

Pronunciation

See *Teacher's tips: helping students with pronunciation* on pages 10–11.

⊟ [16.1] Give students a minute or two to look at the words and decide where they think the stress falls. Then play the recording. Students either mark the stress above the stressed syllable, or choose from the following stress patterns written on the board: ●●●, ●●, ●●●●. Play the words again, or say them yourself, for students to repeat.

> **ANSWERS**
> violence ●●●, violent ●●●; power ●●, powerful ●●●; freedom ●●, free ●; religion ●●●, religious ●●●; tragedy ●●●, tragic ●●; strength ●, strong ●

ADDITIONAL PRACTICE

Workbook: Vocabulary (Wordbuilding), page 94; Vocabulary booster: people in politics, religion and public life, page 95

Listening and vocabulary (PAGE 133)

Imagine

See *Teacher's tips: working with lexical phrases* on pages 12–13, and *making the most of the Mini-dictionary* on page 14.

1 Start by briefly discussing the song *Imagine*. Do students know it/what it's about? Do any of them have it on CD/tape? Do they like it? Then put students in pairs to decide if the pairs of words have the same meaning or not, looking up any unfamiliar ones in their mini-dictionaries. Go through the answers with the class. Ask students to explain whether the meanings are the same, slightly different, or very different.

ANSWERS
All the meanings are different apart from *it's easy/it isn't hard*, and *possessions/things people own*.

2 [16.2] Start by giving students a few minutes to look at the song and predict which words from Exercise 1 go in the gaps. Students then compare their ideas in pairs before listening to the song. Play the song a second time if necessary (or if students want to sing along!).

ANSWERS
1 heaven 2 It's easy 3 below us 4 Above us
5 sky 6 It isn't hard 7 die 8 peace 9 a dreamer
10 join 11 possessions 12 wonder 13 greed
14 hunger 15 Sharing 16 a dreamer 17 join

3 a) Remind students that they have found out information about John Lennon both from the song and from the text on page 132. Direct them to the example in the box, getting them to explain why it is ticked. Then put students in pairs or small groups to discuss their ideas about the other things in the box.

ANSWERS
heaven and hell × (he did not believe in religion)
countries × brotherhood √ (He said, 'It doesn't matter how long my hair is or what colour my skin is, or whether I'm a woman or a man.') living for today √ possessions × (He said, 'If everyone demanded peace instead of another television, then there'd be peace.') greed × hunger × dreamers √

b) Either discuss the ideas as a class (if you feel you will need to guide the discussion and help students to express their ideas about these issues) or put students in small groups.

Language focus 1 (PAGE 134)

Conditional sentences with *would*

Point out that the beginnings of the four sentences are ideas expressed in *Imagine*. Give students a few minutes to underline the endings they agree with. They can underline both endings, or neither of them if they don't agree with them. Put students in pairs to compare and justify their answers.

Grammar analysis

1 Refer students back to the four sentences and give them time, individually or in pairs, to consider questions a–d. As you check the answers, highlight:
● the conditional with *would* is used to talk about imaginary situations (John Lennon's ideas were seen as dreams).
● the verb after *If* is in the past, even though the sentence refers to present or general time (if students have a subjunctive in their language, you could compare it to the past form here).
● *were* is used instead of *was* in the first and third person: *If I were president/If she were president* (although nowadays many native speakers use *was*).
● the form in other part of the sentence is *would(n't)* + verb.
● either clause can begin the sentence (the main clause or the *if* clause).

2 a Elicit the negative and question forms of *would*. Write up a complete table on the board showing positive, negative and question forms.
  b Elicit the contractions. Get students to practise saying the contracted forms by prompting them with different pronouns, for example *Ss: I'd enjoy life more > T: we > Ss: We'd enjoy life more.*

ANSWERS
1 a the sentences are about imaginary situations
  b after *If* the verb is in the Past Simple
  c we find *would* + verb in the main clause
  d the sentences are about the present/general time
2 b you'd he'd she'd it'd we'd they'd

PRACTICE

1 Students work individually before checking answers in pairs and/or with the whole class.

> **ANSWERS**
> **a** were, wouldn't be
> **b** wouldn't need, didn't have
> **c** didn't exist, wouldn't have, could live (would be able to live)
> **d** weren't, would speak
> **e** didn't have, would need
> **f** wouldn't have
> **g** would lose, didn't have
> **h** didn't own, would people wear?, would they sleep?

2 a) Ask students to imagine that they are the president or prime minister of their country and could therefore do things to make it a better place. Direct them to the ideas in the box. Give them a minute or two to decide on four things they would do and two things they wouldn't, and reasons why.

b) Put students in pairs or small groups to compare answers and justify their ideas. Students tell each other their ideas, then one or two report back to the class.

ADDITIONAL PRACTICE

Workbook: *would* and *wouldn't*, page 92; Second conditional, page 92

Language focus 2 (PAGE 135)

Will and *would*

1 Focus students on the picture. They discuss what is happening in pairs. Feed back with the whole class.

2 a) Students work individually to match the words/thoughts in the speech balloons with the people in the picture. They discuss answers in pairs.

b) In pairs, students look at the picture and discuss who says/thinks the items on the list. Feed back with the class.

Grammar analysis

Students can answer questions 1 and 2 individually or in pairs before checking with the class, since both forms have already been covered (*If* + present was covered in Module 9). As you check the answers, highlight:

- *If* + present ..., *will (won't)* + verb is used to talk about a real possibility in the future.

- *If* + past ..., *would (wouldn't)* + verb is used to talk about an imaginary situation and therefore refers to the present/general time.

- the clauses can be reversed in both cases.
- the form of the questions and negatives.

> **ANSWERS**
> **1** **a** the man standing on the boxes
> **b** the boy with the yoyo
> **2** **a** *if* + present = real possibility in the future
> *if* + Past Simple = imaginary situation, present/general time
> **b** *if* + present + *will (won't)*
> *if* + Past Simple + *would (wouldn't)*

PRACTICE

You may wish to do the *Pronunciation* box at this stage, before students practise using both forms.
Focus students on the first sentence and elicit one or two possible endings. Point out that this is a real possibility, so *will (won't)* is needed in the main clause. Words/phrases to check: *change places with a celebrity, invisible, to turn back time*. Give students a few minutes to complete the sentences, then put them in pairs to compare answers.

Pronunciation

See *Teacher's tips: helping students with pronunciation* on pages 10–11.

[16.3] Give students a minute or two to look through the phrases. In some cases they may be able to predict whether the contraction is *'ll* or *'d*, as these are common phrases which students will have heard several times before. Play the recording, twice if necessary, for students to complete the gaps. Play the recording again, or say the phrases yourself, for students to repeat.

> **ANSWERS**
> **1** *'ll* **2** *'ll* **3** *'d* **4** *'ll* **5** *'d* **6** *'d* **7** *'ll* **8** *'d*

Pronunciation: additional suggestion

Put students in pairs. Ask them to choose four of the phrases to put into two or three-line conversations. Give them a few minutes to prepare the conversations. They then act them out for the class. For example:

A: *Have you got any change for the phone?*

B: *I'll have a look. Yes, here you are.*

A: *Thanks.*

Other students guess who/where they are.

ADDITIONAL PRACTICE

Workbook: First and second conditional forms, page 93; *will* or *would* (Exercises 5 and 6), page 94

RB **Resource bank:** 16A *Conditional squares* (Unreal and real conditions), page 177

Choose people to start a space colony

See *Teacher's tips: making speaking Tasks work* on pages 6–7 and *responding to learners' individual language needs* on pages 8–9.

Preparation for task (PAGE 136)

1 Use the pictures to establish the context of space and space travel. Ask students whether they would like to go to travel in space, etc. Then put students in pairs to discuss the questions. Get students to report back for a class discussion.

2 Give students a few minutes to read the text and answer questions a–h. Students compare answers in pairs before checking with the whole class.

> **ANSWERS**
> **a** Because it has water, light, and oxygen, and a similar temperature and air to Earth.
> **b** They are not sure.
> **c** Six people, to start a new human society.
> **d** They won't come back.
> **e** not for 100 years
> **f** They will take enough food tablets for five years, four guns, blankets and space tents.
> **g** ten weeks
> **h** ten

3 Elicit one or two ideas about why someone would be suitable/unsuitable. Then check the following words/phrases: *divorced* /dɪ'vɔːst/, *retired* /rɪ'taɪəd/, *a widower* /ə'wɪdəʊə/, *pregnant* /'pregnənt/, *health* /helθ/, *cancer* /'kænsə/, *a judge* /ədʒʌdʒ/, *an engineer* /ən,endʒɪnɪə/, *an agricultural scientist* /ən'ægrɪ,kʌltʃərəl'saɪəntɪst/, *bravery* /'breɪvərɪ/. Give students plenty of time to read about the candidates and think carefully about their suitability for the project.

Task (PAGE 137)

1 Ask students to choose and make a list of the six best candidates, and to make notes on each one. Direct them to the *Useful language* box for help. Circulate and help with vocabulary queries, etc.

2 **a)** Put students in pairs to compare reasons and try to agree on the same six candidates. Tell them to be ready to justify their choices to other students. As you monitor this stage and the next, note down examples of good language use and/or errors for analysis and correction later.

b) Either put pairs together into groups of four or six, or bring the whole class together to discuss answers and try to agree on a final list.

3 Students discuss these questions as a class, or in small groups.

> **Exercise 3: additional discussion questions**
> ● What problems might the people have on the journey/on Hero?
> ● What would you do if any of these problems happened to you?

> **Task: alternative suggestions**
> a *If you have short lessons:* do the Preparation for task in one lesson. Then ask students to look at the candidates and choose the six best for homework. Do the rest of the Task in the second lesson.
> b *Role-play:* Students work in pairs and role-play one of the following situations:
> ● An interview with one of the chosen volunteers, just before he/she leaves. How is he/she feeling? Why did he/she volunteer? What is he/she hoping/expecting the journey and the planet to be like? etc.
> ● An interview with a scientist from the control station, following reports of some problems with the mission. What exactly are the problems? Have any of the volunteers been hurt? What are they doing to solve the problems? etc.

Creative writing (PAGE 137)

Prepare students for this activity by eliciting language under the four headings, for example:

● **the planet:** *there are lots of beautiful/strange plants/birds/animals/insects; there are (lots of/no) rivers/streams/lakes/forests/mountains; it's (very) warm/cool/quiet/peaceful/isolated/frightening.*

● **the journey there:** *we were/excited/worried/bored during the journey; I slept a lot/couldn't sleep; we had some problems with the engines/the fuel supply and we had to …; we arrived at night/in the morning.*

- **the other people:** *X seems (very) friendly/shy/bossy/ clever/worried/funny; I like/don't like Y because ...; I talked to Y about ...; Z can .../is good at ...ing.*

- **how you feel:** *I feel quite/very/really tired/depressed/ anxious/happy/because ...; I want to ...; I hope ...; I'm glad that ...*

Also elicit some suggestions of how to start/finish the letter, for example *Dear ... Well, here I am on the planet Hero! We've been here for ... days now, and ...* Then ask students to imagine they are one of the volunteers and plan what to put in the letter.

ADDITIONAL PRACTICE

RB **Resource bank:** 16B *Preposition pelmanism* (Revision of prepositions), page 178

Consolidation modules 12–16 (PAGE 138)

ANSWERS

A
Possible answers:
Invest money: make a lot of money/waste money
Furniture: made of wood
Leave a tip: waiter
Corkscrew: tin opener/lighter
Estate agent: lawyer/driving instructor/make a lot of money/wonderful view
Architect: lawyer/driving instructor
Make someone cry: driving instructor/actor
Accessories: sunglasses/gloves
Doctor: patient/honest
Designer goods: lighter/sunglasses/gloves
Make a mistake: honest
Balcony: wonderful view
Sign a contract: lawyer

C
3 See tapescript Consolidation 12–16 on page 168 of the *Students' Book.*

GRAMMAR GAME: ADDITIONAL ACTIVITY

You could use the following game on pages 103–104 as a round up/revision once you have completed the course. Go through the rules of the game with the class, then put students in groups of three to four to play. If you do not have a dice, ask students to write the numbers 1–6 on small slips of paper, and put them in an envelope. Students then draw a number out of the envelope instead of throwing a dice. Students can use different size coins instead of counters. As each student moves to a square, another

student from the group should choose a question from the relevant category (indicated by the symbol on the square) and read it out. Monitor the game, acting as adjudicator if students are not sure about an answer. Make sure students move the correct number of squares or throw again if they answer correctly. The winner is the first person to the finish.

ANSWERS

! = Correct the mistake
1 In my job you have to **be** friendly.
2 I've known him **for** ten years.
3 He hasn't got **any** friends.
4 It's been **raining** all day.
5 A kettle is a machine **that/which** heats water.
6 There isn't **much** nightlife here.
7 Who's sitting next **to** David?
8 She told me/him/her/us/them she was from France.

? = Look at the answer – what was the question?
1 How far is it to X?
2 What shall I buy X (for her birthday)?
3 How long have you had your/that (computer/car, etc.)?
4 What are (your/those gloves/socks, etc.) made of?
5 How long has X been working here?
6 How much are these/those/the ...s? How much do these/those/the ...s cost?
7 Why was X so happy? Why did X (buy champagne for his friends, etc.)?
8 What would you do/buy if you had/won (£XXX)?

* = Mixed questions
1 *some* = an indefinite number of; *a few* = a small number of
2 *on top of* = the object is in contact with the TV; *above* = no contact
3 get off the *bus/train/plane*; come out of the *station/airport*; cross the *road/street/park*
4 *a lot of* = a large amount; *too much* = negative meaning: the amount of noise is a problem
5 you can *spend/save/earn/make/invest/borrow/lend* money
6 *When I got home, he cooked dinner.* = he started cooking dinner when I got home (at the same time)
When I got home, he had cooked dinner. = he cooked dinner before I got home
7 He said he'd be back at nine.
8 *If I feel better, I'll come to the party.* = a future possibility
If I felt better, I would come to the party. = refers to the present, suggests the speaker doesn't feel well enough to go to the party

Language experts

Instructions

- Work in small groups.
- You will need a dice and counters.
- The first person to throw a six starts.
- The symbol on the square tells you which question category you have to answer.
- The other students in the group decide if your answer is correct – check with your teacher if you are not sure!

Questions

ABC = *How do you spell ...?*
Move forward one square if you answer correctly.

1 advertising
2 driving licence
3 imagination
4 experience
5 accountant
6 apartment
7 possession
8 judge

! = *Correct the mistake*
Move forward two squares if you answer correctly.

1 In my job you have to friendly.
2 I've known him since ten years.
3 He hasn't got no friends.
4 It's been rained all day.
5 A kettle is a machine what heats water.
6 There isn't many nightlife here.
7 Who's sitting next David?
8 She told she was from France.

? = *Look at the answer – what was the question?*
Move forward three squares if you answer correctly.

1 About 25 kilometres, I think.
2 You could buy her some flowers.
3 I've had it for five years.
4 They're made of wool.
5 She's been working here since March.
6 They're £10 each.
7 Because he'd won £1,000,000 on the lottery.
8 I'd buy a big house.

* = *Mixed questions*
Throw again if you answer correctly.

1 What is the difference between these sentences?
*There are **some** nice shops.*
*There are **a few** nice shops.*

2 What is the difference between these sentences?
*It's **on top of** the TV.*
*It's **above** the TV.*

3 Finish these phrases for giving directions.
get off the ...
come out of the ...
cross the ...

4 What's the difference between these sentences?
*There's **a lot of** noise.*
*There's **too much** noise.*

5 Think of three things you can do with money.

6 What's the difference between these sentences?
*When I got home, he **cooked** dinner.*
*When I got home, he **had cooked** dinner.*

7 Put this sentence into reported speech.
'I'll be back at nine,' he said.

8 What's the difference between these sentences?
If I feel better, I'll come to the party.
If I felt better, I'd come to the party.

© Pearson Education Limited 2001 **103**

Language experts

© Pearson Education Limited 2001

PHOTOCOPIABLE

Resource bank
Index of activities

Activity	Language point	When to use	Time (minutes)
1A Get to know the *Students' Book*	None	first day of the course	20–30
Learner-training worksheet A	Using the *Mini-dictionary*: introduction	early in the course	20–30
1B Me too!	Present Simple and question words	after Language focus 1, Practice Exercise 2, page 10	15–25
1C Connected lives	Present Simple questions with '*How often ...?*' and adverbs of frequency	after Language focus 2, Practice Exercise 2, page 11	20–30
Learner-training worksheet B	Using the *Mini-dictionary*: irregular verbs – part 1	after the Grammar analysis box, page 16	15–25
2A Dead famous	Past Simple *yes/no* questions and short answers	after Language focus 1, Practice Exercise 3, page 16	15–25
2B The Millionaire's Ball	Past Simple and time phrases	after Language focus 2, Practice Exercise 2, page 17	20–30
2C Invent-a-story	Past Simple and linkers	after Linking ideas in narrative, page 22	20–45
3A The secret of successful language learning	Vocabulary extension (word building)	after Reading and Vocabulary, Exercise 5, page 25	20–30
3B Parents and children	*can, can't, have to, don't have to, should, shouldn't*	after Language focus 2, Practice Exercise 3, page 27	15–25
4A Party guests	Present Continuous and Present Simple	after Language focus 1, Practice Exercise 3, page 33	20–30
4B I'm having lunch with Madonna	Present Continuous (for future arrangements)	after Language focus 2, Practice Exercise 3, page 35	30–40
Learner-training worksheet C	Noticing and recording collocations	any time after the end of Module 4	15–25
5A Put these in order	Comparatives and superlatives	after Language focus 1, Practice Exercise 3, page 40	20–30
5B An alien family	Vocabulary: describing people's appearance	after Language focus 2, Practice Exercise 2, page 43	15–25
Learner-training worksheet D	Recording new vocabulary	any time during or after Module 5	20–30
6A Talk about the future	*going to, would like to, would prefer to, will/won't*	after Language focus 1, Practice Exercise 2, page 48	20–30
6B Holiday crossword	Holiday vocabulary	after Listening and speaking, page 50	20–30
7A Ambition dominoes	Verb/noun collocations	after Vocabulary and speaking, page 56	15–25
7B Life circles	Present Perfect and Past Simple	after Language focus 1, Practice Exercise 1, page 58	20–30
7C Happy verb families	Irregular past tenses and past participles	after Language focus 1, Practice Exercise 2, page 59	15–35
Learner-training worksheet E	Using the *Mini-dictionary*: irregular verbs – part 2	after the Grammar analysis box, page 58	15–25
Learner-training worksheet F	Spelling with double letters	any time after the end of Module 7	15–25

Activity	Language point	When to use	Time (minutes)
8A Article snakes and ladders	Use and non-use of articles	after Language focus 2, Practice Exercise 2, page 68	25–40
Learner-training worksheet G	Noticing and remembering prepositions and articles in phrases	any time after the end of Module 8	20–35
9A In the 2020s	*will, won't, may* and *might* (for future possibility)	after Language focus 1, Practice Exercise 2, page 75	25–40
9B Worried parents	Present tense after *if, when, as soon as* and other time words	after Language focus 2, Practice Exercise 3, page 77	20–30
Learner-training worksheet H	Deducing meaning from context – part 1	any time after the end of Module 9	20–30
10A What can I do for you?	Vocabulary: health problems	after Reading, listening and vocabulary, page 82	15–25
10B The Ghost	*used to* and Past Simple	after Language focus 1, Practice Exercise 2 page 83	20–30
10C Bob's night out	Past Continuous and Past Simple	after Language focus 2, Practice Exercise 3, page 85	25–45
11A The Lovebug Dating Agency	Gerunds; expressions for liking and disliking	after Language focus 1, Practice Exercise 2, page 92	25–40
11B Neither do I	*So do I, Me too, Me neither, Neither do I*, etc.	after Real life, page 96	15–25
Learner-training worksheet I	Using the *Mini-dictionary* to find constructions that follow verbs	any time after the end of Module 11	20–30
12A The Handbag Gang	Past Simple passive	after Language focus 1, Practice Exercise 2, page 101	24–45
12B What's this?	Relative clauses with *that, which* and *who*	after Vocabulary, page 103	15–25
13A Century People	Present Perfect Simple and Continuous (for unfinished past)	after Language focus 1, Practice Exercise 2, page 109	20–30
13B Old friends	Present Perfect Simple and Continuous (for unfinished past)	after Language focus 2, Practice Exercise 3, page 111	20–35
Learner-training worksheet J	Deducing meaning from context – part 2	any time towards the end of the course	25–35
14A The Hungry Hippo café	Quantifiers (*some, any, much, not enough,* etc.)	after Language focus 1, Practice Exercise 2, page 117	25–35
14B Where's the nearest bank?	Language for giving directions	after Real life and Writing, page 120	20–30
14C Building your dream	Vocabulary extension (word building, dependent prepositions and collocations)	after Reading, page 121	15–25
15A Lottery winners	Reported speech	after Language focus 2, Practice Exercise 3, page 127	25–40
15B Get Rich Quick!	Vocabulary: money	after Real life, page 130	25–35
Learner-training worksheet K	Using the *Mini-dictionary* to find dependent prepositions	any time towards the end of the course	15–25
16A Conditional squares	Unreal and real conditionals	after Language focus 2, Practice Exercise, page 135	20–30
16B Preposition pelmanism	Revision of prepositions	any time in the module	15–30

Test one (modules 1–6 pages 179–181   **Test two** (modules 7–11) pages 182–184   **Test three** (modules 12–16) pages 185–187

Instructions for activities pages 107–117   **Resource bank key** pages 188–192

Instructions

1A Get to know the *Students' Book*

You will need: one set of cards for each pair of students

- Shuffle each set of cards. Put students into pairs. Place the sets of cards **face down** in piles at the front of the class and allocate one set of cards to each pair.
- One student from each pair comes up to the front of the class, takes **one** card only from the top of their pile, and goes back to their partner. Then they write the answer to the question **on their card**.
- When a pair has completed a card they take it to the teacher to check their answer. If the answer is correct, they keep the card and take the next card from their pile at the front of the class. If the answer is not correct, they must work out the correct answer.
- The first pair to finish all the cards are the winners.

If it is not possible for students to move around the class freely, follow the following procedure:

- Put students into pairs and give each pair a set of cards face down in a pile. Students turn over the cards one by one and write the answers on the cards.
- When a pair has finished, they hand their pile of cards to the teacher for checking.
- The first pair to finish all the cards correctly are the winners.

Learner-training worksheet A
(Using the *Mini-dictionary:* introduction)

You will need: one copy of the worksheet per student

The *Mini-dictionary* helps students make the transition from bilingual to monolingual dictionaries (see *Making the most of the Mini-dictionary* on page 14 for more details). This worksheet gives students an overview of the type of information contained in the *Mini-dictionary*. Before starting the worksheet check students understand that the *Mini-dictionary* only contains words and meanings used in the *Students' Book*.

1 Students do **a** on their own, then discuss **b** in pairs. The aim is to show students that they don't always have to understand the definition to grasp the meaning – sometimes the example can be more useful.
2 Students work individually before checking answers with the whole class (see **Key**).
3 Students work individually or in pairs before checking answers with the whole class (see **Key**). Make sure that students understand the grammar terms and how verbs and nouns are marked in the *Mini-dictionary* (i.e. noun C, noun U, verb T, verb I).
4 Students work individually, then check answers in pairs or with the whole class (see **Key**).
5 Check that students understand what word stress is, and how it is marked in the *Mini-dictionary,* before they do the exercise individually or in pairs. Check answers with the whole class (see **Key**).

6 Students work individually before checking answers with the whole class.

1B Me too!

You will need: one copy of the worksheet per student

- Pre-teach/check the following vocabulary: *cousin*; *thriller*; *comedy*; *horror film*. Give each student a copy of the worksheet. Students work individually and make sentences about themselves in the first column on the worksheet.
- Students then work in pairs and, on a separate piece of paper, write down the **questions** that correspond to the sentences on their worksheet. Students must write questions for 'you' in the Present Simple, and each one must begin with a question word (*Who, Which, How often*, etc.). For example, for the first sentence on the worksheet students should write: *What time/When do you usually get up on Sundays?* Do the first two as examples with the whole class before they start.
- Students then move around the room asking the questions. When they find someone who has the same answer as them, they say *Me too!* and write the other student's name in the second column on the worksheet. **Students cannot look at each other's worksheets.** Encourage them to talk to as many different people as possible and to ask follow-up questions where appropriate.
- Students discuss their findings in small groups or with the whole class.

1C Connected lives

You will need: one copy of the Student A worksheet *and one copy of the* Student B worksheet *for each pair of students*

- Divide the class into two groups, A and B. Give a copy of Student A worksheet to students in group A, and a copy of Student B worksheet to those in group B. Tell students that the other group has the information that is missing from their worksheets.
- Students work individually, or with someone in their group, and decide what questions they need to ask to complete the worksheet. They must use the Present Simple in their questions, either with *How often …?* or with another question word plus an adverb of frequency. Do the first question on each worksheet with the whole class as examples before they start: (1) *How often does Lola sing at the* Flamingo Club? (a) *When/What time does Lola usually finish work?*
- Put students in pairs, so that one Student A and one Student B are working together. Students then ask each other the questions and complete their own worksheets.
- When they have finished, students discuss in pairs how many connections they can find between the six people before sharing their answers with the whole class.

Learner-training worksheet B
(Using the *Mini-dictionary*: irregular verbs – part 1)

You will need: one copy of the worksheet per student

This worksheet helps students to find the infinitive of irregular past tenses in the *Mini-dictionary*, and introduces some new irregular verbs that appear later in the *Students' Book*.

1 Students do the exercise individually or in pairs. Check answers with the whole class.
2 Check that students understand how irregular verbs are written in the *Mini-dictionary*.
3 Students do the exercise in pairs. Check answers with the whole class. Make sure that students understand the meaning of any new verbs, and know how to pronounce the past tenses.
4 Students work individually. Check answers with the whole class (see **Key**).

2A Dead famous!

You will need: one set of cards per three or four students

- Put students into groups of three or four. Give each group one set of cards **face down**, and ask them to divide them equally among themselves. Allow time for students to read the information on their cards. **They are not allowed to look at each other's cards.**
- Write the following question prompts on the board or on a separate handout. If necessary, check that students can make questions in the Past Simple from these prompts by doing an example with the whole class.
  born in America/Europe?   nationality?
  live in 20th/19th century?   live in Europe/Asia?
  married?   wife/husband famous too?   die young?
  write something?   discover something?
  actor/politician/film star/singer?   rich/poor?
  play a musical instrument?   clever/talented/beautiful?
- Student A chooses one of his/her cards, and the other students have to find out who the famous person on the card is by asking questions, either based on the prompts on the board or their own ideas. However, they are only allowed to ask questions which require **a yes/no answer**. They can ask a maximum of fifteen questions.
- If they haven't guessed after ten questions, Student A reads out the clue at the bottom of the card. If the other students don't discover the person's identity after fifteen questions, Student A can reveal his/her identity.
- Students take it in turns to be asked questions about a famous person until all the cards are finished.

2B The Millionaire's Ball

You will need: one copy of the worksheet and one role card per student

- Give each student a copy of the worksheet. Tell them that the line at the beginning of each sentence corresponds to a person's name.
- Students work individually and complete the time phrases by writing *in, on, at, ago*, on the dotted lines, or

by leaving the line blank. Check answers with the whole class (see **Key**).
- Pre-teach/check the following vocabulary: *to leave someone money in a will; to play cards/poker; caviar.*
- Tell students they are going to a party where everyone is *very* rich! Revise the following 'getting to know you' questions: *What's your name? Where do you live? What do you do? Are you married? Have you got any children?*
- Give each student a role card in random order, and allow time for them to read and understand the information. **They must not look at one another's cards.** (If you have more than ten students, the cards can be duplicated without affecting the outcome of the activity.)
- Tell students that they must talk to all the other guests at the party and write their names in the correct place on the worksheet. Students mingle and have short conversations with one another. Encourage them to introduce themselves and use the 'getting to know you' questions to start the conversation, rather than just ask the questions required to complete the worksheet.
- Students check answers in pairs or with the whole class.

2C Invent-a-story

You will need: one copy of the worksheet per student

- Put students into pairs or small groups. Give each student a copy of the worksheet and tell them that they are going to invent a story. Students must include **at least four** of the items or people at the top of the worksheet in their story.
- The questions on the worksheet provide a framework for the story. Students discuss each question in turn and write their ideas in the appropriate box. Encourage them to write **notes** rather than complete sentences.
- When they have made notes for all the questions, students write their story in their pairs or groups. Encourage them to use the linkers from page 22 of the *Students' Book* (*and, because, but, so* and *then*) when writing their story. Alternatively, the story can be written for homework.
- Students can put their stories up round the classroom and vote on which they like the most.

3A The secret of successful language learning

You will need: one copy of the worksheet per student; a set of monolingual dictionaries (not the Mini-dictionary*)*

- Give each student a copy of the worksheet. Students work through the exercises individually or in pairs before checking answers with the whole class (see **Key**).

3B Parents and children

You will need: one copy of the worksheet per student

- Pre-teach/check the following vocabulary: *to dye your hair; make-up; to do housework.*

- Put students into pairs. If possible, pair one male student with one female student. Give each student a copy of the worksheet and tell them to write their partner's name at the top of the second column.
- Explain that students have to give their opinion on ten statements about parents and children. They also have to guess their partner's opinion, too. Draw students' attention to the scale at the top of the worksheet.
- Students work individually and circle numbers in both columns. They are not allowed to ask their partner anything at this stage.
- Students compare their answers in pairs and see how many of their predictions are correct. Encourage students to justify their opinions, particularly when they don't agree with each other.
- Students tell the whole class how many of their predictions were correct and discuss any differences of opinion they had.

4A Party guests

You will need: *one role card per student; one copy of* Student A worksheet *or* Student B worksheet *per student*

- Tell students that they are at a party where they don't know anyone. Elicit appropriate questions you could ask a stranger at a party and write them on the board. (Useful ones for the activity are: *Where do you live? Do you live near here? What do you do? What do you do in your spare time? Are you enjoying the party?*)
- Give each student a role card, and allow time for them to read and understand the information. **They are not allowed to look at each other's role cards**. (The activity will work with any number of students, but a minimum of eight is preferable. If there are more than twelve students, distribute duplicate role cards.)
- Give half the class Student A worksheet and the other half Student B worksheet. Students must find out who the people on their worksheet are by asking questions in the Present Simple and Present Continuous based on the information provided. **All four pieces of information about each person must match before the student writes down the name.**
- Students move around the room having short conversations and asking one another questions. When they have found someone who **completely** matches the description, they write his/her name in the appropriate place on their worksheet. The activity continues until students have found out who everyone is.
- Students can compare their answers in pairs/groups or with the whole class.

4B I'm having lunch with Madonna

You will need: *one diary per student*

- Check that students know the following language in **bold** for talking about and making arrangements:
  What are you doing on Monday (afternoon)?
  I'm having lunch with my sister. / Nothing special.

Would you like to go out for a drink? / **Let's** have lunch. / **How about** meeting for a coffee?
Yes, I'd love to. / **Yes, why not?** / **I'd rather not, thanks**.

- Brainstorm with the class the types of activities that people arrange together and write them on the board. Include the following: *have lunch/dinner; go to the cinema/the theatre/a concert/a football match; go shopping; go/come to a party; come round for a meal; go out for a drink; meet for a coffee.*
- Give each student one of the diaries and tell them that it contains their arrangements for next week. (If you have more than eight students, use extra copies of the diaries.) Allow time for students to read the information.
- Tell students that they have to make **at least six** new arrangements with their classmates (using the language and ideas previously highlighted) and write them in their diaries. These arrangements can be made **at any time of the day**. Students move around the room making arrangements. When two students have made an arrangement with each other, they must both write it in the appropriate place in their diaries.
- Remind students to express their arrangements in full sentences using the Present Continuous, and not just read out the notes in their diaries.
- If you have more than eight students, tell them to check they have **different** diaries before they start talking. If they have the same diary, they must find a different student.
- When they have finished, students work in pairs or small groups and tell each other about all the arrangements they have made.

Learner-training worksheet C
(Noticing and recording collocations)

You will need: *one copy of the worksheet per student*

The aim of this worksheet is to raise students' awareness of collocation, and to provide them with some useful ways of recording collocations when they come across them in class.
1 Go through the example with the whole class.
2 Students work individually, then check answers with the whole class (see **Key**).
3 Students work individually or in pairs, checking any answers they are not sure of in the *Mini-dictionary*. Check answers with the whole class (see **Key**). All the collocations are taken from Modules 1–4 in the *Students' Book.*
4 Go through the examples of how to record collocations with the whole class. Students discuss the questions at the end in pairs or groups.

5A Put these in order

You will need: *one copy of the worksheet per student*

- Pre-teach/check the following vocabulary: *assassination; to release somebody from prison; recent.*
- Divide the class into teams of three or four. Give each student a copy of the worksheet. Do the example at the top of the page with the whole class.

- Set a time limit of ten or fifteen minutes, and allow students to do the quiz in their teams. They should discuss the answers together and come to a consensus as a team. Encourage students to use comparatives and superlatives while they are deciding on the correct order. For example, *Do you think that Sharon Stone is older than Brad Pitt? / I'm sure Robert DeNiro is the oldest.*
- Check answers with the whole class (see **Key**). Students get one point for each item they have in the correct place. They also get a bonus point if they get all four items correct (a completely correct answer is therefore worth five points). The team with the most points is the winner.
- Students can go through the quiz again in their groups and explain what they got wrong and why, using more comparatives and superlatives: *We thought that the Eiffel Tower was older than the Taj Mahal, but it isn't.*

5B An alien family

You will need: *one copy of* Picture A *and one copy of* Picture B *for each pair of students*

- Put students into pairs and give one student a copy of Picture A and the other a copy of Picture B. Tell students that all the aliens in the picture are members of the same family. **Students are not allowed to look at each other's pictures**.
- Students work in pairs. Student A describes one of the aliens in his/her picture that *hasn't* got a name. He/she must describe the alien's appearance (using the language on page 42 of the *Students' Book*), **not** where the alien is in the picture.
- When Student A has finished the description, Student B tells him/her the name of the alien, which Student A then writes in the correct space on the picture. If Student B is unsure which alien is being described, he/she should ask questions about the alien's appearance to clarify any doubts.
- Students take it in turns until all the aliens are identified. When they have finished, students may look at each other's pictures and check their answers.
- Finally, each pair of students decides how all the aliens are related, giving reasons for their choices. Their ideas can be discussed with the whole class.

Learner-training worksheet D
(Recording new vocabulary)

You will need: *one copy of the worksheet per student*

When recording new vocabulary, students often make lists of new English words next to translations in their own language. The aim of this worksheet is to encourage students to include more information in their lists, therefore making them more useful.

1   Students work in pairs or small groups and make notes on what extra information is included in the second list. Check answers with the whole class. (The second list includes the following **extra information**: part of speech (including putting *to* in front of a verb and *a/an* in front of a countable noun), word stress, regular/irregular verbs, dependent prepositions, transitive and intransitive verbs

(by writing *someone* or *something* after the verb), countable/uncountable nouns, common collocations and examples, common errors in student's own language, phonemic script.)

2   Students rewrite the list in pairs or small groups. Encourage them to use the *Mini-dictionary* to add more information. Check answers with the whole class (see **Key**).

3   Students work on their own before comparing their ideas in groups. Or, this exercise can be set for homework.

6A Talk about the future

You will need: *one copy of the board per three or four students; one dice and three/four counters per group*

- Put students into groups of three or four. Give each group a board, counters and dice. If one student has a watch with a second hand, make him/her the timekeeper.
- Students take it in turns to throw a number. When they land on a future square, they have to talk about the topic or question for twenty seconds without stopping. With a less confident class, you can allow students twenty seconds' thinking time before speaking.
- If a student can't think of anything to say, or stops talking before the twenty seconds are up, then he/she has to move back to his/her previous square.
- The student who reaches the *Finish* square first is the winner.

6B Holiday crossword

You will need: *a copy of each crossword for each pair of students*

- Divide the class into two groups, A and B. Give a copy of Student A crossword to students in group A, and a copy of Student B crossword to those in group B.
- Students work together in their separate groups to check they know the meaning of the words on their half of the crossword. All the vocabulary in this activity is taken from the *Vocabulary and speaking* section on page 49 and the *Listening and speaking* section on page 50 of the *Students' Book*.
- Put students in pairs, so that one Student A and one Student B are working together. **They are not allowed to look at each other's crossword.**
- Students take it in turns to define the words on their half of the crossword. The other student has to guess the words and write them in his/her own crossword. Encourage students to use collocations and examples from the material in the *Students' Book* where possible.
- Students continue until they both have a completed version of the crossword.

7A Ambition dominoes

You will need: *one set of dominoes for each pair of students*

- All the collocations in this activity are taken from the *Vocabulary and speaking* section on page 56 of the *Students' Book*.

- Students work in pairs. Give one set of dominoes to each pair, and ask them to share them out equally.
- One student places a domino in front of them, and the other student has to make a complete sentence by placing one of his/her dominoes at either end of the first domino. The students then take it in turns to put down their dominoes at either end of the domino chain. Encourage students to look at the words in **bold** and consider which words collocate with them.
- If a student thinks his/her partner's sentence is not grammatically correct or doesn't make sense, he/she can challenge the other student. If the students cannot agree, the teacher adjudicates. If the sentence is incorrect, the student must take back the domino and miss a turn.
- If a student cannot make a sentence, the turn passes to his/her partner.
- The game continues until one student has used up all his/her dominoes, or until neither student can make a correct sentence. The student who finishes first, or has the fewest dominoes remaining, is the winner.
- Students who finish early can test each other on the collocations in bold on the cards.

7B Life circles

You will need: one copy of the worksheet per student

- Check/pre-teach the following words: *primary school*; *recently*; *a personal possession.*
- Give each student a copy of the worksheet. Encourage them to answer as many questions as possible, and make sure they write their answers in **random order**. They should write single words, names or short phrases, **not** complete sentences. Set a time limit of five or ten minutes.
- Students work in pairs. They fold their worksheet in half and swap with their partner. Students then have to ask questions to find out why their partner has written the words in the circles: *Why have you written 'Italy' here? Who's Michael?* etc. The other student must reply using the correct tense: Present Perfect or Past Simple.
- For each circle, students must ask their partner two or three suitable follow-up questions on the same topic. For example, for 'someone you've known for over ten years' they could ask: *Where did you meet him/her? What does he/she do? How often do you see him/her?* etc.
- At the end, students report back on the most interesting things they found out about their partner.

7C Happy verb families

You will need: one set of cards for each group of three or four students

- Put students into groups of three or four. Give each group a set of cards and ask them to deal out **seven** cards to each player. The rest of the cards are then placed **face down** in a pile in the middle of the group.

- **The aim of the activity is for students to get rid of all the cards in their hands**. To do this, students must collect 'verb families' of infinitive, past tense and past participle, which they then place face up in front of them.
- Student A begins by asking **one** of the other students (**not** the whole group) if he/she has a particular card that Student A needs for a verb family. For example, if Student A has cards that say *wear* and *wore,* he/she can ask: *Jaime, have you got a card that says 'worn'?*
- If the other student does have the card Student A has asked for, he/she must give it to him/her. If the other student does not have the card, Student A must pick up an extra card from the pile in the middle. The turn then passes to the next student.
- If a student is asked to hand over his/her last card to another student, he/she wins the game. So asking a student for his/her last card is a very silly thing to do!
- When a student gets a verb family, he/she immediately places it face up in front of him/her. The other students should check that the verb family is correct. Only the verbs in **bold** can be counted as part of a verb family. If necessary they can check with you or refer to the table of irregular verbs on page 148 of the *Students' Book*.
- If there are no extra cards left, students continue taking it in turns to ask each other for cards until there is a winner. The winner is the first person with no cards left in his/her hands.
- Groups who finish early can shuffle the cards and play again.

Note: it would be advisable to demonstrate this activity with the whole class before they start playing in groups.

Learner-training worksheet E
(Using the *Mini-dictionary*: irregular verbs – part 2)

You will need: one copy of the worksheet per student

The aim of this worksheet is to raise students' awareness of how irregular verbs are written in dictionaries, and to increase students' speed at using the *Mini-dictionary*.

1 Go through the example dictionary entry.
2 Students work individually and complete the table as fast as possible, using the *Mini-dictionary* when necessary. The student who finishes first, with all the answers spelt correctly, is the winner. Alternatively, students can do the activity in pairs. (Note: students are not allowed to look at the table on page 148 in the *Students' Book*, as the aim of this exercise is to increase dictionary speed.) When they have finished, they can work in pairs to test each other on the verbs. One student says an infinitive and his/her partner has to say the correct past tense and past participle.

Learner-training worksheet F
(Spelling with double letters)

You will need: one copy of the worksheet per student

The aim of this worksheet is to raise students' awareness of double letters in English, and teach them a simple spelling rule.

1   Check students know the meaning of *vowel* and *consonant*, then give out the worksheet. Allow students a minute or two to read the rules on their own. Go through the rule on the board if necessary. (Note that the term *-ing word* is used to avoid having to differentiate between present participles and gerunds.)
2   Students work individually or in pairs. Check answers with the whole class (see **Key**).

8A Article snakes and ladders

You will need: one snakes and ladders *board per group of three students; one set of* Question cards *per group; one dice and three counters per group*

●   Put students into groups of three and give each group a *snakes and ladders* board, a set of *Question cards*, counters and dice. Tell a student to shuffle the *Question cards* before putting them **face down** in a pile.
●   Students take it in turns to throw a number. When they land on a square with a question mark on it, they must take a *Question card* from the top of the pile. The student places the card down next to the board so all the students can see it, then has to answer the question. If the student answers the whole question correctly, he/she stays on the square and the next student takes his/her turn. If the student answers the question incorrectly, he/she must return to his/her original square.
●   If students cannot agree on the correct answer, the teacher adjudicates (see **Key**).
●   If a student lands at the foot of a ladder, he/she must get the question correct **before** he/she is allowed to go up it. If a student lands on the head of a snake, he/she must slide down the snake to its tail.
●   The game continues until one student reaches the *Finish* square (or until the group runs out of *Question cards*).
●   At the end of the game students can discuss the cards they got wrong, and/or go through the *Question cards* they didn't answer.

Learner-training worksheet G
(Noticing and remembering prepositions and articles in phrases)

You will need: one copy of the worksheet per student (detach the picture from the worksheet before the lesson)

The aim of this worksheet is to raise students' awareness of fixed and semi-fixed phrases containing articles and prepositions, and to encourage students to recognize, record and remember these phrases.
1   Students work in pairs. Give each pair a copy of the picture, and allow a few minutes for them to predict what the two teachers are saying. Students discuss their ideas with the rest of the class.
2   Give each student a copy of the second half of the worksheet and allow time for them to check their predictions. Students compare their predictions in pairs or with the whole class.

3   Go through the example phrases with the class, then let students do the exercise individually or in pairs. Check answers with the whole class (see **Key**). All the phrases in the conversation are taken from Modules 1–8 of the *Students' Book*. Note that some of the phrases in this activity are 'fixed' (e.g. *the other day*), while others can change the tense or the pronoun (e.g. *to be not very good at something*). Some of the easier two-word phrases (e.g. *on Friday*) have not been included in subsequent exercises or the key.
4   Students work individually. Suggest they cover the dialogue. Students check answers in pairs, referring back to the dialogue if necessary. Check answers with the whole class (see **Key**). Students can then practice the conversation in pairs. Two or three pairs can 'perform' their dialogue in front of the class.

9A In the 2020s

You will need: one copy of Survey A, B, C *or* D *for each student*

●   Check/pre-teach the following vocabulary: *a survey; 3D; to clone; to be extinct; IQ; to be homeless.*
●   Divide the class into four groups A, B, C and D. Give each student in group A a copy of *Survey A*, each student in group B a copy of *Survey B*, and so on. Tell the class they are going to prepare questions on what life will be like in the 2020s.
●   Students work in their groups and write down questions based on their *Survey* sheets: for example for the prompt *people – have more free time?*, students should write *Do you think people will have more free time (in the 2020s)?* When they have finished, encourage them to write one or two more questions on the same topic.
●   Rearrange the class so that one student from each of the four groups, A, B, C and D, is sitting together. If there are students left over, have some groups of five.
●   Write the following answers on the board: *Yes, definitely. / Yes, probably. / Maybe. / No, probably not. / No, definitely not.* Students then ask each other the questions in turn. When responding, students must use one of the answers on the board, and give reasons for their opinion if possible. **All students must make notes on what their classmates think**, based on the five answers on the board.
●   Students return to their original groups and collate their answers. The members of the group then add their own answers to the survey, so that their results represent the opinion of the whole class.
●   Write the following prompts on the board: *will definitely; will probably; might/may; probably won't; definitely won't.* Each group presents their results to the whole class, using the language highlighted on the board. For example, group A might have found out that: *Five students think that people will definitely have more free time in the 2020s, but four students think that they probably won't.* Alternatively, you can rearrange the class into small groups again (one student from each of

the groups, A, B, C and D) and students can report the results of their survey.

- Students can write up their survey for homework and put the results up round the classroom for others to read.

9B Worried parents

You will need: one copy of Student A worksheet *and one copy of* Student B worksheet *for each pair of students*

- Check/pre-teach the following vocabulary: *to hitchhike; to give somebody a lift; to get lost; to run out of money; to go camping; a tent; a guide; a sleeping bag; to be fully booked* (of a train).
- Divide the class into two groups, A and B. Give a copy of *Student A worksheet* to students in group A, and a copy of *Student B worksheet* to those in group B. Explain that they are going to do **two** role plays: one where they are a son/daughter going on a dangerous holiday, and another where they are the son/daughter's worried parent. Allow time for students to read and understand the information on their worksheets.
- Students work individually or in pairs and, using the prompts on the worksheet, prepare questions to ask when they are the **parent** in the role play. They should use 'you' as the subject of the questions. Do an example with the whole class before they begin: *phone me/as soon as/arrive in Miami? = Will you phone me as soon as you arrive in Miami?* and *what/do/if/get lost? = What will you do if you get lost?*
- Put students in pairs, so that one Student A and one Student B are working together, and tell them to do **role play 1**. Allow time for Student B to read the information on his/her worksheet before they begin.
- When students have finished, they change roles and do **role play 2**.

Learner-training worksheet H
(Deducing meaning from context – part 1)

You will need: one copy of the worksheet per student; a set of Longman Active Study Dictionaries *(optional)*

The aim of this worksheet is to raise students' awareness of the importance of context when faced with unknown vocabulary, and to give them practice in deducing meaning from context.

1 Students read the text individually, then discuss in pairs what they think really happened. Check ideas with the whole class. (The man had put ketchup on his shirt to pretend he was injured, in order to trick a passerby into giving him some money.)
2 Students work individually or in pairs. Check answers with the whole class. (Note that these words do not appear in the *Mini-dictionary*.)
3 Students work individually. Set a time limit of five minutes.
4 Students compare their answers in pairs or small groups. Check answers with the whole class. Although the success rate will vary, most students should be able to guess the exact meaning for **a, b, d, e, f** and **i**, and the

general meaning for **c, g** and **j**. Students are unlikely to be able to guess the meaning for **h**. (Note that these words do not appear in the *Mini-dictionary*, but students can check the meanings in the *Longman Active Study Dictionary* if necessary.)

10A What can I do for you?

You will need: one set of role cards for each pair of students

- Put students into pairs. Give one student a copy of the *Patient A* role card and the other a copy of the *Doctor A* role card. Allow a few minutes for students to prepare their roles. (All the vocabulary used in this activity is taken from the *Reading, listening and vocabulary* section on page 81 of the *Students' Book*.)
- Students act out the role play in their pairs. If there is space in the classroom, rearrange the chairs so that students are facing each other, with room for the doctor and patient to stand up if they wish.
- When each pair finishes, give the *Doctor B* role card to the student who was the patient in the first role play, and the *Patient B* role card to the student who was the doctor. Again, allow a few minutes for them to prepare. Students then act out the second role play in their pairs.
- Finally, students report back to the whole class on the advice/treatment their doctor gave them.

10B The Ghost

You will need: one set of role cards for each pair of students

- Pre-teach the following vocabulary: *to burgle/a burglar; a burglar alarm; a criminal; to get caught.*
- Divide the class into two groups and give one group *The Ghost* role cards and the other group *Journalist* role cards. Allow time for them to read the introduction at the top of the cards, and check they all understand the situation. If there is an odd number of students, include an extra journalist.
- Students with the *Journalist* role cards work individually or in pairs to prepare the questions they need to ask. Encourage them to use *used to* where possible in their questions, as well as the Past Simple. Students with *The Ghost* role cards work individually to prepare their stories by filling in the gaps in the information on the card. Allow about ten or fifteen minutes for this.
- Rearrange the class so that one student with the *Ghost* role card is sitting next to one student with a *Journalist* role card. The journalists then conduct the interview and make notes of their answers.
- Journalists can write an article for the *Famous Criminals* magazine in class or for homework, and burglars can write their life story.

10C Bob's night out

You will need: one set of pictures for each pair of students; one copy of the whole picture story per student (optional)

- Before the class, cut up and shuffle a set of pictures for each pair of students.

- Put students into pairs and give each pair a set of pictures. Tell students that they have the complete story of 'Bob's night out'. Students work together to decide on the correct order of the pictures. Encourage them to discuss their reasons for choosing each picture with their partner while they are working.
- Check the correct order with the whole class (see **Key**). Other orders may be possible, depending on the students' versions of the stories.
- Students work individually or in pairs and write the story in the past, using the Past Simple and Past Continuous where appropriate. The stories can be completed for homework (students will need a copy of all the pictures to take away with them in order to finish the story).
- Students can put up their completed stories round the classroom for other students to read.

11A The Lovebug Dating agency

You will need: *one set of six* Lovebug Dating Agency *cards (either* Men *or* Women*) for each pair of students*

- Put students into pairs (or groups of three). You must have an **even number** of pairs or groups for this activity.
- Check that students understand the concept of a dating agency, and give each pair/group a set of six *Lovebug Dating Agency* cards. Give half the number of pairs/groups the *Men* set of cards, and the other half the *Women* set.
- Tell students to look at the pictures on the cards and fill in the profile with information that they think suits the person's character. Set a time limit of ten or fifteen minutes.
- Group each pair that has *Men* cards with a pair that has *Women* cards. Students tell one another about the people on their cards, then the whole group decides who should go on a date with who, based on the information in the profile. Encourage students to pair up all the men and women if possible, and give reasons for their decisions.
- Students tell the whole class about their most promising dates. Alternatively, the pairs of cards can be put up round the classroom. Students walk around looking at all the pairs of cards and decide which dates they think will be the most successful.

11B Neither do I

You will need: *one copy of the worksheet per student*

- Give each student a copy of the worksheet. Students work individually and fill in the gaps with their own ideas. Set a time limit of five or ten minutes.
- If necessary, check which responses for agreement (*Neither did I, So am I*, etc. – see page 96 of the *Students' Book*) would be correct for each sentence before students do the next stage of the activity.
- Students move around the room saying their sentences to one another. They must try to find one person in the class who agrees with each of their statements. When

one student agrees with another student's sentence, he/she must respond using an appropriate expression and the first student writes his/her name in the second column on the worksheet. For example, Student A says *I really like playing tennis* and Student B responds by saying *Me too / So do I*. Student A then writes Student B's name on the worksheet. **They do *not* need to have written the same sentence**.

- If Student B doesn't agree with the sentence, he/she responds by saying what he/she has written for the same prompt (e.g. *Well, I really like going to the cinema.*), and seeing if Student A agrees with the statement. Encourage students to ask follow-up questions on each topic of agreement if possible.
- When two students have both found something they agree on (and written each other's names on their worksheets) they should move on and find new partners. Each student should try to talk to as many different people as possible. The activity continues until they have all completed the second column on their worksheet.
- Students work in pairs and tell their partner what they have found out, using *Both (Miguel) and I ...* or *Neither (Hiroko) or I ...* to begin their sentences.

Learner-training worksheet I
(Using the *Mini-dictionary* to find constructions that follow verbs)

You will need: *one copy of the worksheet per student*

The aim of this worksheet is to show students how to use the *Mini-dictionary* to find out what grammatical construction follows a verb, as well as to revise some of the verbs they have already met in the *Students' Book*.
1 Go through the dictionary entries with the whole class. Check they understand what a *gerund* is.
2 Students work in pairs or small groups. All the verbs and verb phrases are taken from Modules 1–11 of the *Students' Book*. Check answers with the whole class (see **Key**).
3 Students work individually before checking their answers with the whole class (see **Key**).

12A The Handbag Gang

You will need: *one set of pictures for each pair of students; one copy of the* Vocabulary worksheet *per student; one copy of the whole story per student (optional)*

- Before the class, cut up and shuffle a set of pictures for each pair of students.
- Put students into pairs and give each pair a set of pictures. Tell them that they have the complete story of the Handbag Gang. Students put the pictures in order, giving reasons for their choices. Check the correct order with the whole class (see **Key**), and discuss any variations to the suggested order.
- Give each student a copy of the *Vocabulary worksheet*. Students work in pairs again and match the vocabulary with the appropriate picture(s). Tell students that some

items of vocabulary can go with more than one picture. Check answers with the whole class. Make sure students understand all the words and expressions, and that they know the past participles of the verbs.

- In their pairs, students tell the story orally, using the new vocabulary. They should tell the main part of the story in the Past Simple, and the verbs on the worksheet should be used in the passive form.
- Tell students that they are journalists working for the local newspaper, and they have to write the story for tomorrow's edition. Their report **must** include at least six verbs in the Past Simple passive. Encourage students to think of a headline and lay out the report in newspaper style.
- Students can either write the report in class or for homework. (Note: students will need a copy of all the pictures if they write the story outside class.)
- The finished versions can be displayed round the classroom for other students to read.

12B What's this?

You will need: one set of picture cards per three students

- Put students into groups of three. Give each group a set of picture cards **face down in a pile.** Shuffle the cards beforehand.
- Student A picks up the first card. He/she must define the object or person to the student on his/her right (Student B), using a sentence containing *that*, *which* or *who*. Student B must try to guess what or who Student A is describing. (All the words included in this activity are from *Language focus 2* on page 102 and the *Vocabulary* section on page 103 of the *Students' Book*.) Students are not allowed to say the name of the object or person, or mime in any way – they should fold their arms when they are defining the words!
- If Student B guesses correctly, Student A gives him/her the card. If Student B doesn't know the word, the turn passes to Student C. If neither student can guess the word, the card goes back to the bottom of the pile.
- Students continue taking turns defining the objects on the cards to the student on their right. The student who collects the most cards by the end of the game is the winner.

Note: it would be advisable to demonstrate this activity to the whole class before they begin working in groups.

13A Century People

You will need: one set of role cards for each pair of students

- Divide the class into two groups and give one group *Old person* role cards, and the other group *Interviewer* role cards. Allow time for students to read the introduction on the cards. If there is an odd number of students, include an extra interviewer.
- The old people work individually and fill in the gaps in the information on the role card. Encourage them to be

as inventive as possible and to think of interesting details to add to their life story. The interviewers work individually or in pairs and write down the questions they are going to ask in the interview. Make sure students use the Present Perfect Simple and Continuous in their questions where appropriate. Allow the class about ten or fifteen minutes for this.

- Rearrange the class so that one old person is sitting next to one interviewer and allow students to do the role play.
- When they have finished, the interviewers can tell the whole class about the old people they have just talked to, and the class can decide which old person has had the most interesting life.

13B Old friends

You will need: one role card per student

- Tell students that they are at a party where there are lots of old friends they haven't seen for ten years. Elicit questions they could ask each other, and write them on the board. Useful questions for this activity are: *What have you been doing since I last saw you? What do you do? Where do you live? Are you married? What does your husband/wife do? What do you do in your spare time?* Also elicit a follow-up question with *How long …* for each of the preceding questions.
- Give each student a role card, and allow time for them to read the information. **They are not allowed to look at each other's role cards**. (Role cards 1 to 8 are needed for all students to complete the activity; role cards 9 to 12 are optional. If you have more than twelve students, distribute duplicate role cards.)
- Tell students that they have to find at least four old friends they have something in common with. When they find someone they must write down the name of the person, and what they have in common, on their role card. They should write **notes** (e.g. *architect – 7 years*) in the second column, not complete sentences.
- Students move around the room introducing themselves and asking one another the questions elicited earlier. Encourage students to ask as many *How long …* follow-up questions as possible during the conversations.
- Finally, students work in pairs and tell each other what they have found out, using the notes on their role card as prompts. Again, encourage them to use Present Perfect Simple or Continuous in their answers. For example *Lisa and I live in New York, and we've both been living there since 1990.*

Learner-training worksheet J
(Deducing meaning from context – part 2)

You will need: one copy of the worksheet per student; copies of the Longman Active Study Dictionary *(optional)*

This worksheet follows on from *Learner-training worksheet H* and gives students more practice in deducing meaning from context.

1 Allow students a few minutes to read the story

individually, then put them into pairs to put the story in order. Avoid answering questions about the words in italics at this stage. Check answers with the whole class (see **Key**).

2 Students work in pairs and try to deduce the meaning of the words in italics from the context. Check answers with the whole class. Alternatively, provide the class with copies of the *Longman Active Study Dictionary* and allow them to check their answers themselves. (Note that these words are *not* included in the *Mini-dictionary*.)

3 Students ask and answer the questions in pairs. Encourage both students to answer each question. Students report back to the whole class on their most interesting answers.

14A The Hungry Hippo café

You will need: one copy of Worksheet 1 *or* Worksheet 2 *per student*

- Divide the class into two groups. Give copies of *Worksheet 1* to one group, and copies of *Worksheet 2* to the other. Allow time for students to read the information at the top of the worksheet, and check they understand the situation.
- Students work in pairs with someone who has the **same** worksheet. You need **an equal number of pairs** for this activity, so have one or two groups of three if necessary. Students must look at the menu and the pictures, and make three lists: things they have too much / many of; things they don't have enough of; things they don't have any of. Allow about ten minutes for this.
- Group each pair that has *Worksheet 1* with a pair that has *Worksheet 2*. The students tell/ask each other what they've got too much of, not enough of, etc., and swap items where possible. When they swap items, they tick them off their lists.
- Students report back to the whole class on how much they have swapped, and what they still need. (Note: nobody has any ice cream or any cutlery.)

14B Where's the nearest bank?

You will need: one Map A *and one* Map B *for each pair of students*

- Check that students know how to ask for directions. For example: *Excuse me, where's the nearest bank?*
- Put students into pairs. Give a copy of *Map A* to one student and a copy of *Map B* to the other. **Students are not allowed to look at each other's maps.**
- Check that students know where they are on the map (at the station). Tell them that the places that are shaded (e.g. the bus station) are on *both* maps, so they can refer to them when giving directions.
- Students take it in turns to ask for directions to the places listed in the top right-hand corner of their map. (Students can refer to the *Real life and Writing* section on page 119 of the *Students' Book* for useful words and expressions.) When a student has been given directions

to the place he/she wants to go to, he/she writes the name of the place on his/her copy of the map.

- When both students have found all six places, they can compare their maps and see if they have marked the places correctly.

14C Building your dream

You will need: one set of cards for each pair of students; a set of Longman Active Study Dictionaries (optional)

PROCEDURE 1

- Put students into pairs. Place the sets of cards **face down in piles** at the front of the class, and allocate one set of cards to each pair. Shuffle the cards beforehand.
- One student from each pair comes up to the front of the class and takes **one card only** from the top of their pile. They go back to their partner, read the question and write the answers **on their card**, referring to the *Building your dream* text on page 121 of the *Students' Book* (or a *Longman Active Study Dictionary*) to find the answers.
- When a pair has completed a card, they take it to the teacher at the front of the class to check the answers (see **Key**). If the answers are correct, the student keeps the card and takes the next card from his/her pile at the front of the class. If the answer is not correct, the student has to return to his/her partner and find the correct answer.
- The first pair of students to finish all the cards correctly are the winners.

PROCEDURE 2

If it is not possible for your students to move around the class freely, follow the following procedure:

- Put students into pairs and give each pair a set of cards **face down in a pile**. Students turn over the cards one by one and write the answers on the cards.
- When a pair has finished, they hand their pile of cards to the teacher for checking (see **Key**). The teacher gives back the cards that are not correct and the students correct their mistakes.
- The first pair of students to finish all the cards correctly are the winners.

15A Lottery winners

You will need: one copy of the newspaper article per student; one set of role cards for each pair of students

- Give each student a copy of the newspaper article to read, and check they have understood the main points.
- Divide the class into pairs. Give half the pairs *Lottery winner* role cards and the other half *Reporter* role cards. You need an **even number of pairs** for this activity. If there are extra students, have extra reporters.
- Students prepare questions and answers in their pairs/groups, following the instructions on the card. Make sure that **all** the reporters write down the questions. Allow about ten minutes for this.
- Rearrange the class so that each reporter can interview one lottery winner individually. The reporters need to

make brief notes during the interview, in order to report back later.

- At the end of the interviews, rearrange the class so that each reporter is sitting with another reporter who was not his/her original partner. Similarly, place each lottery winner with another lottery winner who was not his/her original partner.
- The reporters and lottery winners tell their new partners what was said in their interviews, using reported speech.
- Finally, reporters can work with the lottery winners they interviewed and write the newspaper article together.

15B Get Rich Quick!

You will need: one copy of the board and one set of Money cards *per four students; one dice, four counters per group*

- Put students into groups of four. Give each group a copy of the *Get Rich Quick!* board, a set of *Money cards* (shuffled), dice and counters. Tell students to put the *Money* cards **face down** in a pile in the middle of the board, and their counters on the *Start* square. Check that students understand what happens when they land on the non-money squares on the board, and that every time they pass *Start* they automatically receive £10,000.
- If you can make some fake money (in £5,000, £10,000 and £20,000 notes!), distribute it amongst the students and make one member of each group the 'banker'. If not, students can write down their running total as they play the game.
- Students take it in turns to throw a number. If Student A lands on a square with some money on it, **another student** takes a *Money card* from the top of the pile and asks Student A the question on the card. If the student gets the answer right, he/she receives the amount of money on the square and adds it to his/her total. If Student A gets the answer wrong, the other student tells him/her the correct answer, and Student A receives no money. All the questions are based on the vocabulary in Module 15 of the *Students' Book*.
- The game continues until all the *Money cards* are finished. When the last *Money card* has been answered, all the students count up how much money they have. The student who has the most money wins the game.
- Groups that finish early can go through the *Money cards* and test each other.

Learner-training worksheet K
(Using the *Mini-dictionary* to find dependent prepositions)

You will need: one copy of the worksheet per student

The aim of this worksheet is to show students how to use the *Mini-dictionary* to find dependent prepositions that follow certain verbs and adjectives.

1 Go through the dictionary entries with the whole class.
2 Students work individually. They are not allowed to use their *Mini-dictionary* at this stage. Encourage them to guess if they don't know the answers (see **Key**).

3 Students work in pairs and check their answers using the *Mini-dictionary*.
4 Students work individually and check their answers in the *Mini-dictionary* if necessary.
5 Students work in pairs and test each other. Encourage them to repeat the whole phrase (as in the example) as this will help them remember the whole expression.

16A Conditional squares

You will need: one copy of the worksheet per student

- Give each student a copy of the worksheet. Students work individually and answer the questions. Make sure they write their answers in **random order**, and encourage them to answer as many questions as possible. They should write single words or short phrases, **not** complete sentences. Set a time limit of five or ten minutes.
- Students work in pairs and swap worksheets with their partner. Students then have to try and guess why their partner has written the words/phrases in the squares. For example: Student A writes *big house*. Student B asks *Would you buy a big house if you won a lot of money?* Student B writes *seaside*. Student A asks *Will you go to the seaside if the weather's good this weekend?* Students must ask at least one follow-up question on each topic. For example: *What other things would you buy? / Where do you usually go at the weekend?*
- At the end of the activity, students report back to the class on the most interesting things they found out about their partner.

16B Preposition pelmanism

You will need: one complete set of cards per three students

- Put students into groups of three and give each group a set of cards. **Shuffle the cards before the class**. Tell the students to spread the cards out in front of them **face down**, with the bigger cards on one side and the smaller cards on the other.
- Students take it in turns to turn over one big card and one small card. If the preposition is the correct one to fill the gap in the sentence, they keep the cards as a 'trick' and have another turn. If the cards do not match, they must put them back **in exactly the same place**. If students cannot agree, the teacher adjudicates.
- The activity continues until all the cards are matched up. The student with the most tricks is the winner.
- If one group finishes early, they can test each other on the prepositions.

1A Get to know the *Students' Book*

A

Which two pages contain a summary of everything in the *Students' Book?*

Pages . . . . and . . . .

B

Where can you find a **pronunciation table**?

. . . .

C

What colour are the **Grammar analysis** boxes in Module 2?

. . . .

D

What topic do you study in the **Real life** section in Module 12?

. . . .

E

On which page is the **Language summary** for Module 10?

Page . . . .

F

What do you write in the empty box on page 94?

. . . .

G

On which page is the **Do you remember?** section of Module 8?

Page . . . .

H

Where are the **tapescripts** for Module 15?

Pages . . . . and . . . .

I

Which word is studied in the **Wordspot** in Module 4?

. . . .

J

How many **Pronunciation boxes** are there in Module 5?

. . . .

K

What colour is the **Useful language** box in Module 6?

. . . .

L

On which page is there a list of **irregular verbs**?

Page . . . .

© Pearson Education Limited 2001   PHOTOCOPIABLE

Learner-training worksheet A

Using the *Mini-dictionary:* introduction

MEANING

1 **a)** Look up the following words in your *Mini-dictionary* and read the definitions and examples.

- to gamble
- a witness
- to interrupt

b) Do you understand from the *Mini-dictionary* what these words mean? What helped you most – the definition, the example, or both?

2 The words underlined in the following sentences have more than one meaning. Look them up in the *Mini-dictionary* and write down the number of the dictionary definition that is used in each sentence.

a My mother keeps old Christmas cards in a box under the bed. ....
b They run a restaurant in the centre of town. ....
c I dream of living on a beautiful tropical island. ....

GRAMMAR

3 Match the words in bold in this paragraph with the correct grammatical description below.

Mark **woke up** and looked at the alarm clock next to his **bed**. It was 11 o'clock, and he was **late** for **work**. He jumped out of bed, **quickly** got dressed, then **opened** the front door and got into his car. Then he realised it was Sunday!

a an adjective ....
b an adverb ....
c a countable noun ....
d an uncountable noun ....
e a transitive verb ....
f an intransitive verb ....

4 Look in your *Mini-dictionary* and find out what part of speech these words are.

a pullover ....
b spacious ....
c protect ....
d hesitate ....
e fame ....
f immediately ....

PRONUNCIATION

Word stress is marked like this in the *Mini-dictionary*:

Stress mark

musical /ˈmjuːzɪkl/ *adj.*

5 Look up the following words in the *Mini-dictionary* and mark the stress.

- economics
- newsagent's
- independent

6 How do you pronounce these words? (There is a pronunciation table on the inside front cover of the *Mini-dictionary* to help you.)

- chaos
- receipt
- pigeon

 © Pearson Education Limited 2001

1B Me too!

Present Simple and question words

YOUR ANSWERS	NAME
1 I usually get up at .... on Sundays.	
2 I go to the cinema once / twice / .... times a week / month.	
3 My favourite food is	
4 My journey home from school takes .... minutes.	
5 At the weekend I usually	
6 I want to learn English because	
7 I've got .... cousins.	
8 I like action films / thrillers / comedies / romantic films / horror films / science-fiction films.	
9 My favourite actor is	
10 I usually go to bed at .... during the week.	
11 I like winter / spring / summer / autumn the most.	
12 I go shopping for new clothes once / twice / .... times a week / month / year.	

1C Connected lives

Present Simple questions with *How often ...?* and adverbs of frequency

Student A worksheet

Lola is a nightclub singer, and sings at the *Flamingo Club* (1) ....
She usually finishes work at 3 a.m., and always takes a taxi home. She plays tennis with her best friend (2) .... times a week, but loses every time! She goes to the seaside once a year, and stays in a hotel called *The Sea View*.

Molly is a student, and goes to university (3) .... days a week. On Wednesday evenings she always goes to her dance class. She meets her new boyfriend for lunch (4) ...., and plays tennis with her best friend three times a week (Molly always wins!).

Tim and Karen own *The Sun Cafe* in the centre of town. They get up early (5) .... and always open the cafe at 7 o'clock. They go on holiday (6) .... times a year, and usually stay in *The Sea View Hotel*.

Paul works for a computer company, and meets his new girlfriend for lunch in *The Sun Cafe* (7) .... When he's at work he e-mails her twelve times a day! They go out together (8) ...., and usually go to the *Flamingo Club*.

Bill is a taxi driver, and he usually works (9) .... On Sundays he always gets up at about lunchtime. In the afternoon he usually (10) .... His sister is a dance teacher, and he sees her about once a week.

© Pearson Education Limited 2001

Student B worksheet

Lola is a nightclub singer, and sings at the *Flamingo Club* three nights a week. She usually finishes work at (a) ...., and always takes a taxi home. She plays tennis with her best friend three times a week, but loses every time! She goes to the seaside (b) .... a year, and stays in a hotel called *The Sea View*.

Molly is a student, and goes to university four days a week. On Wednesday evenings she always (c) .... She meets her new boyfriend for lunch every day, and plays tennis with her best friend (d) .... times a week (Molly always wins!)

Tim and Karen own *The Sun Cafe* in the centre of town. They get up early every morning (except Sundays) and always open the cafe at (e) .... o'clock. They go on holiday three times a year, and usually stay in (f) ....

Paul works for a computer company, and meets his new girlfriend for lunch in *The Sun Cafe* every day. When he's at work he e-mails her (g) .... times a day! They go out together every night except Wednesday, and usually go to (h) ....

Bill is a taxi driver, and he usually works at night. On Sundays he always gets up at (i) .... In the afternoon he usually watches football on TV. His sister is a dance teacher, and he sees her (j) ....

Learner-training worksheet B

Using the *Mini-dictionary*: irregular verbs – part 1

1 Look at the following sentence and answer the questions below. When you have finished, check your answers in the *Mini-dictionary*.

Sally didn't want to go to school yesterday, so she <u>hid</u> under the bed.

a What tense is the verb <u>underlined</u>? ....
b Is this a regular or irregular verb? ....
c What's the infinitive? ....
d Do you know the meaning of this verb? If not, can you guess?

2 Notice how irregular verbs are written in the *Mini-dictionary*.

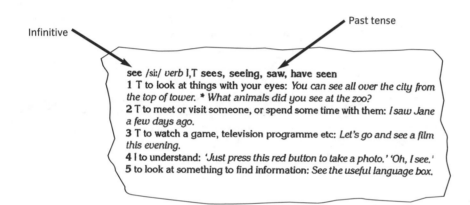

Infinitive

Past tense

see /siː/ *verb* I,T sees, seeing, saw, have seen
1 T to look at things with your eyes: *You can see all over the city from the top of tower.* * *What animals did you see at the zoo?*
2 T to meet or visit someone, or spend some time with them: *I saw Jane a few days ago.*
3 T to watch a game, television programme etc: *Let's go and see a film this evening.*
4 I to understand: *'Just press this red button to take a photo.' 'Oh, I see.'*
5 to look at something to find information: *See the useful language box.*

3 What's the infinitive of these irregular past tenses? Use your *Mini-dictionary* to find the answers or check your spelling.

INFINITIVE	PAST TENSE	INFINITIVE	PAST TENSE
	brought		taught
	fell		wore
	left		drove
	caught		bought
	rang		broke

4 Fill in the gaps with one of the irregular past tenses from the table above.

a Last summer we .... around Europe in a BMW.
b My grandfather .... English when he was younger.
c Lots of people .... presents to his birthday party.
d Last night Jane .... her favourite dress to the wedding.
e I .... a new computer yesterday.
f I .... my leg when I .... off the roof of my house.
g The phone .... ten times last night.
h We .... the restaurant at 10.30 and .... the last bus home.

© Pearson Education Limited 2001

2A Dead famous

Past Simple *yes/no* questions and short answers

Name: John Lennon
Born: 1940, Liverpool, England.
Died: December 1980, aged 40.
He was shot outside his New
York home by Mark Chapman.
Famous for: Member of the
Beatles, and then a solo singer/
songwriter. One of his songs
(*Imagine*) was voted 'best song
of the 20th Century'.
Lived in: Liverpool and New
York.
Family life: Married twice. His second wife was the
musician and artist Yoko Ono.

Clue: His first guitar cost him £17.

Name: Elvis Presley
Born: 1935, Mississippi, USA.
Died: 1977. He was found dead
on the toilet in his Gracelands
home. He died of a heart
attack.
Famous for: 'The King of Rock
and Roll'. He sold millions of
records around the world, and
also starred in many
Hollywood films.
Lived in: Memphis, Tennessee,
USA.
Family life: Married Priscilla (who starred in the TV
series *Dallas*), but they separated in the 1970s.

Clue: He spent two years in the army.

Name: William Shakespeare
Born: 1564, Stratford-upon-
Avon, England.
Died: 1616. He was 52.
Famous for: He wrote 37 plays,
including *Romeo and Juliet*,
Hamlet and *Macbeth*. Thought to
be the best English writer in
history. He became very rich,
and lived in a big house in the
centre of London.
Lived in: Stratford and London.
Family life: He married Anne Hathaway when he
was 18.

Clue: He used to be an actor.

Name: Princess Diana
Born: 1961, Norfolk, England.
Died: 1997, in a car accident
in Paris. She was 36. Her
boyfriend, Dodi Fayed, also
died in the crash.
Famous for: Princess of
Wales, wife of Prince Charles.
She also did a lot of charity
work.
Lived in: London.
Family life: Married Prince Charles in 1981. They
had two children, William and Harry. They
separated in 1992.

Clue: She used to be a kindergarten teacher.

Name: Marie Curie
Born: 1867, Warsaw, Poland.
Died: 1934, aged 67, of
leukaemia caused by exposure
to radium.
Famous for: Discovered
radioactivity and radium.
Despite her discoveries she was
poor all her life.
Lived in: Paris.
Family life: Married Pierre
Curie, who was also a famous scientist, in 1895.

Clue: She was the first woman to win the Nobel Prize
twice.

Name: Albert Einstein
Born: 1879, Ulm, Germany.
Died: 1955, aged 76. He died
in his sleep.
Famous for: A brilliant
scientist and mathematician.
Discovered the Theory of
Relativity, which changed
how we see the world.
Lived in: Zurich, Berlin, and
the USA.
Family life: He was married twice. The second time
he married his cousin, Elsa.

Clue: Mathematics was the only school subject he
was good at.

PHOTOCOPIABLE

Name: Mahatma Gandhi
Born: 1869, Porbandar, India.
Died: 1948 in New Delhi. A Hindu who didn't agree with Gandhi's political view assassinated him. He was 79.
Famous for: Non-violent leader of Indian Independence from British rule.
Lived in: India, England (he did a Law degree in London) and South Africa.
Family life: He married when he was 13 and had four children.

Clue: He never wore any shoes.

Name: Christopher Columbus
Born: 1451, Genoa, Italy.
Died: 1506, in Spain. He was 55.
Famous for: He was a sailor and explorer. He went on four long journeys by boat and was the first European to discover South America. He also went to Cuba and the Caribbean.
Lived in: Italy, Portugal and Spain.
Family life: He was married and had one son, named Diego.

Clue: A country is named after him.

Name: Mother Teresa
Born: 1910, Albania.
Died: 1997, of a heart attack. She was 87.
Famous for: In 1950 she started a hostel for the sick and dying in Calcutta, India. She spent her life there and established The Missionaries of Charity, which looks after poor people in over 50 countries.
Lived in: Calcutta, India.
Family life: She became a nun in 1931. She was never married.

Clue: She won the Nobel Peace Prize in 1979.

Name: Marilyn Monroe
Born: 1926, Los Angeles, USA.
Died: 1962, aged 36, from an overdose of drugs. Maybe she killed herself or someone else killed her.
Famous for: Movie star. She made 29 films in 16 years.
Lived in: New York and Hollywood, USA.
Family life: She was married four times. Her second (and fourth!) husband was Joe DiMaggio, a famous baseball player.

Clue: Her real name was Norma Jean.

Name: Wolfgang Amadeus Mozart
Born: 1756, Salzburg, Austria.
Died: 1791, aged 35 of typhoid fever.
Famous for: Composer and musician. He started composing music when he was five, and composed over 600 works during his short life.
Lived in: Vienna, Italy.
Family life: He was married, but had no children. Despite his talent, he never made any money and died a poor man.

Clue: There is a film about his life.

Name: Cleopatra
Born: 69 BC, Egypt.
Died: 30 BC, when she was 39. She killed herself by allowing a poisonous snake to bite her.
Famous for: Queen of Egypt, and for being extremely beautiful and intelligent.
Lived in: Egypt and Syria.
Family life: She married her ten-year-old brother when she became Queen of Egypt. Later she was the lover of Julius Caesar, and then Mark Antony.

Clue: She liked cats.

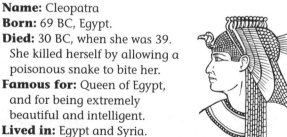

2B   The Millionaire's Ball

Past Simple and time phrases

WHO'S WHO AT THE MILLIONAIRE'S BALL?

1 _____ married someone very rich .... New Year's Day this year.

2 _____ was a very successful film director .... the 1970s.

3 _____ spent $200,000 on a ring .... yesterday afternoon.

4 _____ sold his company for a billion dollars three weeks ....

5 _____ became a millionaire at midnight .... last night.

6 _____ bought an island in the Caribbean three months ....

7 _____ won fifty million pounds .... Saturday night.

8 _____ bought the biggest house in the world .... March last year.

9 _____ invited 10,000 guests to his/her birthday party .... January 9th.

10 _____ sold 10 million copies of his/her first CD .... 1996.

© Pearson Education Limited 2001

Role card 1

You live in New York with your new husband/wife, who is a *very* famous pop star (you decide who he/she is!). You met him/her in a restaurant last year, where you worked as a waiter/waitress. The wedding took place in Hawaii on New Year's Day this year, and you went to Paris on your honeymoon.

Role card 2

You are now retired and live in a big house in Hollywood. In the 1970s you were a famous film director, and your most successful film, *Bus Driver*, made over $100 million and won seven Oscars. Now you live with your wife (who was an actress in *Bus Driver*) and your three children.

Role card 3

You are a famous actor/actress, and have three houses (you decide where). Last week you started making your new film and fell in love with another actor/actress. Yesterday afternoon you bought a *very* expensive ring (it cost $200,000!) and tomorrow night you're going to ask him/her to marry you.

Role card 4

You are a very successful businessman/woman and live in New York. You aren't married. Ten years ago you started a computer company called *Grey Box*, and now it's one of the biggest companies in the world. Three weeks ago you sold your company to Microsoft for $1 billion.

Role card 5

You live in a small flat and work at *McDonald's*. Your grandfather owned an oil company and was very rich. He died when you were a child, and left you a million pounds in his will – but he also said you couldn't have the money until you were 21. Today is your 21st birthday, so now you're a millionaire!

Role card 6

You are a famous tennis player, and last year you won three big tennis tournaments. You make a lot of money, of course, and three months ago you bought an island in the Caribbean! Now you live on the island with your family, and spend the days swimming and sunbathing on the beach.

Role card 7

You are very rich and live in a big house in the south of France, but you've never worked in your life! You make all your money playing poker. Last Saturday you won fifty million pounds in one game! Tomorrow you're going on holiday with your girl/boyfriend – to Las Vegas!

Role card 8

You own a big car company and have *a lot* of money. In March last year you bought the biggest house in the world, where you now live with your wife/husband and six children. It has 420 bedrooms (each with its own bathroom), 80 living rooms, 65 kitchens and 17 swimming pools!

Role card 9

You are a successful lawyer and live in California with your husband/wife. It was your 30th birthday on January 9th. You invited 10,000 guests to your party, which cost over $1 million. The guests drank 5,000 bottles of champagne and ate 100 kilos of caviar!

Role card 10

You are a famous singer and you live in South America. Your first CD, called *I Want Lots of Money*, sold 10 million copies in 1996. Your second album, *I Love Being Rich*, sold nearly 15 million copies two years later. Now you live by the beach, and have fifteen cars and three boats.

 © Pearson Education Limited 2001 **127**

2C Invent-a-story

Past Simple and linkers

Invent a story which includes at least **FOUR** of the following:

A GUN $10,000 IN CASH **A WOMAN CALLED KATE**

A LARGE BROWN PARCEL **THE POLICE** **PLANE TICKETS**

A DIAMOND **A FALSE PASSPORT** **A MAN CALLED DYLAN**

Discuss the questions in groups and write your ideas in the box. Then write the complete story in groups, using *and, so, because, but* and *then*.

	WRITE YOUR IDEAS HERE
1 Why was Mark late home from work? How did he feel? Why?	
2 How did his wife Laura feel? Why? What did she do?	
3 What two things did Mark do when he got home?	
4 Mark went into the bedroom and telephoned someone. Who was it? What did they say?	
5 How did Mark feel after the phone call? What did he decide to do? Why?	
6 What did he have in his briefcase? What did he do with it/them?	
7 Laura walked into the bedroom. Why was she angry?	
8 What did Mark say to her? Did she believe him? Why (not)?	
9 Somebody knocked at the front door. Who was it? What did he/she do or say?	
10 Mark left with the person at the door. Where did they go? Why?	
11 How did Laura feel after Mark left? Who did she telephone? Why?	
12 What happened at the end of the story?	

PHOTOCOPIABLE

3A The secret of successful language learning
Vocabulary extension (word building)

1 The following words all come from the magazine article *What's the secret of successful language learning?* on page 25 of the *Students' Book*. Find the words in the text and <u>underline</u> them.

a important (para. 1)   c imagine (para. 1)   e successful (para. 6)

b believe (para. 1)   d enjoyable (para. 6)

2 Are the words above verbs, nouns or adjectives? Write them in the correct column of the table. (Make sure you keep the words **in the same order** as above).

	VERB	NOUN	ADJECTIVE
a			
b			believable
c			
d			
e			

3 Complete the rest of the table with the verb/noun/adjective forms of the words as appropriate. Use an English–English dictionary to help you. Mark the stress on each word, as in the example.

4 Complete the gaps in the following questions with a word from the table. (Note that the questions do not follow the same order as the words in the table.)

a If you want to s............................ in business, what do you have to do?
b Can you think of something i............................ you have to do tomorrow?
c Do you b............................ that UFOs exist? Why (not)?
d Can you name someone who has a very good i............................?
e What was the most e............................ thing you did last year?
f Can you think of a film or book that is very i............................ .
g Do you think it is important to marry someone with the same religious b............................ ?
h I............................ that you are 100 years old. What do you think the world will be like?
i What kind of things do you e............................ doing in your spare time?
j Can you name a businessman or businesswoman who is very s............................ in your country?

5 Ask another student the questions above, and discuss the answers together.

3B Parents and children

can, can't, have to, don't have to, should, shouldn't

Read these statements about parents and children. Decide whether you agree or disagree with the statement and circle a number in the **first** column. Then guess your partner's opinion about the same statement and circle a number in the **second** column.

1 = agree strongly   2 = agree   3 = not sure   4 = don't agree   5 = disagree strongly

		You	Partner's name: _____
1	Children under 10 shouldn't watch more than 1 hour of TV a day.	1 2 3 4 5	1 2 3 4 5
2	Girls over the age of 12 can wear make-up if they want to.	1 2 3 4 5	1 2 3 4 5
3	Children can get up when they want to at the weekends.	1 2 3 4 5	1 2 3 4 5
4	Teenage boys can stay out later than girls of the same age.	1 2 3 4 5	1 2 3 4 5
5	Parents shouldn't tell their children what clothes to wear.	1 2 3 4 5	1 2 3 4 5
6	Teenagers can dye their hair without their parents' permission.	1 2 3 4 5	1 2 3 4 5
7	Girls should do more housework than boys.	1 2 3 4 5	1 2 3 4 5
8	Girls shouldn't go out on their own in the evening before they are 18.	1 2 3 4 5	1 2 3 4 5
9	Children over 10 years old can decide what time they go to bed.	1 2 3 4 5	1 2 3 4 5
10	Children over 16 years old don't have to tell their parents where they're going at night.	1 2 3 4 5	1 2 3 4 5

4A Party guests

Present Continuous and Present Simple

Role Card 1

You live in Amsterdam.
You go to Paris every weekend.
You're studying French in the evenings.
You're enjoying the party a lot.

Role Card 2

You live in Amsterdam.
You're staying in a hotel around the corner.
You're doing a course in photography.
You like going to the gym.

Role Card 3

You work for a television company.
You spend a lot of time surfing the Internet.
You're writing a book in your spare time.
You're enjoying the party a lot.

Role Card 4

You work for a television company.
You're learning how to play the guitar.
You're doing a course in photography.
You're waiting for your wife/husband to arrive.

Role Card 5

You write for a national newspaper.
You're studying French in the evenings.
You go to Paris every weekend.
You're waiting for a taxi – you want to go home.

Role Card 6

You write for a national newspaper.
You're working in London at the moment.
You're writing a book in your spare time.
You like going to the gym.

Role Card 7

You have a big house in the country.
You're staying in a hotel around the corner.
You spend a lot of time surfing the Internet.
You're waiting for a taxi – you want to go home.

Role Card 8

You have a big house in the country.
You're working in London at the moment.
You're learning how to play the guitar.
You're waiting for your wife/husband to arrive.

Role Card 9

You live in Amsterdam.
You're working in London at the moment.
You spend a lot of time surfing the Internet.
You're learning how to play the guitar.

Role Card 10

You work for a television company.
You're studying French in the evenings.
You like going to the gym.
You're waiting for a taxi – you want to go home.

Role Card 11

You write for a national newspaper.
You're staying in a hotel around the corner.
You're enjoying the party a lot.
You're waiting for your wife/husband to arrive.

Role Card 12

You have a big house in the country.
You go to Paris every weekend.
You're doing a course in photography.
You're writing a book in your spare time.

Student A worksheet

You have to find these six people at the party. When you find them, write down their names. Make sure that the person **completely** matches the description.

Person A ....
... has a big house in the country.
... is staying in a hotel around the corner.
... spends a lot of time surfing the Internet.
... is waiting for a taxi – he/she wants to go home.

Person B ....
... works for a television company.
... spends a lot of time surfing the Internet.
... is writing a book in his/her spare time.
... is enjoying the party a lot.

Person C ....
... lives in Amsterdam.
... goes to Paris every weekend.
... is studying French in the evenings.
... is enjoying the party a lot.

Person D ....
... writes for a national newspaper.
... is studying French in the evenings.
... goes to Paris every weekend.
... is waiting for a taxi – he/she wants to go home.

Person E ....
... writes for a national newspaper.
... is staying in a hotel around the corner.
... is enjoying the party a lot.
... is waiting for his wife/her husband to arrive.

Person F ....
... lives in Amsterdam.
... is working in London at the moment.
... spends a lot of time surfing the Internet.
... is learning how to play the guitar.

Student B worksheet

You have to find these six people at the party. When you find them, write down their names. Make sure that the person **completely** matches the description.

Person G ....
... works for a television company.
... is learning how to play the guitar.
... is doing a course in photography.
... is waiting for his wife/her husband to arrive.

Person H ....
... lives in Amsterdam.
... is staying in a hotel around the corner.
... is doing a course in photography.
... likes going to the gym.

Person I ....
... writes for a national newspaper.
... is working in London at the moment.
... is writing a book in his/her spare time.
... likes going to the gym.

Person J ....
... has a big house in the country.
... is working in London at the moment.
... is learning how to play the guitar.
... is waiting for his wife/her husband to arrive.

Person K ....
... has a big house in the country.
... goes to Paris every weekend.
... is doing a course in photography.
... is writing a book in his/her spare time.

Person L ....
... works for a television company.
... is studying French in the evenings.
... likes going to the gym.
... is waiting for a taxi – he/she wants to go home.

4B I'm having lunch with Madonna

Present Continuous (for future arrangements)

DIARY A	
Monday 19th	Thursday 22nd
3 p.m. coffee – David Bowie (his house)	
Tuesday 20th	Friday 23rd
lunch – Madonna – 1 p.m. Hilton Hotel	dance class – 2–5 p.m.
Wednesday 21st	Saturday 24th
	shopping with Elton John (a.m.)
party – Spice Girls' house! 9 p.m. to ???	

DIARY B	
Monday 19th	Thursday 22nd
party – Leonardo DiCaprio's house 8 p.m.	8 p.m. Cinema – premiere of Leonardo's new film
Tuesday 20th	Friday 23rd
	1 p.m. – lunch with Steven Spielberg
Wednesday 21st	Saturday 24th
9 a.m. – breakfast – Sheraton Hotel – Jodie Foster	
	8.25 p.m. – fly to Hollywood

DIARY C	
Monday 19th	Thursday 22nd
8.30 a.m. – arrive back from Bali	10–12 – meet accountant
Tuesday 20th	Friday 23rd
9 a.m. – collect new Rolls Royce	7 p.m. dinner – US Embassy (with the President)
Wednesday 21st	Saturday 24th
	fly to Monte Carlo (7.40 a.m.)

DIARY D	
Monday 19th	Thursday 22nd
	1 p.m. – lunch with Frank Einstein (Albert's son)
Tuesday 20th	Friday 23rd
	9–12 – Philosophy class
Chinese class (evening)	
Wednesday 21st	Saturday 24th
2–5 p.m. – take exam (Nuclear Physics)	1–3 p.m. – visit National Science Museum

© Pearson Education Limited 2001

DIARY E	
Monday 19th	Thursday 22nd
American Open tennis final (New York) arrive back 10.20 p.m.	9–12 – play tennis with Andre Agassi (his house)
Tuesday 20th	Friday 23rd
lunch – Maradona (Charlie's Restaurant)	
Wednesday 21st	Saturday 24th
8 a.m. till ??? - run marathon	3 p.m. football – England v Germany

DIARY F	
Monday 19th	Thursday 22nd
10 a.m. - buy new clothes for Rome trip	meet Russian President – 1 p.m.
Tuesday 20th	Friday 23rd
fly to Rome – 6.30 a.m. in Rome all day – interview Pope 3–4 p.m. arrive back 11 p.m.	
Wednesday 21st	Saturday 24th
dinner party – my house – 8 p.m.	a.m. – do TV interview with Tony Blair

DIARY G	
Monday 19th	Thursday 22nd
afternoon - go shopping - Harrods!	theatre – 7.30 p.m. (with Prince Charles)
Tuesday 20th	Friday 23rd
Breakfast at the Ritz with Tony (Blair)	opera – 8 p.m. (with Charles again)
Wednesday 21st	Saturday 24th
Queen of England coming round for tea	

DIARY H	
Monday 19th	Thursday 22nd
engagement party – 9 p.m. – parents' house	
Tuesday 20th	Friday 23rd
restaurant – Alex and parents – 7.30 p.m.	a.m. – buy wedding dress/suit
Wednesday 21st	Saturday 24th
afternoon – shopping (for honeymoon)	get married today!! party at The Palace Hotel – 8 p.m.

Learner-training worksheet C

Noticing and recording collocations

1 If you want to improve your vocabulary, learning single words is not enough. You often need to learn words that 'go together'. These are called **collocations**.

The *Mini-dictionary* includes many common collocations for you to learn. They are usually written in **bold**.

> **holiday** /ˈhɒlɪdi, -deɪ/ *noun* C **1** time you spend in a different place, in order to rest and enjoy yourself: *a beach/camping holiday* • *Where would you like to* **go on holiday**? • *We didn't* **have a holiday** *this year.* **2** a day when people do not go to work or school, and businesses, shops, and banks are closed because of a national celebration: *May 1st is a* **national holiday** *in many countries.*

2 There are many different types of collocations. Look at the collocations <u>underlined</u> in these sentences and match them with the grammatical descriptions.

1   I always <u>listen to</u> the radio when I'm getting up in the morning.
2   Anne <u>works hard</u> all week, so she usually sleeps a lot at the weekends.
3   Why don't we <u>have a party</u> this weekend?
4   This is <u>a true story</u> about life in the 1960s.

a   verb + noun
b   verb + preposition
c   adjective + noun
d   verb + adverb

3 One common type of collocation is *verb + noun* (e.g. to play football, to watch TV). Which words are missing in these collocations? Use your *Mini-dictionary* to help you.

a   to surf the _ _ _ _ _ _ _ _
b   to _ _ _ _ _ a mistake
c   to rob a _ _ _ _
d   to _ _ your homework

e   to guess the _ _ _ _ _ _
f   to _ _ _ _ _ your e-mail
g   to _ _ _ _ _ for a meal
h   to _ _ _ _ _ a video

RECORDING COLLOCATIONS

4 It is important to write down collocations when you see them. Look at the following examples from students' notebooks, then discuss the questions below with another student.

A
to ride a bicycle
to drive a car
to ride a motorbike
to take a taxi

B
to do
to take
to pass
to fail
} an exam

C
to have a party **not** ~~to make a party~~
to make a mistake **not** ~~to do a mistake~~

D
to stay up all night e.g. Last New Year's Eve we stayed up all night!

- Which do you think is the most useful way to record collocations? Which methods do you use already?
- Find some examples of collocations you have written in your notebook on this course.
  How did you write them down?

© Pearson Education Limited 2001

5A Put these in order

Comparatives and superlatives

Example: Put these animals in order, starting with the **biggest**.
☐ a cow ☐1 an elephant ☐ a mouse ☐ a dog

A Put these countries in order, starting with the **smallest**.
☐ Peru ☐ Japan ☐ France ☐ Spain

F Put these planets in order, starting with the one **furthest** from the sun.
☐ Earth ☐ Mars ☐ Pluto ☐ Mercury

B Put these oceans in order, starting with the **largest**.
☐ The Atlantic Ocean
☐ The Pacific Ocean
☐ The Indian Ocean
☐ The Arctic Ocean

G Put these world events in order, starting with the **most recent**.
☐ the first man on the moon
☐ the assassination of John F Kennedy
☐ the fall of the Berlin Wall
☐ Nelson Mandela's release from prison

C Put these countries in order, starting with the one that has **the highest population**.
☐ Poland ☐ Spain
☐ India ☐ Brazil

Put these in order!

H Put these film stars in order, starting with the **youngest**.
☐ Julia Roberts
☐ Robert de Niro
☐ Brad Pitt
☐ Sharon Stone

D Put these famous buildings in order, starting with the **oldest**.
☐ The Colosseum
☐ The Eiffel Tower
☐ The Taj Mahal
☐ The Sydney Opera House

I Put these rivers in order, starting with the **longest**.
☐ The Mississippi ☐ The Amazon
☐ The Rhine ☐ The Nile

E Put these cities in order, starting with the one **nearest** to the North Pole.
☐ London ☐ New York ☐ Moscow
☐ Tokyo

J Put these films in order, starting with the one that made **the most money**.
☐ E.T. ☐ Titanic ☐ Jurassic Park
☐ Star Wars

5B An alien family

Vocabulary: describing people's appearance

Picture A

Picture B

NEEK LEMMY FREEMA SEELA ANNE BINT DRONGO

© Pearson Education Limited 2001 PHOTOCOPIABLE

Learner-training worksheet D

Recording new vocabulary

1 Students often write new vocabulary in lists, with a translation into their own language. Look at these two lists of words from Modules 1 and 2 of the *Students' Book*. What **extra** information about the English words is included in List B?

LIST A

sunbathe	=	tomar sol
racket	=	raqueta
experienced	=	experto (en)
explain	=	explicar
nervous	=	nervioso
check	=	verificar
rubbish	=	basura
write down	=	anotar

LIST B

to sunbathe (reg) (*not 'to take sun'!)	=	tomar sol
a (tennis/squash) racket (also spelt 'racquet')	=	raqueta
experienced (adj) (e.g. an experienced teacher)	=	experto (en)
to explain something to somebody	=	explicar
nervous (adj) /n‰...v´s/ to be / feel nervous about something (e.g. an exam)	=	nervioso
to check something (e.g. the meaning of a word)	=	verificar
rubbish (noun U)	=	basura
to write something down (e.g. in a notebook) (write / wrote / written)	=	anotar

2 Look at this list of vocabulary a Polish student has made. Write the list again so that it is more useful. Include as many points as possible from Exercise 1. Use your *Mini-dictionary* to help you if necessary, and write the translations in your own language.

detective	=	detektyw
steal	=	ukraść
rob	=	okradać
journey	=	podróż
wedding	=	ślub
embarrassed	=	zakłopotany
dress up	=	przebierać sie
earn	=	zarabiać

3 Look in your vocabulary notebook (or your notes from this course) and see how you wrote down new vocabulary. What extra information can you add to help you use the vocabulary correctly?

 © Pearson Education Limited 2001 **139**

6A Talk about the future

going to, would like to, would prefer to, will/won't

Which of these places would you prefer to go to? *India Australia The Caribbean* 6	**a country you'd like to visit** 7	**GO BACK ONE SPACE** 20	somewhere you'd like to go on holiday 21	**FINISH**
GO FORWARD TWO SPACES 5	how your town/city will change in the next ten years 8	**your plans for this evening** 19	five things that definitely won't happen to you this year 22	what you'll buy next time you go shopping 33
something you'd like to buy 4	a place where you'd like to live when you're old 9	**GO FORWARD THREE SPACES** 18	**someone famous you'd like to meet** 23	**MISS A TURN** 32
your plans for next month 3	**MISS A TURN** 10	what the world will be like in a hundred years' time 17	something a friend is going to do soon 24	*how you'll celebrate your next birthday* 31
THROW AGAIN! 2	**your plans for next week** 11	what you think your children (or grandchildren) will look like 16	**THROW AGAIN!** 25	something a member of your family is going to do soon 30
a job you'd really like to do 1	Which of these jobs would you prefer to do? *doctor teacher police officer* 12	**something you're planning to buy** 15	**a job you *wouldn't* like to do** 26	**GO BACK TWO SPACES** 29
START	a film or play you'd like to see again 13	**GO BACK THREE SPACES** 14	your plans for the weekend 27	Which of these places would you prefer to go to tonight? *restaurant club cinema* 28

6B Holiday crossword

Holiday vocabulary

Student A

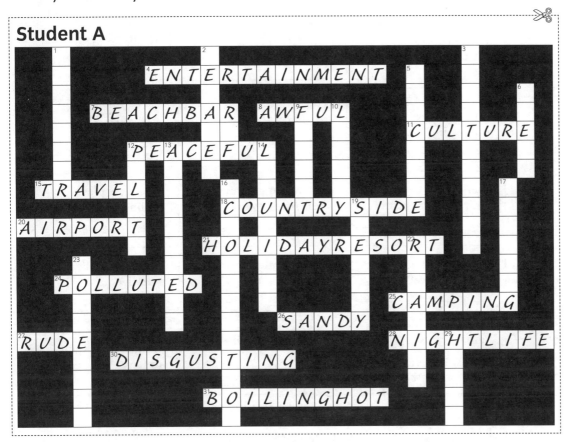

Student B

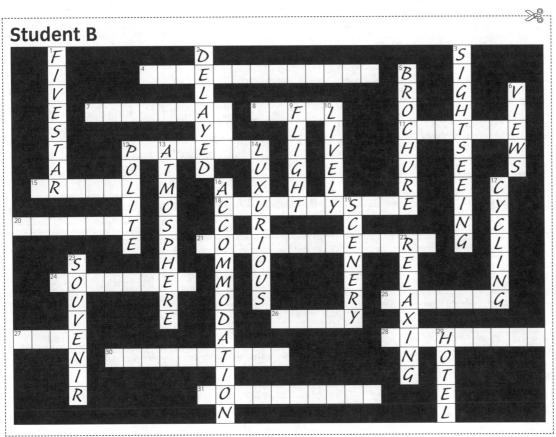

© Pearson Education Limited 2001

7A Ambition dominoes

Verb/noun collocations

… rock **band** when he was younger.	I'm going to start **learning how to** …	… **drive** next weekend.	People go to university to **get** …
… **a degree**.	It's hard to **get an interesting** …	… **job** without any experience.	Marilyn Monroe **became** …
… more **famous** after she died.	Tim's new girlfriend **speaks** …	… five **languages** really well.	My uncle **plays** violin **in** …
… the London Philharmonic **Orchestra**.	My best friend is going to **travel** …	… **around the world** next year.	Would you like to **go and live** …
… **in the country** when you're older?	Sidney wants to **go to** …	… **university** when he leaves school.	Nowadays many women don't want to **have** …
… **children** until they're in their thirties.	Would you like to **go and live** …	… **in an exciting city** like London or New York?	It was always Frank's dream to **appear** …
… **on TV** before he died.	It took Chris eight years to **write** …	… his first **novel**.	I'd like to **go** …
… **abroad** in the summer.	If you want to **become really good at** …	… **the guitar**, you need to practise every day.	You don't need much money to **start your own** …
… **business** on the Internet.	We don't want to **have** …	… **a large family**. We think two children is enough.	Michael Jackson **became** …
… **a millionaire** when he was a teenager.	David Beckham and Victoria Adams **got** …	… **married** in 1999.	Jack and Sally **bought** …
… **their own home** last year.	When they first fell in love they **wrote** …	… **poems** to each other all the time.	Al Pacino **appeared in** …
… all three *Godfather* **films**.	Mark **is really bad at** …	… **football**. He always misses the ball!	My Dad **played in a** …

PHOTOCOPIABLE

7B Life circles

Present Perfect and Past Simple

Write down **short** answers to the following points in the circles below. Write your answers in any circle you want, but **not** in the same order as the points. You do not have to answer every question, but try to answer at least **ten**.

- the name of someone you've known for over ten years (but not a family member)
- a film you've seen recently (either in the cinema or on TV/video)
- a place you went to on holiday when you were a child
- a personal possession you've had for more than five years
- the name of your best friend when you were at primary school
- a city or country you've been to that you didn't like
- something you got for Christmas last year
- a place you've been to that's very beautiful
- a job you've had in your life that you didn't like
- a film you saw last year that you really enjoyed
- something you've wanted to buy for a long time
- the name of someone you've talked to on the phone this week

FOLD

7C Happy verb families

Irregular past tenses and past participles

I'm going to **wear** my favourite dress tonight.	Michael **wore** the same pair of socks all last week!	I've only **worn** these trousers twice, and there's already a hole in them.
I'm planning to **make** a cake for your birthday.	All the students **made** a lot of mistakes in their homework.	My brother has **made** a lot of money this year.
My parents want to **grow** vegetables in their garden.	Rebecca **grew** over five centimetres last year.	These plants haven't **grown** much this summer.
I'd like to **become** a doctor when I'm older.	Kevin **became** ill when he was on holiday.	He's **become** a very good tennis player, hasn't he?
Can you **write** it down for me, please?	Shakespeare **wrote** over forty plays.	I've already **written** to the electricity company.
Will you **take** me home? I'm tired.	George **took** a long time to finish the exercise.	I've **taken** two aspirin and now I'm going to bed.
You have to **tell** him about losing your job.	On Thursday he **told** his girlfriend that he was leaving her.	Have you **told** your father about the car accident yet?
They were planning to **steal** the Mona Lisa!	The boys **stole** sweets from the shop every day.	Help! Someone has **stolen** my handbag!
Will you **send** me a copy of the report?	Aunt Mary **sent** me a letter two weeks ago.	I've just **sent** Mr Robinson an e-mail about the meeting.

Be quiet for a minute. I need to **think**.	They all **thought** that Susan and Tim were married.	Have you ever **thought** of leaving your job?
She's planning to **teach** English in Japan.	I **taught** all my children how to swim.	I've never **taught** children before. I'm scared!
I have to go and **cut** the grass.	Nancy **cut** herself while she was playing in the garden.	I've never **cut** my own hair. Have you?
I'm going to **spend** the weekend with my parents.	Yesterday my girlfriend **spent** over £300 on a dress!	I haven't **spent** much money this month.
Can you **put** that bag on the table?	Polly carefully **put** the injured animal on the table.	Where have you **put** my glasses?
I want to **see** Leonardo DiCaprio's new film.	Everybody **saw** that he was drunk when he arrived at the party.	He hasn't **seen** his brother for years.
My sister is going to **meet** the Prime Minister next week.	Nick **met** his ex-girlfriend at a party last weekend.	I've never **met** that man before.
I'd like to **lose** some weight this year.	Italy **lost** the 1994 World Cup Final on penalties.	Oh no! I've **lost** my keys!
We're planning to **leave** on Sunday.	She **left** home at 10, and arrived at the office at 11.	Laura has **left** her husband and married his best friend!

Learner-training worksheet E

Using the *Mini-dictionary:* irregular verbs – part 2

1 Notice how irregular verbs are shown in the *Mini-dictionary*.

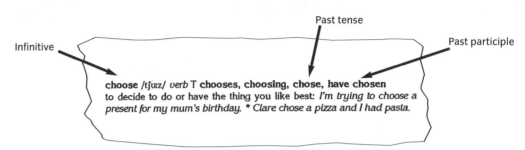

Infinitive
Past tense
Past participle

choose /tʃuːz/ *verb* T chooses, choosing, chose, have chosen
to decide to do or have the thing you like best: *I'm trying to choose a
present for my mum's birthday.* * *Clare chose a pizza and I had pasta.*

2 Complete the table as quickly as possible to find out who's the fastest *Mini-dictionary*-user in the class!
(Note: You must spell all the words correctly to win!). Then test your partner on the verbs.

INFINITIVE	PAST TENSE	PAST PARTICIPLE
shoot		
ring		
catch		
fly		
bring		
teach		
stand		
fight		
build		
wake up		

Learner-training worksheet F

Spelling with double letters

1 When you make **past tenses** and **past participles** of regular verbs, and **-ing words** of all verbs, you
sometimes need to double the last letter. Here's a rule to help you for **one-syllable verbs**.

a If the verb ends in **consonant + vowel + consonant**, you **double** the final consonant.
  ● STOP → STO**PP**ED ● SWIM → SWI**MM**ING
b All other one-syllable verbs **don't** double the final consonant.
  ● CLEAN → CLEANED ● WALK → WALKING
c Verbs that end in **y** and **w** are an exception to this rule.
  ● SHOW → SHOWING ● PLAY → PLAYED
d This rule is also true for **comparatives** and **superlatives** from **one-syllable** adjectives.
  ● BIG → BI**GG**ER ● FAT → FA**TT**EST **but** ● LONG → LONGER ● WEAK → WEAKEST

2 Look at the following words and put a double letter if necessary.

1	run_ing	5	beat_ing	9	shut_ing	13	shout_ed	17	cool_er
2	steal_ing	6	hit_ing	10	start_ed	14	stay_ed	18	bright_est
3	shop_ing	7	grow_ing	11	drop_ed	15	short_er	19	thin_est
4	cut_ing	8	win_ing	12	pass_ed	16	slim_er	20	flat_est

PHOTOCOPIABLE

8A Article snakes and ladders

Use and non-use of articles

Question cards

---

1 Which is correct?

Tom is 13, and is still at
a / *the* / Ø school, but
Jim is now at *a* / *the* / Ø
university studying
English.

---

2 Find *two* mistakes with
articles and correct them.

I live in a flat in city
centre, very close to the
Oxford Street.

---

3 Fill in the gaps with *a*, *an*,
the or Ø.

He went to Italy on
.... holiday, and
spent a week in
.... north of
.... country.

---

4 Is this sentence right or
wrong? (If it's wrong,
correct it.)

I usually go to work by
the train, but yesterday I
went by the bus.

---

5 Which of these should
begin with *the*?

Indian Ocean
Mediterranean
Lake Ontario
Amazon

---

6 *The* or no article?

He's usually at *the* / Ø
college in *the* / Ø
morning, and at *the* / Ø
work in *the* / Ø
afternoon.

---

7 Is this sentence right or
wrong? (If it's wrong,
correct it.)

In the USA most people
go to work by car.

---

8 Fill in the gaps with *a*, *an*,
the or Ø.

I met .... Queen
of .... England
when I was in ....
UK.

---

9 Is this sentence right or
wrong? (If it's wrong,
correct it.)

El Paso is on border of
Mexico and United
States.

---

10 Which is correct?

I've got two cars, *a* / *the*
Porsche and *a* / *the*
BMW.
A / *The* Porsche is much
faster, but I usually drive
a / *the* BMW.

---

11 Find *two* mistakes with
articles and correct them.

Madras is in the south of
the India, on east coast.

---

12 *The* or no article?

The / Ø Lake Titicaca is
in *the* / Ø Peru, and it's
the / Ø highest lake in
the / Ø world.

© Pearson Education Limited 2001

Question cards

13 Find *two* mistakes with articles and correct them.

John is standing on left, and Susan is standing in the middle, next to Headmaster.

14 *The* or no article?

The / Ø French people love going out at *the* / Ø night, but *the* / Ø English people prefer staying at *the* / Ø home.

15 Which is correct?

Sally lives at *the* / Ø top of *a* / *the* block of flats in *a* / *the* / Ø centre of *the* / Ø Madrid.

16 *A*, *the* or no article?

Mark couldn't find *a* / *the* / Ø job because he was in *a* / *the* / Ø prison for ten years.

17 Fill in the gaps with *a*, *an*, *the* or Ø.

When I was at .... school I lived outside .... London in .... suburbs.

18 Is this sentence right or wrong? (If it's wrong, correct it.)

I think dogs are more intelligent than cats, but horses are the most intelligent animals I know.

19 Which is correct?

They found *a* / *the* / Ø Titanic at *a* / *the* / Ø bottom of *the* / Ø Atlantic Ocean.

20 Find *two* mistakes with articles and correct them.

I bought a picture and a carpet this morning. I've put a picture on the bathroom wall and the carpet on kitchen floor.

21 Fill in the gaps with *a*, *an*, *the* or Ø.

He lives in .... town centre, on .... Park Road, and his house is on .... left.

22 Which of these should begin with *the*?

Andes
Mount Everest
Himalayas
Mount Fuji

23 Is this sentence right or wrong? (If it's wrong, correct it.)

Loch Ness is most famous lake in Scotland, because of Loch Ness Monster.

24 Find *two* mistakes with articles and correct them.

I really hate the mice, but I love spiders. I have a tarantula at home, and it lives on ceiling!

Learner-training worksheet G

Noticing and remembering prepositions and articles in phrases

1 Look at this picture of two English teachers having a break in the teachers' room. What do you think they are talking about?

✂- - - - -

2 Read the following conversation and see if your predictions were right.

MATTHEW: Hi Jill, <u>have you got a light</u>?

JILL: Yes, here you are. Are you feeling OK?

MATTHEW: Yes, I'm just tired, that's all. I went to a party <u>in the city centre</u>, and didn't get home until three.

JILL: So that's why you didn't <u>arrive on time</u> this morning!

MATTHEW: Er, yes. But you were late for work the other day.

JILL: That was because I went to the doctor, not because I stayed out late!

MATTHEW: Yes, well, I'm not very good at getting up early.

JILL: That's probably why you're always in a bad mood!

MATTHEW: I'm not! Anyway, what are you doing at the weekend?

JILL: I'm going out for a meal with some friends on Saturday. On Sunday I might go for a walk in the countryside. What about you?

MATTHEW: I've got the day off on Friday, so I'm going to visit an old friend who lives on the coast.

JILL: That sounds fun. Look, we're going to be late for our classes. Let's go.

MATTHEW: What, already? Where did I put my books ...?

3 There are lots of phrases in English that are always the same, or only change a little. These phrases often include **articles** (*a*, *an*, *the*) and **prepositions** (e.g. *to*, *for*). Look at the conversation above again and <u>underline</u> all the phrases that contain articles and/or prepositions. The first three are done for you.

4 It is useful to write down and learn these phrases as one item of vocabulary. Here are some of the phrases in the conversation. Write in the missing words.

a .... light?
b .... city centre
c to arrive ....
d to be .... work
e .... day
f to go .... doctor
g to stay .... late
h to be (not very) .... doing something

i to get .... early
j to be .... bad mood
k .... weekend
l to go .... meal
m to go .... walk
n .... countryside
o to have the day ....
p .... coast

PHOTOCOPIABLE

9A In the 2020s

will, *won't*, *may* and *might* (for future possibility)

SURVEY A

HOLIDAYS AND FREE TIME

Write questions based on the following prompts.

In the 2020s ...

- people – have more free time?
- people – have longer holidays?
- all films – be in 3D?
- people – still read books?
- everyone – spend more time watching TV?
- people – be able to go on holiday to the moon?
- computer games – be more popular than television?

When you have finished, add one or two

SURVEY B

HOMES AND LIFESTYLES

Write questions based on the following prompts.

In the 2020s ...

- robots – do all the housework?
- people – still shop in supermarkets?
- everyone – have videophones in their homes?
- more people – be homeless?
- cars – use water instead of petrol?
- clothes – look completely different?
- students – have robot teachers?

When you have finished, add one or two questions of your own.

SURVEY C

FAMILIES AND CHILDREN

Write questions based on the following prompts.

In the 2020s ...

- people – have smaller families?
- parents – be able to choose the colour of their baby's eyes?
- parents – be able to choose their baby's IQ?
- a lot more people – live to be over 100 years old?
- fewer people – get married?
- men – be able to have babies?
- governments – make laws about how many children you can have?

When you have finished, add one or two questions of your own.

SURVEY D

WORLD NEWS

Write questions based on the following prompts.

In the 2020s ...

- scientists – be able to clone human beings?
- tigers – be extinct?
- there – be a nuclear war?
- a woman – become president of the USA?
- we – make contact with life on other planets?
- China – be the most powerful country in the world?
- we – have enough food to feed the world?

When you have finished, add one or two questions of your own.

9B Worried parents

Present tense after *if*, *when*, *as soon as* and other time words

Student A

ROLE PLAY 1

Your son/daughter is planning to hitchhike across the USA. He/She is flying to Miami, then going to New Orleans, Las Vegas and San Francisco. You are very worried about him/her and have lots of questions to ask.

1 phone me / as soon as / arrive in Miami?
2 what / do / if / nobody / give / you a lift?
3 what / do / if / get lost?
4 where / stay / when / get to New Orleans?
5 what / do / when / run out of money?
6 what / do / if / lose all your money in Las Vegas?
7 where / stay / when / arrive in San Francisco?
8 visit me / as soon as / get back home?

ROLE PLAY 2

You're going to the north of India. You're flying to Delhi – you've already booked a hotel there – then getting a train (or a bus) to the Himalayas. You want to go camping in the mountains, and you're planning to find a local guide to come with you. You're going to take a lot of medicine, a tent, some chocolate for emergencies – and a very good sleeping bag!

Your mother/father is very worried about you and is going to ask you lots of questions about the holiday. Use the information above (or your own ideas) to answer the questions, and try to make him/her feel more relaxed!

Student B

ROLE PLAY 1

You're going to hitchhike across the USA. You're planning to fly to Miami, then hitchhike to New Orleans, Las Vegas and San Francisco. You haven't got enough money for the whole trip, but you've got friends in New Orleans who own a restaurant – you think that you can get a job there. You also have friends in San Francisco. You're planning to take a tent, your credit card, and a very big map!

Your mother/father is very worried about you, and is going to ask you lots of questions about the holiday. Use the information above (or your own ideas) to answer the questions, and try to make him/her feel more relaxed!

ROLE PLAY 2

Your son/daughter is planning to go camping in the north of India. He/She is flying to Delhi, then going by train to the Himalayas. You are very worried about him/her, and have lots of questions to ask.

1 where / stay / when / arrive in Delhi?
2 how / get to the Himalayas / if / the trains / be / fully booked?
3 what / do / if / get / very cold in the mountains?
4 what / do / if / get lost?
5 what / eat / if / can't find any food?
6 call me / as soon as / get back to Delhi?
7 what / do / if / get ill?
8 buy me a present / before / leave India?!

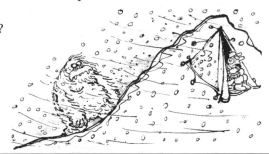

   PHOTOCOPIABLE

Learner-training worksheet H

Deducing meaning from context – part 1

1 Read the following text and decide what really happened!

> When Mark was walking home, he noticed a man sitting on the **pavement** with his head in his hands. Mark saw that there was blood all over the man's shirt, so he walked over to him and **tapped** him on the shoulder.
>
> 'Are you OK?' asked Mark.
>
> 'Three men have just **beaten** me **up** and stolen all my money,' said the man. 'Can you lend me five pounds so that I can get home?'
>
> 'Of course,' said Mark, and he took out his **wallet** and gave the man a five-pound note.
>
> 'Thanks a lot,' said the man with a **grin**. He stood up and handed Mark a brown paper bag. 'This is for you,' he said, then **sprinted** across the road before Mark could say anything. Mark watched him disappear, then **shrugged** his shoulders and opened the bag. The only thing inside was an empty bottle of tomato ketchup …

2 Look at the words in **bold** in the text above, and answer the following questions.

a   Can you guess the meaning of these words from the context?

b   Which words can you guess the *exact* meaning of, and which can you only guess the *general* meaning?

c   What other words in the text helped you guess the meaning? Are there any words in **bold** that you can't guess the meaning of?

d   When you find a word you don't know in a text, do you always have to know the exact meaning, or is the general meaning sometimes enough?

3 Look at the vocabulary <u>underlined</u> in the following sentences.

Which words   • can you guess the **exact** meaning of?
              • can you guess the **general** meaning of?
              • **can't** you guess the meaning of?

a   He walked down the stairs to the <u>cellar</u> and came back with two bottles of red wine.

b   I went to a party last week and <u>bumped into</u> an old friend from school.

c   I didn't like him at all. I thought he was very <u>arrogant</u> and unfriendly.

d   Sally <u>blushed</u> when her brother started telling his friends about the silly things she did when she was a little girl.

e   Frank decided <u>to dig</u> a big hole at the bottom of the garden and put the dead body in it.

f   Nobody slept very well because the dogs <u>barked</u> all night.

g   Wilf drank nearly a whole bottle of whisky, then <u>staggered</u> out of the pub to look for a taxi.

h   Tim walked into the shop and bought a new <u>hammer</u>.

i   The bomb <u>went off</u> at exactly 3.47 p.m.

j   Tom walked into the room wearing a T-shirt and <u>flares</u>.

4 Discuss your answers with another student. Do you both agree? Which words in the sentence helped you guess the meaning?

10A What can I do for you?

Vocabulary: health problems

Patient A

You have these health problems. Write down what they are in the boxes.

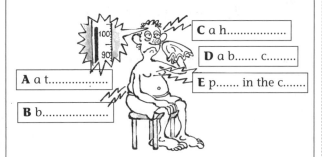

C a h...................

D a b....... c.........

A a t.................

E p....... in the c.......

B b...................

Decide **when** you get problems D and E, and **how long** you've had all your problems.

You also cut yourself! (You decide **what** happened.)

You saw your doctor about problems A and B last week. He told you to stay in bed and keep warm, but didn't give you anything to take. Now you are going to see him/her again.

Tell the doctor about your problems **one at a time**.

Doctor A

This patient came to see you last week with a bad cold and a headache. You told him/her to stay in bed and keep warm, but didn't give him/her anything to take. Now the patient is back and doesn't look very well!

Look back at the quiz in the *Students' Book* on page 81 and try to remember all the different treatments and advice you can give.

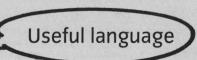

Useful language

'Hello, what can I do for you?'

'How long have you had (this problem)?'

'Have you taken anything for it?'

'You should ...'

'You must ...'

Patient B

You have these health problems. Write down what they are in the boxes.

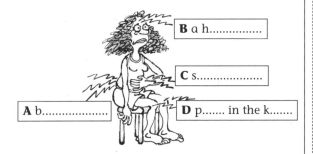

B a h...............

C s...................

A b.................

D p....... in the k.......

Decide **when** you get problems C and D, and **how long** you've had all your problems.

You also burnt yourself this morning! (You decide **how** and **where** you burnt yourself.)

You think you are very ill and want the doctor to send you to hospital (or at least give you a letter saying that you don't have to go to work tomorrow!).

Tell the doctor about your problems **one at a time**.

Doctor B

This patient has been to see you quite often. Sometimes he/she has real health problems, but sometimes you think the patient is telling lies so that he/she doesn't have to go to work!

You cannot tell the patient that you think he/she is lying, but you must ask lots of questions about the illnesses to make sure that they are real.

Look back at the quiz in the *Students' Book* on page 81 and try to remember all the different treatments and advice you can give.

Useful language

'Hello, what can I do for you?'

'How long have you had (this problem)?'

'Have you taken anything for it?'

'You should ...'

'You must ...'

10B The Ghost

used to and Past Simple

The Ghost role card

You are a world-famous burglar called The Ghost. You've spent your life stealing from the houses of rich and famous people all over the world, but last year the police caught you in the middle of a robbery. Now you're in prison! A journalist from the magazine *Famous Criminals* is coming to interview you. Look at the following information and prepare your life story.

The first thing you stole in your life was .... (what?) when you were .... years old.
You started burgling houses in .... (when?). You used to sell burglar alarms to rich and famous people.
Then you went back to the house at night, switched off the burglar alarm, and stole anything you wanted!
You used to steal .... , ... , and .... (what kind of things?) from the houses.
You always used to wear .... and ....
You used to leave .... (what?) in every house to tell them The Ghost was there.
You burgled ....'s house two years ago, and you stole .... from it.
You spent all the money on .... and ....
One night you got caught! You went to burgle ....'s house – but they had a *new* burglar alarm!!

When you've finished, think of some more houses of famous people that you burgled, and what you stole from them!

Journalist role card

You are a journalist from the magazine *Famous Criminals*. You are going to interview The Ghost, a world-famous burglar. The Ghost used to steal from the houses of rich and famous people all over the world, but last year the police caught him/her in the middle of a burglary. Now he/she is in prison.

Look at the following ideas and write down the questions you are going to ask The Ghost in your interview. Use both *used to* and the Past Simple in your questions.

- the first thing / steal in your life? Age?
- when / start burgling rich people's houses?
- how / get into / the houses?
- what / steal?
- what / wear?
- what / leave / in the houses you burgled?
- whose house / you burgle two years ago?
- what / steal from him/her?
- what / do with all the money?
- how / get caught?

When you've finished, add some more questions of your own.

10C Bob's night out

Past Continuous and Past Simple

© Pearson Education Limited 2001

PHOTOCOPIABLE

11A The Lovebug Dating Agency

Gerunds; expressions for liking and disliking

Men cards

♥ *Lovebug Dating Agency* ♥

Client A Name: ....

'I really like ....
and ....,
and I'm very keen on ....
.... I think ....
.... is
good fun, and I quite like ....
.... I don't mind .... ,
but I can't stand .... !'

♥ *Lovebug Dating Agency* ♥

Client B Name ....

'I love .... and
............................., and I'm
very interested in ....
I really enjoy .... ,
and I quite like ....
.... as well.
I don't mind .... , but I absolutely loathe
.... !'

♥ *Lovebug Dating Agency* ♥

Client C Name: ....

'I'm crazy about ....
I also like .... and
.... I also find
.... very relaxing.
I think .... can be fun,
but I don't like ....
And I really hate .... !'

♥ *Lovebug Dating Agency* ♥

Client D Name: ....

'I'm mad about .... ,
.... and I also enjoy
.... and
.... I find ....
.... very interesting,
and I like .... too.
.... can be really boring, and I
can't stand ....'

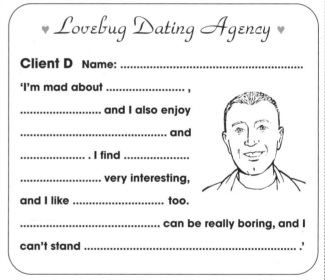

♥ *Lovebug Dating Agency* ♥

Client E Name: ....

'I'm very keen on ....
and .... I also
love .... , and I
really enjoy I
think .... is
very relaxing, and I don't mind
.... ,
but I really hate ....'

♥ *Lovebug Dating Agency* ♥

Client F Name: ....

'I'm mad about ....
and .... I also
really like I
think .... is very
interesting, but I find ....
.... incredibly boring.
I don't mind .... , but I absolutely
loathe .... !'

PHOTOCOPIABLE

Women cards

♥ *Lovebug Dating Agency* ♥

Client 1 Name: ....

'I don't really like .... ,

but I love .... I'm

also very interested in ....

.... and ....

.... I find ....

relaxing, but I loathe ....

.... Oh, and I'm crazy about ....

.... !'

♥ *Lovebug Dating Agency* ♥

Client 2 Name: ....

'I'm very keen on .... ,

and I love .... at

the weekends. I also really like

.... and

....

I think .... can be

great fun, and I don't mind .... – but I

can't stand ....'

♥ *Lovebug Dating Agency* ♥

Client 3 Name: ....

'I really enjoy .... and

.... , and I find

.... very

interesting. I'm also keen on

.... , and I quite

like .... too. I think

.... is good fun, but I really

hate .... !'

♥ *Lovebug Dating Agency* ♥

Client 4 Name: ....

'I like ....

and .... , but I

can't stand ....

I'm mad about .... ,

and I really enjoy ....

I think .... can

be very boring, and I absolutely loathe ....

....'

♥ *Lovebug Dating Agency* ♥

Client 5 Name: ....

'I'm very keen on ....

.... , and I also really like

....

I find ....

very relaxing, and I quite like

.... and ....

.... I don't mind ....

.... , but I really hate ....

....'

♥ *Lovebug Dating Agency* ♥

Client 6 Name: ....

'I'm mad about .... ,

and I really like .... as

well. I think ....

can be fun, and I also enjoy

.... and ....

I don't really like ....

and I find .... incredibly boring.'

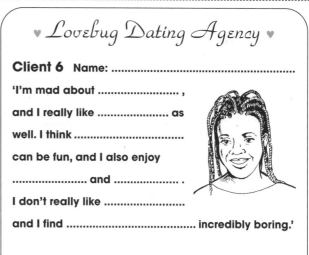

© Pearson Education Limited 2001

11B Neither do I

So do I, Me too, Me neither, Neither do I, etc.

YOUR IDEAS	STUDENT'S NAME
1 I'm .... tomorrow evening.	
2 I don't usually .... at the weekends.	
3 When I was a child I really hated ....!	
4 I really like	
5 I didn't .... last weekend.	
6 I'm not very keen on	
7 I love .... in my spare time.	
8 I'm not very interested in	
9 When I was a child I didn't like	
10 I'm very .... at the moment.	
11 I went to .... last month.	
12 I don't like .... very much.	

Learner-training worksheet I

Using the *Mini-dictionary* to find constructions that follow verbs

1 Notice how the *Mini-dictionary* shows which grammatical construction follows a verb.

> **love** / / **1** verb T to like something very much: '*Do you like beer?*' '*Yes I love it*' *Lucy **loves singing**. **2** verb T.
>
> **try** / / [**tried, have tried**] verb I, T to make an attempt to do something: I try to learn a few new English words every day. She tried hard to forget about Rob. Ms Wood always **tries to make** the lesson interesting.
>
> **should** / / modal verb used to give someone advice and say what the best thing to do: You **should stop** smoking. *Do you think I should call a doctor?*

2 Look up the following verbs and verb phrases in your *Mini-dictionary*, and put them in the correct column in the table below.

want	have to	enjoy	would prefer	arrange
stop	might	hate	would like	could
learn	intend	don't mind	plan	must

VERB + GERUND	VERB + INFINITIVE WITH *TO*	VERB + INFINITIVE WITHOUT *TO*
	want	

3 Are the following sentences correct? If not, can you correct them?

a I've arranged meeting my brother this evening. ....

b I must to go to the dentist this afternoon. ....

c Stop watching television and do your homework! ....

d Do you enjoy play tennis? ....

e Would you prefer have Chinese food or Indian food? ....

f Jim is learning to drive at the moment. ....

g I'd like to live in France when I'm older. ....

h I hate get up early. ....

i We're planning go to New York for our holidays. ....

j I don't mind looking after the children tonight. ....

12A The Handbag Gang

Past Simple passive

PHOTOCOPIABLE

The Handbag Gang – Vocabulary

Match these words and expressions with the correct pictures. There could be more than one correct answer.

1   to pull out a gun ....

2   to steal money ....

3   to rob a bank ....

4   to arrest someone ....

5   a wig ....

6   a cashier ....

7   to order someone to do something ....

8   to send someone to prison ....

9   to be disguised as women ....

10 a number plate ....

11 a shopping trolley ....

12B What's this?

Relative clauses with *that*, *which* and *who*

13A Century People

Present Perfect Simple and Continuous (for unfinished past)

Old person role card

You are over 100 years old! You are going to be interviewed for a TV programme called *Century People*. Before the interview, fill in the gaps in the information below. Use your imagination!

You are .... years old!
You live in .... (where?).
You moved there in .... (which year?).
You got married in .... (when?)
    to .... (name?).
He/She is .... years old.
You have .... children, ... grandchildren and ....
    great-grandchildren (how many?).
Your oldest friend is .... (who?).
You met him/her in .... (when?).
Your favourite hobby is .... (what?).
You started doing this in .... (when?).
You are studying .... (what?) in the evenings.
You started this .... (when?).
Your oldest possession is .... (what?).
You were given it in .... (when?) by .... (who?).
What is the secret of long life? ....

When you've finished, add more details to the topics above to talk about in the interview.

Interviewer role card

You are an interviewer for the TV programme *Century People*, which every week looks at the life of someone who is over 100 years old. You are going to interview someone for next week's programme. Look at the information below and write questions to ask him/her. Be careful of the tenses you use.

- how old ?
- where / live? how long / live there?
- married? how long / be married?
- children? grandchildren? great-grandchildren?!
- oldest friend? how long / know him/her?
- what do / spare time? how long / do that?
- study anything now? what? how long / study it?
- what / oldest possession? how long / have it?
- what / be / the secret of long life?

When you've finished, think of three or four more questions to ask.

13B Old friends

Present Perfect Simple and Continuous (for unfinished past)

Role card 1

You've been an architect for seven years.
You live in New York, and you've been living there since 1990.
Your wife/husband has been a primary school teacher for five years.
You study Chinese, but you've only been studying it for two weeks.

Name	What we have in common

Role card 2

You've been an architect for seven years.
You live in Rome, but you've been staying at the Ratz Hotel this week.
Your wife/husband is a waiter/waitress in an Italian restaurant, and he/she has worked there since January.
You go horse riding, and you've had your horse since last April.

Name	What we have in common

Role card 3

You're a lawyer for a computer company. You've been working for them since 1998.
You've been living in London since 1997.
Your wife/husband has been a primary school teacher for five years.
You do yoga, and you've been doing it for nearly three years.

Name	What we have in common

Role card 4

You're a lawyer for a computer company. You've been working for them since 1998.
You live in a flat in the centre of town. You've had the flat for eight years.
Your wife/husband is a waiter/waitress in an Italian restaurant, and he/she has worked there since January.
You love sailing. You've been sailing since you were a child.

Name	What we have in common

Role card 5

You've been studying to be a doctor for three years. You want to become a GP.
You live in New York, and you've been living there since 1990.
You've been married for exactly one year – it's your wedding anniversary today!
You love sailing. You've been sailing since you were a child.

Name	What we have in common

Role card 6

You've been studying to be a doctor for three years. You want to become a GP.
You live in Rome, but you've been staying at the Ratz Hotel this week.
You're getting married tomorrow, but you've only known your boyfriend/girlfriend for a few weeks!
You do yoga, and you've been doing it for nearly three years.

Name	What we have in common

PHOTOCOPIABLE

Role card 7

You're an actor/actress. You've been appearing in *Romeo and Juliet* since last March.
You've been living in London since 1997.
You've been married for exactly one year – it's your wedding anniversary today!
You go horse riding, and you've had your horse since last April.

Name	What we have in common

Role card 8

You're an actor/actress. You've been appearing in *Romeo and Juliet* since last March.
You live in a flat in the centre of town. You've had the flat for eight years.
You're getting married tomorrow, but you've only known your boyfriend/girlfriend for a few weeks!
You study Chinese, but you've only been studying it for two weeks.

Name	What we have in common

Role card 9

You've been an architect for seven years.
You've been living in London since 1997.
You're getting married tomorrow, but you've only known your boyfriend/girlfriend for a few weeks!
You love sailing. You've been sailing since you were a child.

Name	What we have in common

Role card 10

You're a lawyer for a computer company. You've been working for them since 1998.
You live in Rome, but you've been staying at the Ratz Hotel this week.
You've been married for exactly one year – it's your wedding anniversary today!
You study Chinese, but you've only been studying it for two weeks.

Name	What we have in common

Role card 11

You've been studying to be a doctor for three years.
You want to become a GP.
You live in a flat in the centre of town. You've had the flat for eight years.
Your wife/husband has been a primary school teacher for five years.
You go horse riding, and you've had your horse since last April.

Name	What we have in common

Role card 12

You're an actor/actress. You've been appearing in *Romeo and Juliet* since last March.
You live in New York, and you've been living there since 1990.
Your wife/husband is a waiter/waitress in an Italian restaurant, and he/she has worked there since January.
You do yoga, and you've been doing it for nearly three years.

Name	What we have in common

Learner-training worksheet J

Deducing meaning from context – part 2

1 Put the following story in order, starting with paragraph **D**.

THE BOX

A 'Michael!' said Jennifer when she opened the door. 'What are you doing here?'
Michael took off his hat and *undid* his coat. 'It's Sally,' he said. 'She found the letters. Not surprisingly, she was furious.'

B 'I ... I can explain ...' began Michael.
'Get out, and don't ever come back!' *yelled* Susan. Then she *slammed the door* and ran to the bedroom.

C 'This is going to be a wonderful holiday,' she thought as she started *packing*. Soon she had everything she needed, except for one thing – sun cream. She went to the bathroom to look for some, and when she pulled open the bottom *drawer* she found a small box.

D One afternoon Sally was getting ready to go on holiday. She was going to Jamaica with her husband Michael to celebrate their tenth wedding anniversary, and was looking forward to lying in the sun on a beautiful beach.

E She took the box out of the drawer and opened it. It was full of letters. She lifted the box to her nose and *sniffed* – the letters smelt of expensive perfume! Sally sat on the *edge* of the bath and started reading.

F Michael stood outside the house for a few minutes, then started walking into the centre of town. It was raining hard, and when he arrived at Jennifer's house he was completely *soaked*.

G 'Oh no!,' said Jennifer. 'What are we going to do now?'
Michael put his arms around her and *hugged* her. Then he put his hand into his coat pocket and took out a white envelope. Inside the envelope were two plane tickets.
'Let's go to Jamaica,' he said with a smile.

H Two hours later Michael came home from work. 'Hello darling!' he said as he opened the front door. Sally was waiting for him.
'I *came across* these when I was packing,' she said, and threw the box of letters at him. 'I know all about you and Jennifer.'

2 With a partner, try to work out the meaning of the words in *italics*, from the context. (Don't use a dictionary.)

3 Ask and answer these questions in pairs or groups.

a What do you always **pack** when you're going on holiday?
b Who was the last person you **hugged**?
c What do you keep in the **drawers** in your house/flat?
d Think of two reasons why people **sniff**.
e Think of three things that have **edges**.
f Have you ever **come across** some old letters or photos in your house?
g Think of two reasons why people **yell**.
h If someone **slams the door**, how do they feel?
i When was the last time you were **soaked**?
j Think of three things you can **undo**.

© Pearson Education Limited 2001

14A The Hungry Hippo café

Quantifiers (*some*, *any*, *much*, *not enough*, etc.)

Worksheet 1

THE HUNGRY HIPPO CAFÉ

NORTH STREET BRANCH

You are the new managers of this branch of the Hungry Hippo café. You want to open the café **tomorrow**! Look at the menu and the pictures, and decide:

- what you have too much/many of
- what you don't have enough of
- what you don't have any of.

MENU

DRINKS		HOT FOOD	
Tea	80p	Hamburger	£2.40
Coffee	£1.00	Cheeseburger	£2.90
Coke	90p	Pizza	£3.20
Orange juice	£1.00	Chips	£1.20
SANDWICHES		**DESSERTS**	
Egg	£1.30	Chocolate cake	£1.70
Cheese	£1.60	Ice cream	£1.50

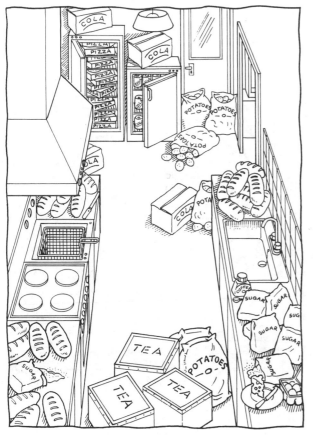

© **Pearson Education Limited 2001**

Worksheet 2

THE HUNGRY HIPPO CAFÉ

SOUTH STREET BRANCH

You are the new managers of this branch of the Hungry Hippo café. You want to open the café **tomorrow**! Look at the menu and the pictures, and decide:

- what you have too much/many of
- what you don't have enough of
- what you don't have any of.

MENU

DRINKS		HOT FOOD	
Tea	80p	Hamburger	£2.40
Coffee	£1.00	Cheeseburger	£2.90
Coke	90p	Pizza	£3.20
Orange juice	£1.00	Chips	£1.20
SANDWICHES		**DESSERTS**	
Egg	£1.30	Chocolate cake	£1.70
Cheese	£1.60	Ice cream	£1.50

14B Where's the nearest bank?

Language for giving directions

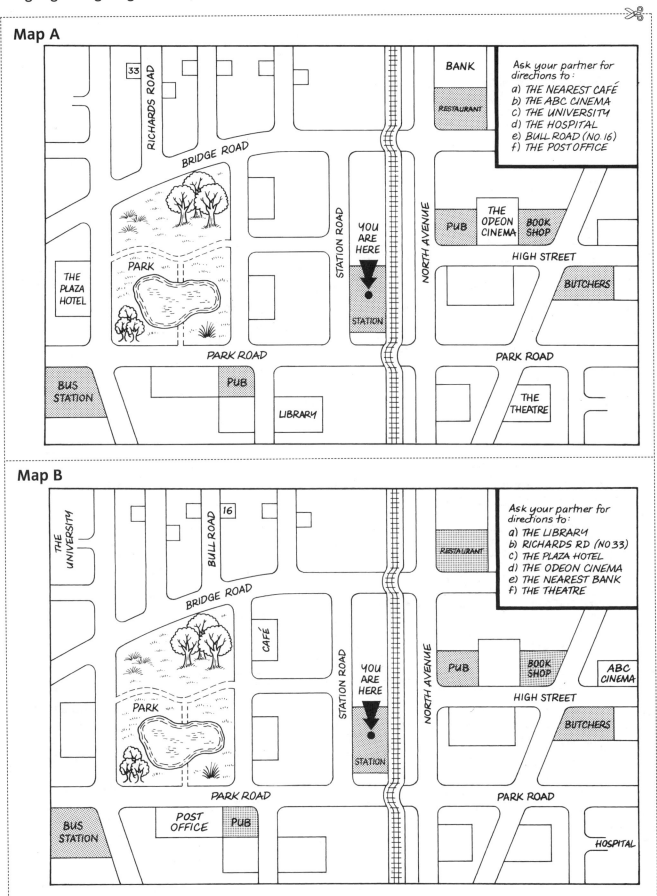

Map A

Ask your partner for directions to:
a) THE NEAREST CAFÉ
b) THE ABC CINEMA
c) THE UNIVERSITY
d) THE HOSPITAL
e) BULL ROAD (NO. 16)
f) THE POST OFFICE

Map B

Ask your partner for directions to:
a) THE LIBRARY
b) RICHARDS RD (NO 33)
c) THE PLAZA HOTEL
d) THE ODEON CINEMA
e) THE NEAREST BANK
f) THE THEATRE

14C Building your dream

Vocabulary extension (word building, dependent prepositions and collocations)

1 a Which **preposition** is used in paragraph 1 with this expression:

to find the right combination .... (something and something else)

b What is the **verb** from *combination*? Write it in the space below.

2 a Find a **noun** in paragraph 1 which means *the ability to form ideas in your mind.*

Write it here ....

b Complete the 'word family' for this noun.

verb ....

adjective ....

3 Which **prepositions** are used with these verbs and phrases in paragraph 2?

a to be made .... something (e.g. metal)

b .... the press .... a button

c east .... a town or city (e.g. Madrid)

d to be similar .... something

4 a Is *surprisingly* (at the beginning of paragraph 3)

– a **noun**?
– an **adjective**?
– an **adverb**?

b What is the **verb**? Write it in the space below.

5 Which **prepositions** are used with these verbs and phrases in paragraph 3?

a to be surrounded .... something

b .... the top floor

c compared .... something

d to spend money .... something

6 a Find a **verb** in paragraph 4 which means *to make people want to visit a place.*

Write the infinitive here ....

b What is the **noun** from this verb? Write it in the gap in the following sentence.

The Pyramids are the most popular tourist .... in Egypt.

7 a Which **verb** in paragraph 4 means *to make the inside of a building more attractive by painting it?*

Write the infinitive here ....

b What is the **noun** from this verb? Write it in the space below.

8 Match a word from column **A** with a word from column **B**. If you aren't sure, look back at the text.

A	B
a dream	bathroom
to turn off	pitch
a football	presents
to wrap	visitors
to attract	home
an upstairs	the TV

15A Lottery winners

Reported speech

FIRST TIME LUCKY!

MILLIONS OF PEOPLE in Britain buy a lottery ticket every week, but never win a penny.

Some people, however, are just born lucky. Last Saturday Chris Simpson and Alex Kelly bought a lottery ticket for the very first time – and won £5 million! Yesterday afternoon Chris and Alex were presented with the cheque by Ivor Lott, the Managing Director of the Con-a-Lot Lottery Company, outside the Bank of England. They said it was the happiest day of their lives!

Tomorrow we will have an exclusive interview with one of the lucky winners – only in the *Daily Planet*!

Chris and Alex celebrating their lottery win in London yesterday

Reporter's role card

You are going to interview Chris Simpson or Alex Kelly. With your partner(s), write down some of the questions you are going to ask. Try to write at least **twelve** questions.

Make sure you include questions to find out the following information. Remember to ask about the other lottery winner too!

- personal details (age, where they live, married/single, etc.)
- relationship with other lottery winner
- jobs / where they work
- how they chose the lottery numbers
- how they heard about the win
- what they did to celebrate
- what their family / work colleagues think
- what they will do with the money
- other plans for the future
- do lottery again next week?!

Lottery winner's role card

You are Chris Simpson / Alex Kelly, and you're going to be interviewed by a reporter from the *Daily Planet*. With your partner, make brief notes to help you in your interview.

Here are some things you could be asked about. Remember that the reporter will ask you about each other too!

- personal details (age, where you live, married/single, etc.)
- relationship with each other
- jobs / where you work
- how you chose the lottery numbers
- how you heard about the win
- what you did to celebrate
- what your family / work colleagues think
- what you will do with your money
- other plans for the future
- do lottery again next week?!

15B Get Rich Quick!

Vocabulary: money

GIVE HALF YOUR MONEY TO THE PERSON ON YOUR RIGHT!

£15,000

£10,000

£25,000

£5,000

DOUBLE YOUR MONEY!

£5,000

£10,000

£20,000

£25,000

£15,000

£20,000

GET RICH QUICK!

MONEY CARDS

THROW AGAIN!

MISS A TURN!

£5,000

£15,000

£25,000

£5,000

£5,000

£10,000

START (EVERY TIME YOU PASS THIS SQUARE YOU GET £10,000 FREE)

£10,000

£15,000

£20,000

£5,000

GIVE HALF YOUR MONEY TO THE PERSON ON YOUR LEFT!

PHOTOCOPIABLE

Money cards

1 Q: What's the word for someone who bets on horses or goes to casinos? A: *a gambler*	**2** Q: Which preposition? 'I'd like to change a hundred pounds .... dollars.' A: *into*	**3** Q: If you owe somebody money, what should you do as soon as possible? A: *pay him/her back*
4 Q: Which word is missing? 'I'd like to go to Italy on holiday, but I can't .... it.' A: *afford*	**5** Q: Which verb is correct? 'I *win / earn* about £1,000 a month.' A: *earn*	**6** Q: Which of these three verbs is irregular, and what is the past tense and past participle? **save waste bet** A: *bet (bet, bet)*
7 Q: Which verb is correct? 'If you buy that car, you're *spending / wasting* your money. It's over 20 years old!' A: *wasting*	**8** Q: Which preposition? 'He invested all his money .... a new Internet company.' A: *in*	**9** Q: Which word is missing? (at a restaurant) 'Excuse me, is service .... ?' A: *included*
10 Q: Which of these three verbs is irregular, and what is the past tense and past participle? **borrow lose change** A: *lose (lost, lost)*	**11** Q: What do you call money that is round and made of metal? A: *coins*	**12** Q: Which verb is correct? 'Could you *borrow / lend* me some money until tomorrow?' A: *lend*
13 Q: Which preposition? 'Excuse me, could you tell me the price .... that computer?' A: *of*	**14** Q: Which of these three verbs is irregular, and what is the past tense and past participle? **invest win earn** A: *win (won, won)*	**15** Q: Which preposition? 'Frank bets .... football matches every weekend.' A: *on*
16 Q: Which preposition? 'I spend a lot of money .... clothes.' A: *on*	**17** Q: Which preposition? 'John is always very careful .... money.' A: *with*	**18** Q: If you move to a new country and want to put your money in a bank, what do you need to do? A: *open a bank account*
19 Q: Which *two* words are missing? 'Can I pay for this .... card?' A: *by credit*	**20** Q: Which preposition? 'I borrowed £10 .... my brother.' A: *from*	**21** Q: Which of these three verbs is irregular, and what is the past tense and past participle? **lend pay owe** A: *lend (lent, lent)*
22 Q: What do you call the money you leave for a waiter at the end of a meal? A: *a tip*	**23** Q: How do you spell 'businessman'? A: *B-U-S-I-N-E-S-S-M-A-N*	**24** Q: Which of these can't be used with the word 'money'? **earn spend can't afford win** A: *can't afford*

© Pearson Education Limited 2001

Learner-training worksheet K

Using the *Mini-dictionary* to find dependent prepositions

1 Notice how the *Mini-dictionary* shows which preposition follows some verbs and adjectives.

> **depend** / / verb 1 if one thing **depends** (on) another, it can change, or be decided by the second thing: There are lots of . . . etc.
> **frightened** / / adjective feeling worried and afraid of something: Jack is **frightened** (of) dogs, etc.

2 Circle the correct prepositions in the following sentences.

a Do you ever **worry** *for / about / on* getting old?
b Put this hat on. It'll **protect** you *by / of / from* the sun.
c I'm very **annoyed** *about / with / from* what happened yesterday.
d He lost control of the car and **crashed** *against / into / onto* a tree.
e Her opinion of the film was very **similar** *for / to / about* mine.
f If you **click** *on / at / onto* this, then you can save your document.
g How much have you **spent** *with / on / for* food this week?
h She's always **arguing** *with / to / for* her boyfriend.
i Jack's aunt **died** *with / of / in* a heart attack last weekend.
j My son **is very good** *for / at / in* playing tennis.

3 Check your answers using the *Mini-dictionary*. How many did you get right?

4 Fill in the gaps with a preposition from the box. Check your answers in the *Mini-dictionary* if necessary.

a If you eat chocolate every day you'll **put** .... **weight.**
b You should eat more fruit. It's very **good** .... you.
c Don't talk to Tom, he's .... **a bad mood** at the moment.
d Lots of children are **afraid** .... the dark.
e I saw a great film .... **video** last night.
f In England lots of people **complain** .... the weather.
g What's the **difference** .... British English and American English?
h Bruce wrote to me last month, but I haven't **replied** .... him yet.
i Who did you **vote** .... in the last election?
j What are the **disadvantages** .... working at home?

on	for
of	to
about	in
between	on
for	of

5 Test your partner on the prepositions in Exercises 2 and 4, like this:

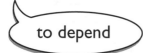 to depend

to depend on something

16A **Conditional squares**

Unreal and real conditionals

Write **short** answers to the following questions in the squares below. You can write your answers in any square you like, but **not** in the same order as the questions. Answer as many questions as you can.

- If you won a lot of money, what would you buy *first*?
- What will you do this weekend if the weather's good?
- If you could go anywhere in the world tomorrow, where would you go?
- If you have enough money for a holiday this year (or next year), where will you go?
- If you could choose one famous person to have dinner with, who would it be?
- If you study English next year, which school will you go to?
- If you could change one part of your body, what would you change?
- If there was a fire in your house, what would be the first thing you'd take outside?
- If you could have any job in the world, what would you like to be?
- If the teacher gives you homework tonight, will you definitely do it?
- If you could only watch one film again in your life, which film would it be?
- What would you do if the doctor told you that you only had two days to live?

16B Preposition pelmanism
Revision of prepositions

He **invested** all his money .... his friend's business.	**IN**	Sometimes it's really nice to be .... **your own**.	**ON**
Hello, doctor. I've got a terrible **pain** .... **my knee**.	**IN**	When we were in London we **went** .... **a tour** of the city.	**ON**
He didn't get married until he was .... **his forties**.	**IN**	Is your new coat **made** .... leather?	**OF**
Can I **change** these yen .... dollars, please?	**INTO**	I**'m really frightened** .... spiders.	**OF**
Mark's **really bad** .... speaking Spanish.	**AT**	We're **going out** .... **a meal** this evening.	**FOR**
Their address is .... **the top** of the letter.	**AT**	I often **go** .... **a walk** after lunch.	**FOR**
Stop **looking** .... **the window** and pay attention!	**OUT OF**	I've **borrowed** £100 .... my brother.	**FROM**
E-mail is a good way of **keeping in touch** .... friends who live abroad.	**WITH**	I**'m looking forward** .... going on holiday.	**TO**
The best thing .... living here is the park opposite.	**ABOUT**	What are you doing **the day** .... **tomorrow**?	**AFTER**
Susannah **knows a lot** .... computers.	**ABOUT**	I went to the theatre **the day** .... **yesterday**.	**BEFORE**

Test one

modules 1–6

Ⓐ Present Simple/Continuous and Past Simple

Complete the gaps in the following sentences with the correct form (Present Simple/Continuous or Past Simple) of the verb in brackets.

For example:

The average American ..*watches*.. *(watch)* more than three hours television a day.

1 I .... *(send)* Stuart a card last Tuesday.
2 Josh normally .... *(practise)* tennis for about four hours a day.
3 I'm sorry, I can't send you an e-mail now because my brother .... *(use)* the computer.
4 All of the students .... *(take)* the exam next week.
5 Anna isn't here. She .... *(go)* out about an hour ago.
6 A good teacher always .... *(correct)* our mistakes.
7 Joan Lloyd .... *(have)* lunch with the Korean President the day after tomorrow.
8 David .... *(live)* with some friends this month, but next month he's going to move into his new flat.

[8]

Ⓑ Vocabulary

Circle the correct verb in the following sentences.

For example:

play/*go* tennis

1 *do / make* a mistake
2 *go / do* shopping
3 *miss / lose* a bus
4 *pass / succeed* an exam
5 *say / tell* a story
6 *have / go* a party
7 *lose / miss* your wallet
8 *earn / win* a competition

[8]

Ⓒ Comparing things

Four of the sentences below are correct. Tick (✓) the correct ones and correct the others.

For example:

She's ~~more old~~ than me.   *older*

1 It's the biggest city of the world.
2 Ruth's more organised than me.
3 My English is badder than Paolo's.
4 Vanessa's friendlyer now than she was a year ago.
5 That man looks as Tom Cruise!
6 German is very different from Italian.
7 Her computer is the same like mine.
8 I'm going to spend more time with my children.
9 Which is better, video or DVD?
10 My surname's similar than yours.

[10]

Ⓓ Prepositions

Complete the gaps in the following sentences with a preposition from the box.

~~in~~	with	at	off	down	at
with	out	on			

For example:

She started her job ....*in*.... 1989.

1 It happened .... Thursday afternoon.
2 Rachel spends a lot of time .... her new boyfriend.
3 Jim had three weeks .... work last month because he broke his leg.
4 I'm sure I wrote .... Sally's telephone number, but now I can't find it.
5 Your driving test will be .... the beginning of June.
6 You shouldn't stay .... late during the week because you have to get up to go to school.
7 Carmen and Hans communicate .... each other by e-mail.
8 I'll be home .... about seven o'clock tonight.

[8]

© Pearson Education Limited 2001   **179**

E Questions

Look at the answer and write the question in the correct tense. Pay attention to the underlined part of the answer and use a question word from the box

~~Where~~	Which	When	How often	Why
How many	What kind	How long	What ... like?	

For example:

Where did you go last night?
We went to the cinema last night

1 I like rock and jazz music.
2 Karen goes to Spain once a month.
3 Nicolai speaks three languages.
4 I prefer the black boots.
5 Sylvie's going home because it's late.
6 It will take about five minutes to find the information.
7 It was very snowy.
8 I last used my credit card yesterday.

| 8 |

F Pronunciation

Put the words below in the correct column of the table according to their word stress.

~~improve~~	enjoy	appearance	relaxed	Internet	
crowded	prefer	embarrassed	frightened		
relative	ambition	foreign	photograph		
surprised	attractive	scenery	happened		

○ ●	● ○	● ○ ○	○ ● ○
improve			

| 8 |

G Vocabulary

Complete the gaps with the missing word.

For example:

Did you buy any s o u v e n i r s of your holiday?

1 I haven't got a pen. Can I _ _ _ _ _ _ yours?
2 A: Who's your _ _ _ _ _ _ _ _ _ actor?
   B: Tom Hanks. What about you?
3 A: Did you do much _ _ _ _ _ _ _ _ _ _ while you were in Moscow?
   B: Yes, we went to Red Square and we visited lots of museums.
4 A: What's the matter?
   B: I feel really _ _ _ _ _ _ _ because I've got a history exam this afternoon.
5 I'm sorry I can't hear you because the baby is _ _ _ _ _ _ .
6 A: How was your flight?
   B: Terrible. The plane was _ _ _ _ _ _ _ by five hours and we didn't leave the airport until 2.00 in the morning.
7 Could you _ _ _ _ _ _ the phone Pat? I'm in the bath.
8 I'm so sorry. I feel really _ _ _ _ _ _ _ _ _ _ , but I can't remember your name.

| 8 |

H *will / won't / going to / planning to / would like to / would prefer to*

Complete the gaps in the following sentences with of a phrase from the box.

'd like to	~~'m going to~~	'll have to	'd prefer to
won't	'm planning to	'll be able to	

For example:

I *'m going to* call my baby Louise.

1 I .... speak to Miss Stacey please.
2 I'm sure you .... find a hotel easily.
3 I .... to travel the world after university.
4 Just a minute. I .... be long!
5 A: Would you like to go out for a drink?
   B: Actually, I .... go for a meal.
6 I'm afraid you .... wait. There are ten people before you.

| 6 |

I Phrases with articles

Complete the following phrases with *a*, *an*, *the* or nothing.

For example:

She's *an* architect.

1 Jenny started playing .... piano when she was very young.
2 Wayne generally goes swimming three times .... week.
3 You should never look directly at .... sun.
4 Laurence is slim and has got .... dark hair.
5 There was .... beautiful beach right outside the apartment.
6 The children stayed with their grandmother .... last week.
7 .... first time Pablo went to a football match was when he was seven.
8 What kind of .... entertainment was there in the hotel?

☐ 8

J can / have to / should / shouldn't

Circle the correct form in the following sentences.

For example:

Can I/ Do I have to / Should I smoke in here?

1 I'm sorry, Sir, but you *don't have to / can't / should* go through that door. It's private.
2 A: I've got a terrible headache and I feel sick.
   B: I think you *should / can / have to* go to bed.
3 You *don't have to / can / have to* wear jeans or trousers at work if you want to.
4 You *shouldn't / can't / don't have to* speak English for this job, but it's very useful when you're travelling.
5 You *shouldn't / don't have to / can* smoke if you want to be healthy .
6 Passengers *can / have to /should* go through security before they get on the plane.

☐ 6

K Irregular verbs

Write the Past Simple tense of the following irregular verbs.

For example:

write ...*wrote*...

1 meet ....
2 wear ....
3 feel ....
4 steal ....
5 tell ....
6 cost ....
7 think ....
8 ride ....
9 buy ....
10 lose ....

☐ 10

L Opposites

Complete the gaps with the opposite word.

For example:

to lose money   to ...*win*... money

1 a dry day   a .... day
2 a polite woman   a .... woman
3 I'm interested   I'm ....
4 to spend money   to .... money
5 to have an awful time to have a .... time
6 to be tidy   to be ....

☐ 6

M Pronunciation

Look at the underlined sounds in these words. Match a word in column A to a word with the same sound in column B.

	A		B
1	n<u>o</u>rmally	a	t<u>y</u>pical
2	g<u>ue</u>ss	b	h<u>ai</u>r
3	w<u>i</u>ndy	c	c<u>ou</u>rse
4	f<u>a</u>mous	d	he<u>a</u>lthy
5	h<u>eigh</u>t	e	entert<u>ai</u>nment
6	w<u>ear</u>	f	y<u>ear</u>
7	ch<u>ee</u>rs!	g	pr<u>i</u>mary school

☐ 6

TOTAL ☐ 100

 © Pearson Education Limited 2001   **181**

Test two

modules 7–11

A Present Perfect or Past Simple?

Complete the gaps in the following sentences with the correct form of the verb in brackets.

For example:

Patrick .....*sent*..... (*send*) me an e-mail yesterday.

1 Luke Harker .... (*work*) for Unifax from 1993 to 2000.
2 Oh no! I .... (*not buy*) a present for Philip yet.
3 When .... Julie and Pierre .... (*get married*)?
4 The plane to Mexico .... (*leave*) ten minutes ago.
5 .... you .... (*ever go*) to China?
6 This looks delicious! I .... (*never eat*) sushi before.
7 How long .... you .... (*live*) in your present apartment?
8 Where .... (*be*) your children born?

☐ **8**

B Pronunciation: word stress

Put the words below in the correct column of the table according to their word stress.

~~modern~~	temperature	stomachache	bandage
disease	cathedral	electrical	degree	facilities
politics	mountain	canal	deliver

● ○	○ ●	● ○ ○	○ ● ○	○ ● ○ ○
modern				

☐ **6**

C Vocabulary

Read the definitions below and complete the puzzle to find the hidden word.

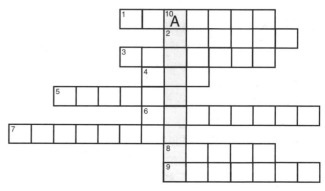

1 If you cut your finger, you can put a .... on it.
2 A job you do for many years: She had a successful .... in banking.
3 You get this piece of paper when you buy something in a shop.
4 You often give this extra money to a waiter or a taxi driver.
5 If you go to another country, you go ....
6 A long hot bath is very ....
7 Islam, Buddhism and Christianity are all types of ....
8 That ice-cream looks nice! What does it .... like?
9 The areas near a city where a lot of people live.
10 Hidden word is ....

☐ **10**

D Agreeing

Put the dialogue in the correct order.

a Good idea, but I don't want anything too expensive. ....
b I'm feeling hungry now. ....
c So did I. ....
d Okay, there's a Pizza place over there. ....
e That was a great film! I really liked it. ....1....
f Neither do I. How about a pizza? ....
g So am I. Shall we go somewhere to eat? ....

☐ **6**

E Verb forms

Circle the correct verb form in the following sentences.

For example:
I *used to see* / *saw* / *was seeing* Abdul at the station today.

1   Jerry and Meg *used to go* / *have been* / *went* to Goa for their holidays last year.
2   Debra *was playing* / *played* / *used to play* tennis when she slipped and broke her leg.
3   I *was living* / *'ve lived* / *used to live* in Seattle all my life, and I'm not going to move now!
4   *Did you used to like* / *Were you liking* / *Did you use to like* Oasis when you were younger?
5   The hotel gave us dinner as soon as we *have arrived* / *arrived* / *were arriving*.
6   Mikako *has had* / *was having* / *used to have* long hair when she was a child.
7   The football match *wasn't finishing* / *didn't finish* / *hasn't finished* yet.
8   Mark cut his hand while he *has cooked* / *was cooking* / *cooked*.

[8]

F will / won't / may / might

Reorder the words to make sentences. The first word is <u>underlined</u>.

For example:
you/night/may/<u>I</u>/tomorrow/see
I may see you tomorrow night.

1   will/race/<u>Coulthard</u>/definitely/win/the
    ....
2   might/late/<u>I</u>/tonight/be
    ....
3   probably/down/<u>Computer</u>/go/will/prices
    ....
4   rain/<u>It</u>/definitely/tomorrow/won't
    ....
5   to/may/Jayne's/not/come/<u>We</u>/party
    ....
6   ten/won't/father/o'clock/<u>My</u>/probably/before/arrive
    ....

[6]

G Articles

Complete the gaps with *the*, *a*, *an* or nothing.

For example:
I can't put pictures on ...*the*.... wall in my room.

1   Budapest is on .... River Danube.
2   What time are we having .... breakfast?
3   Gary's working as .... waiter in Copenhagen.
4   In London you should stand on .... right on escalators.
5   It's easy to book holidays on .... Internet.
6   What's .... best film you have ever seen?
7   Do you want to fly or go by .... boat?
8   Max lives in .... apartment in Madrid.

[8]

H Gerunds and infinitives

Circle the correct form in the following sentences.

For example:
Chris might *phone* / *to phone* / *phoning* tonight.

1   You can't *smoke* / *to smoke* / *smoking* in here.
2   Does your sister enjoy *teach* / *to teach* / *teaching*?
3   I can't stand *drive* / *to drive* / *driving* in the city.
4   You shouldn't *put* / *to put* / *putting* butter on a burn.
5   Sarah says she'd like *go* / *to go* / *going* dancing.
6   Anna usually plays computer games instead of *do* / *to do* / *doing* her homework.
7   A: How would you like *pay* / *to pay* / *paying*?
    B: By credit card.
8   When did Alan learn *sing* / *to sing* / *singing* so well?

[8]

I Vocabulary

Circle the odd one out in the following groups.

For example:
headache cold toothache *relationship*

1   river   beach   ocean   canal
2   cathedral   island   monument   castle
3   resident   customer   healthy   patient
4   friendly   suddenly   eventually   immediately

[4]

Prepositions

Complete the gaps in the following sentences with a preposition from the box.

~~on~~	at	over	about	at	of	into	on	in

For example:

We've got a summer house ..*on*.. the coast.

1 I used to be quite good .... athletics.
2 Are you interested .... modern art?
3 Pablo and I were .... school together.
4 You should put a plaster .... that cut.
5 I'll just change .... something more comfortable.
6 My son Rick is crazy .... American football.
7 A lot of people are frightened .... snakes.
8 William fell .... and hurt himself.

$\boxed{8}$

Past participles

Write the past participles of the following words.

For example:

bring / teach .*brought*.

1	make	9	pay ....
2	win	10	do ....
3	break	11	take ....
4	drink	12	think ....
5	read	13	say ....
6	catch	14	buy ....
7	write	15	eat ....
8	know	16	fly ....

$\boxed{8}$

if / when / before / as soon as

Three of the sentences below are correct. Tick (✓) the correct ones and correct the others.

For example:

If it snows tomorrow, we'll probably stay in. √

1 We can leave as soon as Kevin will find his car keys.
2 If you want to, we could go to the beach tomorrow.
3 Before you leave, don't forget to give me your telephone number.

4 When the film is ending, why don't we go for a meal.
5 Yasmin wants to go back to India before she will die.
6 Could you e-mail me the report when you finish it?

$\boxed{6}$

Vocabulary: collocations

Complete the following sentences with a word from the box.

~~change~~	keep	become	get	change	start	take

For example:

I want to ....*change*.... my e-mail address

1 When did you .... your business?
2 When I .... famous, I'm going to buy a much bigger house.
3 What are you going to do after you .... your degree?
4 I'd like to .... my mind about the car. I'll have it in blue, not green.
5 You should go to bed and try to .... warm.
6 Go home and .... these tablets three times a day.

$\boxed{6}$

Missing words

There is one word missing from each of the sentences below. Put one word from the box in the correct place in each sentence.

~~in~~	for	just	already	yet	last	ago	when
never							

For example:

The first men went to the moon ....*in*... 1969.

1 Jose started learning English four months.
2 Oh no, I've lost all my work on the computer!
3 I've used a DVD player before. Can you help me?
4 We spoke on the phone week.
5 Lee and Oliver have known each other ten years.
6 A: Julie, this is John.
   B: Actually, we've met. Hello again!
7 Chris left school he was sixteen.
8 Mel hasn't heard the results of her exam.

$\boxed{8}$

TOTAL $\boxed{100}$

Test three

modules 12–16

A Vocabulary

Complete the gaps with the missing word. You are given the first letter of each word.

For example:

If the weather is a.*wful*., it's very bad.

1 You can keep money in a w........................ .
2 If you have a problem and someone listens and is very kind, he or she is s........................ .
3 You can use a t........................ to dry yourself after a shower.
4 If someone lends you £10 then you o........................ them £10.
5 There are nine p................. which go round the sun.
6 If children are playing with paint and water they usually make a m........................ .
7 If you disagree with the government you can go on a d........................ in the street.
8 In Britain, when a man gets married his best friend usually makes a s........................ at the party.

$$\boxed{8}$$

B Verb forms: Past Simple / Present Perfect / Present Perfect Continuous

Circle the correct verb form in the following sentences.

For example:

Shakespeare wrote / has written over thirty plays.

1 Yesterday it *rained / has rained* all day!
2 Tom and I are good friends. We *have known / have been knowing* each other for six years.
3 Hi! I *tried / 've been trying* to phone since three o'clock. How are you?
4 How long *have you had / have you been having* your car?
5 Between 1998 and 2000 The Juice Bar *opened/ has been opening* over 200 new shops around the world.
6 I *shopped / 've been shopping* all morning! Let's have lunch.

$$\boxed{6}$$

C Quantifiers

Four of the sentences below are correct. Tick (√) the correct ones and correct the others.

For example:

Are there any special celebrations at New Year? √

1 Henman didn't win no matches in the last championship.
2 There aren't many beaches in the south.
3 A lot people play computer games just to relax.
4 We had to cancel the concert because not enough people bought tickets.
5 People shouldn't spend too many time on their computers without a break.
6 A few students knew the answer, but not many.
7 I'm having days off next week.
8 There's some beautiful scenery in Tuscany.

$$\boxed{8}$$

D Active or passive?

Put the verb in brackets in the correct active or passive form. Make sure that you use the correct tense (Present Simple, Past Simple or the future with *will*).

For example:

The film *Gladiator* *was directed*. (direct) by Ridley Scott.

1 The new art gallery .... (*finish*) before the end of next year.
2 We .... (*tell*) Redman the bad news yesterday.
3 In Japan, kimonos .... (*wear*) for special occasions, for example when a woman gets married.
4 Two people........................ (*hurt*) when their car went over a bridge last night.
5 My parents remember where they were when John F. Kennedy .... (*kill*).
6 The Government .... (*build*) three new hospitals next year.
7 I'm sorry I'm late. My train .... (*delay*).
8 Thanksgiving Day .... (*celebrate*) in the USA in November every year.

$$\boxed{8}$$

© Pearson Education Limited 2001

E Sentences with *that / which / who*

Match the beginnings of these sentences to the endings and join them with *that*, *which* or *who*.

1   A customer is someone   a   you give to waiters
    and taxi-drivers

2   A souvenir is something   b   is not polite

3   A tip is extra money   c   you get when you buy
    something in a shop

4   A ruler is a thing   d   buys things in shops

5   A rude person is someone   e   you take when you
    are ill

6   A receipt is a piece of paper   f   wears very modern
    clothes

7   Medicine is stuff   g   helps you to draw a
    straight line

8   A passenger is someone   h   you buy from another
    country to help you
    remember it

9   A fashionable person is   i   travels on a bus, a
   someone   plane or a train

1 ....*who*.......... 2....................... 3...........................

4 .... 5....................... 6...........................

7 .... 8 .... 9 ....

8

F Pronunciation

Put the words below in the correct column of the table according to their word stress.

decade   afford   accountant   religion   honest
protest (noun)   divorced   well-mannered   account
suitable   qualified   tragedy   pregnant   balcony
exchange   designer   borrow

●○	○●	●○○	○●○
decade			

8

G Past Perfect or Past Simple?

Look at the Past Simple verbs in bold in the text. Some of them should be in the Past Perfect. Tick (√) the ones that are correct, and change the others into the Past Perfect.

Last year we [1] **went** on holiday to Buenos Aires. We [2] **were** very tired and quite dirty when we [3] **arrived** because the plane [4] **left** six hours late. When we [5] **got** to the city centre we [6] **looked** at the map which the travel agent [7] **gave** us in London. We [8] **walked** along the street and [9] **found** our four-star hotel.

'McDonald,' I said to the receptionist.

'No,' she said. 'Go out of the hotel and take the second street on the left. McDonald's restaurant is on the right.'

When she realised she **made** a mistake she **was** very embarrassed!

1........✔.............. 2........................ 3........................

4...................... 5........................ 6........................

7...................... 8........................ 9........................

10...................... 11 ....

10

H Prepositions

Complete the gaps with a suitable preposition. Do not use *in* or *on*.

For example:

A lot of people put their televisions .*in the corner*. of their living rooms.

1   You shouldn't leave your dog .... a car on a very hot day.

2   In the alphabet, B is .... A and C.

3   The temperature is two degrees celsius, just .... freezing point.

4   At the start of a chess game the black pieces are .... the white ones.

5   The *Titanic* was found ....
    .... the sea.

6   In Switzerland there's snow ....
    .... some mountains in Summer!

7   If you are standing in a queue there are people .... you and ....
    .... you.

8

I Vocabulary: word formation

Complete each sentence with the correct form of the word in capitals.

For example:

People in America were very ...*helpful*.... HELP

1 Sam Taylor hasn't got very much ....
IMAGINE
2 Has anybody seen my .... licence? DRIVE
3 It's very .... here by the sea. PEACE
4 Have you got a tin ....? OPEN
5 People have too many .... POSSESS
6 Lianne is an .... teacher. EXPERIENCE
7 Robin is a .... He works in Chicago. LAW
8 She died because she wanted .... for her people. FREE

| 8 |

J Pronunciation

Are the underlined sounds the same (S) or different (D)?

For example:

furniture   waste D

1 patient   tissues
2 violent   licence
3 enough   storey
4 heaven   jeweller
5 building   profit
6 purse   earn

| 6 |

K Prepositions

Circle the correct preposition in the following sentences.

For example:

How about going out (for)/to a meal?

1 The World Health Organisation spent $20 million dollars *on/for* AIDS research last year.
2 Don't ask me! I'm not very good *in/with* numbers.
3 I lent my copy of the book *to/from* John.
4 It took our grandparents twenty years to save up *with/for* an apartment.
5 We don't think this job would be suitable *for/to* you.
6 Mary often borrows things *from/to* me but she never gives them back!
7 Chris is applying *for/on* a new job.
8 The supermarket is *in/on* the right, next to the bank.

| 8 |

L Conditionals

Complete the gaps with a suitable form of the verb in brackets. Think about whether the situation is real or imaginary.

For example:

If I *had* (have) more money *I'd move* (move)

1 If you .... (give) me your e-mail address, I .... (send) you the information.
2 If I .... (have) my mobile phone with me I .... (ring) them now.
3 What .... you .... (do) if you .... (win) the lottery?
4 If I .... (knew) the answer I .... (tell) you!
5 If you .... (leave) your telephone number I .... (ask) Steve to call you later.
6 If I .... (not be) so tired I .... (go out) tonight.
7 If I .... (be) seventeen again I .... (do) a lot of things differently.
8 If we .... (wake up) early tomorrow, we .... (go) swimming.

| 8 |

M Reported speech

Rewrite the following sentences in reported speech.

For example:

'I'm at Tom's house.'
You told me *you were at Tom's house.*

1 'I'll phone you.'
He told her ....
2 'I lost all my money on the train.'
I told him ....
3 'I have a lot of homework.'
She told me ....
4 'I don't want to watch television.'
You told me ....
5 'I didn't speak to Mr Clinton.'
He told them ....
6 'I won't be late.'
You told me ....

| 6 |

TOTAL | 100 |

© Pearson Education Limited 2001

Resource bank key

1A Get to know the *Students' Book*

A pages 4 and 5   B in the front of the *Mini-Dictionary*   C pink   D making suggestions
E page 154   F personal vocabulary
G page 71   H pages 167 and 168   I day
J three   K pink   L page 148

Learner-training worksheet A

2 a meaning 1   b meaning 2   c meaning 3

3 a late   b quickly   c bed   d work   e open
f woke up

4 a countable noun   d intransitive verb
b adjective   e uncountable noun
c transitive verb   f adverb

5 economics   newsagent's   independent

1B Me too!

1 **What time/When** do you usually get up on Sundays?
2 **How often** do you go to the cinema?
3 **What**'s your favourite food?
4 **How long** does your journey home from school take?
5 **What** do you usually do at the weekend?
6 **Why** do you want to learn English?
7 **How many** cousins have you got?
8 **What kind of** films/movies do you like?
9 **Who**'s your favourite actor?
10 **When/What time** do you usually go to bed during the week?
11 **Which** season do you like the most?
12 **How often** do you go shopping for new clothes?

Learner-training worksheet B

4 a drove   b taught   c brought   d wore
e bought   f broke; fell   g rang   h left; caught

2B The Millionaire's Ball

1 on   2 in   3 –   4 ago   5 –   6 ago
7 on   8 in   9 on   10 in

3A The secret of successful language learning

2 and **3**

	VERB	NOUN	ADJECTIVE
a		importance	important
b	believe	belief	believable
c	imagine	imagination	imaginative
d	enjoy	enjoyment	enjoyable
e	succeed	success	successful

4 a succeed   f imaginative / important
b important   g beliefs
c believe   h imagine
d imagination   i enjoy
e enjoyable   j successful

Learner-training worksheet C

2 1 b   2 d   3 a   4 c

3 a Internet   b   c bank   d do
e answer   f check   g go out   h rent

5A Put these in order

A 1 Japan (377,000 sq km)
2 Spain (505,000 sq km)
3 France (551,000 sq km)
4 Peru (1,285,000 sq km)
B 1 The Pacific Ocean
2 The Atlantic Ocean
3 The Indian Ocean
4 The Arctic Ocean
C 1 India (1 billion)
2 Brazil (160 million)
3 Spain (40 million)
4 Poland (36.6 million)
D 1 The Colosseum
2 The Taj Mahal
3 The Eiffel Tower
4 The Sydney Opera House

E 1 Moscow (latitude 56°)
   2 London (latitude 51.5°)
   3 New York (latitude 41°)
   4 Tokyo (latitude 36°)
F 1 Pluto (5,900 million km from the sun)
   2 Mars (228 million km from the sun)
   3 Earth (150 million km from the sun)
   4 Mercury (56 million km from the sun)
G 1 Nelson Mandela's release from prison (February 1990)
   2 the fall of the Berlin Wall (November 1989)
   3 the first man on the moon (July 1969)
   4 the assassination of John F Kennedy (November 1963)
H 1 Julia Roberts (born 28th October 1967)
   2 Brad Pitt (born 18th December 1963)
   3 Sharon Stone (born 10th March 1958)
   4 Robert de Niro (born 17th August 1943)
I 1 The Nile (6,741 km)
   2 The Amazon (6,440 km)
   3 The Mississippi (3,780 km)
   4 The Rhine (1,390 km)
J 1 Titanic ($515 million)
   2 Star Wars ($460 million)
   3 E.T. ($399 million)
   4 Jurassic Park ($356 million)

Learner-training worksheet D

2 *Example answer*

> **a detective** =
> (also 'a detective story')
> **to steal** something (steal/stole/stolen) =
> (you steal things and money)
> **to rob** someone/somewhere (reg) =
> (you rob people and banks)
> **a journey** /dʒɜːni/ =
> (to go **on** a journey)
> **a wedding** =
> (to go **to** a wedding)
> **embarrassed** (adj) =
> to be/feel embarrassed **about** something
> **to dress up** (reg) (e.g. for a party, to go out for a meal) =
> **to earn** /ɜːn/ (money by doing a job) (reg) =

Learner-training worksheet F

2
1 ru**nn**ing	8 wi**nn**ing	15 shorter
2 stealing	9 shu**tt**ing	16 sli**mm**er
3 sho**pp**ing	10 started	17 cooler
4 cu**tt**ing	11 dro**pp**ed	18 brightest
5 beating	12 passed	19 thi**nn**est
6 hi**tt**ing	13 shouted	20 fla**tt**est
7 growing	14 stayed	

8A Article snakes and ladders

1 Ø; Ø
2 I live in a flat in **the** city centre, very close to ~~the~~ Oxford Street.
3 Ø; the; the
4 I usually go to work by ~~the~~ train, but yesterday I went by ~~the~~ bus.
5 The Indian Ocean; The Mediterranean; The Amazon
6 Ø; the; Ø; the
7 The sentence is correct.
8 the; Ø; the
9 El Paso is on **the** border of Mexico and **the** United States.
10 a; a; The; the
11 Madras is in the south of ~~the~~ India, on **the** east coast.
12 Ø; Ø; the; the
13 John is standing on **the** left, and Susan is standing in the middle, next to **the** Headmaster.
14 Ø; Ø; Ø; Ø
15 the; a; the; Ø
16 a; Ø
17 Ø; Ø; the
18 The sentence is correct.
19 the; the; the
20 I bought a picture and a carpet this morning. I've put **the** picture on the bathroom wall and the carpet on **the** kitchen floor.
21 the; Ø; the
22 The Andes; The Himalayas
23 Loch Ness is **the** most famous lake in Scotland, because of **the** Loch Ness Monster.
24 I really hate ~~the~~ mice, but I love spiders. I have a tarantula at home, and it lives on **the** ceiling!

Learner-training worksheet G

3
MATTHEW: Hi Jill, <u>have you got a light</u>?
JILL: Yes, here you are. Are you feeling OK?
MATTHEW: Yes, I'm just tired, that's all. I went to a party <u>in the city centre</u>, and didn't get home until three.
JILL: So that's why you didn't <u>arrive on time</u> this morning!
MATTHEW: Er, yes. But you <u>were late for work the other day</u>.
JILL: That was because I <u>went to the doctor</u>, not because I <u>stayed out late</u>!
MATTHEW: Yes, well, <u>I'm not very good at getting up early</u>.
JILL: That's probably why you're always <u>in a bad mood</u>!

189

MATTHEW: I'm not! Anyway, what are you doing <u>at the weekend</u>?

JILL: I'm <u>going out for a meal</u> with some friends on Saturday. On Sunday I might <u>go for a walk</u> in the countryside. What about you?

MATTHEW: <u>I've got the day off</u> on Friday, so I'm going to visit an old friend who lives <u>on the coast</u>.

JILL: That sounds fun. Look, we're going to be late for our classes. Let's go.

MATTHEW: What, already? Where did I put my books ...?

4
a **Have you got a** light?
b **in the** city centre.
c to arrive **on time**
d to be **late for** work
e **the other** day
f to go **to the** doctor
g to stay **out** late
h to be (not very) **good at** doing something
i to get **up** early
j to be **in a** bad mood
k **at the** weekend
l to go **out for a** meal
m to go **for a** walk
n **in the** countryside
o to have the day **off**
p **on the** coast

10C Bob's night out

The correct order is: E, C, I, A, H, F, D, J, B, G.

Learner-training worksheet I

2

VERB + GERUND	VERB + INFINITIVE WITH *TO*	VERB + INFINITIVE WITHOUT *TO*
enjoy	would prefer	have to
stop	arrange	might
hate	would like	could
don't mind	learn	must
	intend	
	plan	

3
a I've arranged **to meet** my brother this evening.
b I must **go** to the dentist this afternoon.
c correct
d Do you enjoy **playing** tennis?
e Would you prefer **to have** Chinese food or Indian food?
f correct
g correct
h I hate **getting** up early.
i We're planning **to go** to New York for our holidays.
j correct

12A The Handbag Gang

The correct order is E, H, B, F, J, A, D, I, G, C.

Learner-training worksheet J

The correct order is: D, C, E, H, B, F, A, G.

14C Building your dream

1 a of   b to combine
2 a imagination   b to imagine; imaginative
3 a of   b at; of   c of   d to
4 a an adverb   b to surprise (someone)
5 a by   b on   c to   d on
6 a to attract   b attraction
7 a to decorate   b decoration
8 a dream home; to turn off the TV; a football pitch; to wrap presents; to attract visitors; an upstairs bathroom

Learner-training worksheet K

2
a about   f on
b from   g on
c about   h with
d into   i of
e to   j at

4
a on   f about
b for   g between
c in   h to
d of   i for
e on   j of

Test one (modules 1–6)

A

1 sent   2 practises   3 is using   4 are taking
5 went   6 corrects   7 is having   8 is living

B

1 make   2 go   3 miss   4 pass   5 tell   6 have
7 lose   8 win

C

1 It's the biggest city **in** the world.
2 correct
3 My English is **worse** than Paolo's.
4 Vanessa's **friendlier** now than she was a year ago.
5 That man looks **like** Tom Cruise.
6 correct
7 Her computer is the same **as** mine.
8 correct
9 correct
10 My surname's similar **to** yours.

D

1 on   2 with   3 off   4 down   5 at
6 out   7 with   8 at

E

1 What kind of music do you like?
2 How often does Karen go to Spain?
3 How many languages does Nicolai speak?
4 Which boots do you prefer?
5 Why is Sylvie going home?
6 How long will it take to find the information?
7 What was the weather like?
8 When did you last use your credit card?

F (*half a mark each*)

o●   enjoy, relaxed, prefer, surprised
●o   crowded, frightened, foreign, happened
●oo Internet, relative, photograph, scenery
o●o appearance, embarrassed, ambition, attractive

G

1 borrow   2 favourite   3 sightseeing
4 nervous   5 crying   6 delayed   7 answer
8 embarrassed

H

1 'd like to   2 'll be able to   3 'm planning
4 won't   5 'd prefer to   6 will have to

I

1 the   2 a   3 the   4 –   5 a   6 –
7 The   8 –

J

1 can't   2 should   3 can   4 don't have to
5 shouldn't   6 have to

K

1 met   2 wore   3 felt   4 stole   5 told   6 cost
7 thought   8 rode   9 bought   10 lost

L

1 wet   2 rude   3 bored   4 save   5 wonderful
6 untidy

M

2 d   3 a   4 e   5 g   6 b   7 f

Test two (modules 7–11)

A

1 worked   2 haven't bought   3 did … get married
4 left   5 Have … ever been   6 've never eaten
7 have … lived   8 were

B (*half a mark each*)

●o   bandage, mountain
o●   disease, degree, canal
●oo   temperature, stomachache, politics
o●o   cathedral, deliver
o●oo electrical, facilities

C

1 plaster   2 career   3 receipt   4 tip   5 abroad
6 relaxing   7 religion   8 taste   9 suburbs
10 accidents

D

a 5   b 3   c 2   d 7   e 1   f 6   g 4

E

1 went   2 was playing   3 've lived
4 Did you used to like   5 arrived   6 used to have
7 hasn't finished   8 was cooking

F

1 Coulthard will definitely win the race.
2 I might be late tonight.
3 Computer prices will probably go down.
4 It definitely won't rain tomorrow.
5 We may not come to Jayne's party.
6 My father probably won't arrive before ten o'clock.

G

1 the   2 –   3 a   4 the   5 the   6 the   7 –
8 an

H

1 smoke   2 teaching   3 driving   4 put   5 to go
6 doing   7 to pay   8 to sing

I

1 beach   2 island   3 healthy   4 friendly

J

1 at   2 in   3 at   4 on   5 into   6 about
7 of   8 over

K

1 made   2 won   3 broken   4 drunk   5 read
6 caught   7 written   8 known   9 paid
10 done   11 taken   12 thought   13 said
14 bought   15 eaten   16 flown

L

1   We can leave as soon as Kevin **finds** his car keys.
2   correct
3   correct
4   When the film **ends**, why don't we go for a meal.
5   Yasmin wants to go back to India before she **dies**.
6   correct

M

1 start   2 become   3 get   4 change   5 keep
6 take

N

1   Jose started learning English four months **ago**.
2   Oh no', I've **just** lost all my work on the computer!
3   I've **never** used a DVD player before.
4   We spoke on the phone **last** week.
5   Lee and Oliver have known each other **for** ten years.
6   A: Julie, this is John.
    B: Actually, we've **already** met. Hello again!
7   Chris left school **when** he was sixteen.
8   Mel hasn't heard the results of her exam **yet**.

Test three (modules 12–16)

A

1 wallet   2 sympathetic   3 towel   4 owe
5 planets   6 mess   7 demonstration   8 speech

B

1 rained   2 have known   3 've been trying
4 have you had   5 opened   6 've been shopping

C

1   Henman didn't win **any** matches …
2   correct
3   A lot **of** people play …
4   correct
5   People shouldn't spend too **much** time …
6   correct
7   I'm having **a few** days off …
8   correct

D

1 will be finished   2 told   3 are worn
4 were hurt   5 was killed   6 will build
7 was delayed   8 is celebrated

E

2h that / which   3a that / which   4g that / which
5b who   6c that / which   7e that / which
8i who   9f who

F (half a mark each)

●○   honest, protest, pregnant, borrow
○●   afford, divorced, account, exchange
●○○   suitable, qualified, tragedy, balcony
○●○   accountant, religion, well-mannered, designer

G

2 ✓   3 ✓   4 had left   5 ✓   6 ✓   7 had given
8 ✓   9 ✓   10 had made   11 ✓

H

1 inside   2 between   3 above   4 opposite
5 at the bottom of   6 on top of
7 behind, in front of (2 marks)

I

1 imagination   2 driving   3 peaceful   4 opener
5 possessions   6 experienced   7 lawyer
8 freedom

J

1 S   2 S   3 D   4 D   5 S   6 S

K

1 on   2 with   3 to   4 for   5 for   6 from
7 for   8 on

L

1 give, 'll send   2 had, would ring
3 would … do, won   4 knew, 'd tell
5 leave, 'll ask   6 wasn't, would go out
7 were, would do   8 wake up, 'll go

M

1   he would phone her
2   I had lost all my money on a train
3   she had a lot of homework
4   you didn't want to watch television
5   he hadn't spoken to Mr Clinton
6   you wouldn't be late